The Seven Story Tower

A Mythic Journey through Space and Time

The Seven Story Tower

A Mythic Journey through Space and Time

Curtiss Hoffman

PERSEUS
PUBLISHING

The author gratefully acknowledges the use of the following materials:

Joseph Campbell, excerpts from *The Hero with a Thousand Faces*. Copyright © 1949 by Bolligen Foundation Inc., renewed 1976 by Princeton University Press. Reprinted by permission of Princeton University Press.

Joseph Campbell, excerpt from *Masks of God: Primitive Mythology* Copyright © 1953, 1969, renewed 1987 by Joseph Campbell. Reprinted by permission of Viking Penguin, a division of Penguin Putnam Inc.

Carl G. Jung, excerpt from *Psychology and Alchemy*. Copyright © 1953 by Bolligen Foundation Inc. New material © 1968 Bolligen Foundation Inc. Reprinted by permission of Princeton University Press.

Carl G. Jung, excerpt from *The Archetypes and The Collective Unconscious*. Copyright © 1959, 1969 by Princeton University Press. Reprinted by permission of Princeton University Press

Claude Levi-Strauss, except from *Kuniba, Cashinawa, and Arapaho Myths from The Origin of Table Manners: Introduction to a Science of Mythology, Volume 3*. Copyright © 1968 by Librarie Plon; English Translation Copyright © 1978 by Jonathan Cape Ltd. and Harper and Row, publishers, Inc. Reprinted by permission of HarperCollins Publishers, Inc.

Adrian Recinos, except from *Popul Vuh: The Sacred Book of the Ancient Quiche Maya* (translated by Delia Goetz and Sylvanus Morley). Copyright © 1950 by University of Oklahoma Press. Reprinted by permission of University of Oklahoma Press.

J.R.R. Tolkien, map from *The Silmarillion*. Copyright © 1977 by George Allen and Unwin (Publishers), Ltd. Reprinted by permission of Houghton Mifflin Company.

J.R.R. Tolkien, excerpt from *The Letters of J.R.R. Tolkien*, edited by Humphrey Carpenter. Copyright © 1981 by George Allen and Unwin (Publishers), Ltd. Reprinted by permission of Houghton Mifflin Company.

J.R.R. Tolkien, excerpt from *The Lost Road and Other Writings*. Copyright © 1987 by Frank Richard Williamson and Christopher Reuel Tolkien as Executors of the Estate of J.R.R. Tolkien. Reprinted by permission of Houghton Mifflin Company.

J.R.R. Tolkien, excerpt from *Morgoth's Ring: The Later Silmarillion*. Copyright © 1993 by Frank Richard Williamson and Christopher Reuel Tolkien as Executors of the Estate of J.R.R. Tolkien. Reprinted by permission of Houghton Mifflin Company.

Frances Toor, excerpt from *A Treasury of Mexican Folkways*. Copyright © 1947 by Crown Publishers, Inc. Reprinted by permission of Crown Publishers, Inc.

Frank Waters, excerpt from *Book of the Hopi*. Copyright © 1963 by Frank Waters. Repritned by permission of viking Penguin, a division of Penguin Putnam, Inc.

Library of Congress Cataloging-in-Publication Data is available.

ISBN 0-7382-0595-8

Perseus Publishing is a member of the Perseus Books Group.

Find us on the World Wide Web at http://www.perseuspublishing.com

Perseus Publishing books are available at special discounts for bulk purchases in the U.S. by corporations, institutions, and other organizations. For more information, please contact the Special Markets Department at the Perseus Books Group, 11 Cambridge Center, Cambridge, MA 02142, or call (800) 255-1514 or (617)252-5298, or e-mail j.mccrary@perseusbooks.com

First paperback printing, December 2001

1 2 3 4 5 6 7 8 9 10—03 02 01

"Tell me your myth that the whole world may turn to myth."

—Nikos Kazantzakis, *The Odyssey: A Modern Sequel*
[Translated by Kimon Friar (New York: Simon and Schuster, 1958), Book XXI, 1. 1277.]

CONTENTS

FOREWORD

While I was reading *The Seven Story Tower* in manuscript, I tried to describe its unusual quality to a friend, who remarked, "It sounds more like an experience than a book." I agreed, but then felt even more acutely the difficulty of introducing this beguiling and involving book. Its form and content are particularly inextricable.

The author takes his title from the image of a tower in which the ascending person sees views of increasing complexity and significance through the windows.

But I was looking for a supplementary overall metaphor—something organic, lush, proliferating, bizarre, but not ultimately chaotic. I had in mind Hoffman's remark that we resist letting myth impact our lives seriously, because this archetypal domain is threatening. Here, those hidden fears surface which we would rather not acknowledge, let alone confront—or befriend.

I've settled for the rather unoriginal comparison of the reader as traveler. He sets forth, rather vague as to his goal, on a trek through a territory perhaps larger and more strange than he had expected. Part jungle, part cultivated, it plunges him into beauty and horror, danger and delight.

Fortunately, the apprehensive tourist has Hoffman at hand as a tranquil, observant interpreter. At each stage of the journey (seven "key" tales forming the basic structure of the book) the author has the situation well in hand. Harking back to the experiences just past, he explains, supplements, enriches, compares, connects, reassures, hints, and warns. Looping forward in time, he prepares us for what lies ahead and connects it to what has occurred.

"Hey, I'm beginning to get it!" says the traveler. For the result of this complicated interweaving is that somehow the contours of the country begin to emerge. Though perhaps they will always be somewhat shifty, moveable, evasive.

More important, the voyager begins to perceive that though the goal may never be clearly defined—though the central mystery may remain forever more or less obscure—the journey is not only worthwhile, but essential. Thus the traveler is encouraged and equipped to proceed, though perhaps hoping he may not have to cope with still another boar-tusked lady or a severed head talking as it rolls.

Looming against the sky line are three vast stone shapes, like well-meaning Easter Island statues: Campbell, Lévi–Strauss, and Jung. They have done their best to map the territory. And here perhaps is a good time to shrink the stone shapes down to human-scholar size and to attempt a more prosaic summing up.

In generously acknowledging the influence of these writers and many others, Hoffman never accepts any one point of view uncritically. Nor does he indulge in dogmatic condemnations. Everyone who has approached mythology may have a piece of the truth. Gentleness and respect are essential, and the doors must be left open for further research, speculation, and insight.

The seven key stories give the reader a sense of structure, yet of flowing movement in space and time. The last of them is a modern one and of special interest in helping us to understand the whole. This tale comes from the mythology created by J.R.R. Tolkien, author of *The Lord of the Rings.* Hoffman's analytic and synthetic approach to the first six stories equip the reader to understand and evaluate his claim that in Tolkien's work we have a real secondary world, a valid myth.

Myth, as Campbell says, forms the interface between what can and cannot be expressed. It's a marvelous territory for exploration.

Bon voyage!
Edith Gilmore, Ph.D.

PREFACE

The Seven Story Tower is an introduction to the fascinating world of myth, explored in cross-cultural context. It is designed to provide the reader with the conceptual tools essential for the analysis and appreciation of myth as a vital function of human cultural expression. I approach the subject of myth from a social sciences perspective, combining the insights of cultural anthropology and analytical psychology. On one level, the purpose of the book is to guide the reader in the use of both analytical and synthetic methods: analytical, because each myth is considered within its specific cultural context; synthetic, because by comparing myths from different cultures around the world it becomes possible to formulate general conclusions about the role of myth in human society, including our own. On another level, its multilayered stories work to stimulate the reader's emotional appreciation of myth's power today over our lives and societies. Each chapter introduces specific structures that occur within myths: transformation, inversion, substitution and recombination, ætiology, family structure, and ethical dualism. Other themes of importance are explored, such as the significance of names and numbers; relationships to cultural ideas about the plants, animals, and heavenly bodies, as well as the structure of the human body; social tensions between church and state, men and women, old and young, culture and nature; and especially the process of individual maturation in a social context. The latter theme is expected to be of particular appeal to younger readers, who are undergoing the same inevitable social consequences of assuming adult responsibility in a complex world which are central to so many of the myths in this book.

In his brilliant, but nearly forgotten novel *A Voyage to Arcturus,* David Lindsay depicts a tower comprised of seven stories, each with an embrasure window through which a climber can look out upon the world. Lindsay, who died young, was a member of the Inklings, a circle of British fantasy writers which included J.R.R. Tolkien, C.S. Lewis, and Charles Williams. His protagonist Maskull's dark double, Nightspore, is directed to ascend the spiral staircase within the tower. At each stage, the view becomes more distant and abstract, but also more philosophically profound, until Nightspore reaches the summit of the tower and realizes that the responsibility for the fate of the imperiled world lies, at least partially, in his hands.[1] This powerful image came to mind once I realized that the number of key myths in this exploratory venture would be seven, and I knew at once what the title of the book must be. For I also offer the reader seven views upon the world, through mythic windows, which I have chosen because they display great diversity through space and time, yet have a remarkable thematic similarity. These represent the Irish, Greek, Sumerian, Indonesian, Amazonian, and Inuit cultures, and the fantasy world of J.R.R. Tolkien. By the time the seventh stage is reached, I hope it will be clear that there is indeed an inevitable linkage between myth and social responsibility.

A few words of introduction about my approach to myth are in order. I am an archæologist by profession, and my academic training was in the archæology of the Near East, especially of Mesopotamia. For most of the past twenty-five years, however, I have concentrated on the pre-European cultures of my home region, northeastern North America. This is a region in which the environment and its early inhabitants conspired to leave behind only scant traces of human activity, mostly in the form of stone tools. These Native peoples never developed a system of written communication, and the Europeans who arrived here in the seventeenth century were rather effective in eliminating nearly all overt traces of the Native belief system, which they viewed as inferior to their Puritan brand of Christianity. Some of the Native myths and practices have survived, but after 350 years of political and religious persecution many of the people have become so assimilated that they have forgotten the larger cultural system to which the stories once belonged, and they are understandably reluctant to share with outsiders what they do retain. Thus, most of my work has been a study of a culture whose myths are almost irretrievable.

The reader may wonder how, as an archæologist with such a narrow research specialty, I have come to write a book on world myth. First, I would suggest that mythological analysis and archæological investigation are not so distant from one another in their intellectual requirements as one might think. C.G. Jung, a psychoanalyst whose views on the inner dimensions of myth will be quoted frequently in this book, dreamed when young of becoming an archæologist, and maintained a passion for this field throughout his life.[2] I have elsewhere compared the practice of archæology to the spiritual discipline of meditation, for it requires both infinite patience and sharp attention to detail as well as an ability to synthesize a larger picture from what is often very fragmentary evidence.[3]

But aside from this, I have been fascinated by myth since I was a child. My first exposure to the systematic study of myth from the psychological dimension was at the age of fourteen, through a series of lectures on public television given by that redoubtable *doyen* of myth, Joseph Campbell. While pursuing my undergraduate and graduate studies in archæology, I studied the myths of ancient Mesopotamia and Syro-Palestine in close detail, often in the original languages.

I want to make it clear at this point that I regard the material I use in this book that is derived from the Old and New Testaments to be as valuable as the myths of any other culture, that is, neither more nor less true but just as useful as a rich source of mythological thought. I feel that my position outside the orthodoxy of any religion gives me license to do this. I was brought up in the Reformed branch of the Jewish faith, but became disaffected from the religion (not the ethnicity) by the age of seventeen. I do not mean that I am trying to deprecate Western religion by associating it with myth—far from it. Instead, I contend that the canonical writings of the Jewish, Christian, and Muslim religions and the oral and written traditions of other cultures contain the same striving toward the truth, the same uncannily accurate observations about the human condition, and some strikingly similar conclusions about what might be done to attain the former or improve the latter. The same, in my opinion, is true of the best works of the science fiction and fantasy génre of the twentieth century. For this reason, I feel justified in borrowing a motif from that génre as the theme of this book, and in including a tale from the pen of a modern fantasy writer, J.R.R. Tolkien, among the more traditional stories I treat here.

For my doctoral dissertation, I applied my interest in myth to the study of a particular iconographic problem in Mesopotamian archæology: the meanings of the animal motifs which occur with great frequency on stone cylinder seals. After performing exhaustive statistical analyses of motif frequency and position, I examined a series of hypotheses about the invariances I observed in the iconography of the motifs. I concluded that their symbolism reflected ancient observations about the human psychological constitution and its relationship to the perceived world.[4] Already by this time (much to the dismay of my professors, I fear) I was branching out beyond the narrow field of Assyriology, in which I was trained, into anthropology and psychology, particularly the works of Claude Lévi–Strauss and Carl G. Jung, which are frequently cited in this book.

It was also during this period that I spent seven years of study at the feet of a spiritual teacher, Mr. Anthony Bonello. His teachings were highly eclectic, and combined eastern yogic disciplines with western Qabbalah, as well as many other sources. Participating in a community based upon several interrelated traditional systems of symbols gave me a rare opportunity to observe both the relativity of the systems we humans tend to create and the degree to which these systems are capable of being mapped onto one another from culture to culture without a significant loss of meaning. There is nothing particularly new about this observation. The Hellenistic Greeks—particularly the Gnostics and the Neoplatonists—were busily syncretizing the varied mythic systems of Alexander's far-flung empire by the second century B.C., and it was out of this heady mix that Christianity arose. The Provençal Crusaders of the twelfth century A.D. brought back many eastern ideas from the Islamic world and incorporated these into their Albigensian observances. But it is really only in the twentieth century that it has become possible to integrate mythological systems on a global scale. This method of cross-cultural comparison is at the core of this book.

I began teaching at the adult education level in 1973, shortly before receiving my doctorate, and my first offerings were courses both in archæology and in myth. I have taught both subjects side by side ever since. At Bridgewater State College, where I have taught since 1978, I have created college level courses in Myth and Culture, Anthropology of Religion, Myths and Peoples of the Ancient Near East, and Culture and Consciousness, and they are among my favorite courses to teach. The material in this book derives directly from my class notes for the first third of the former course.

More than this, myth has been for me personally a revelatory, participatory experience since the age of seventeen. My studies with Mr. Bonello provided me with a personal familiarity with the states of consciousness which myths both describe and entail, and I am moreover conversant with the ability of myth to speak across the barriers of space, time, and culture to the modern day. I consider myself a storyteller in the traditional sense. I have selected the stories in this book with some care from among the tens of thousands of myths available in the published record, and I have presented them in a deliberate sequence and with a deliberately symbolic number of stages in order to enhance their cumulative effect upon the reader. But I also understand the importance of letting the story tell itself while keeping my personal opinions out of the way—at least until the story is told. The power of mythic story derives not solely from its tellers, though they can certainly enhance it by proper delivery and attention to detail, but from the subject itself as a representation of the unchanging truths about the human condition. If the seven stories at the heart of this volume have this effect upon the reader, then I will perhaps have earned my supper, though I must acknowledge that the credit is not mine alone, but that of the stories themselves.

As I said above, this book approaches the subject of myth from the perspective of the social or behavioral sciences, particularly anthropology and psychology. My aim is to illustrate many of the important elements of myth, to demonstrate it to be a function operating in all cultures, and to describe mythology as a means of studying that function. As a social scientist, I am particularly interested in elucidating patterns of similarity among myths and exploring their causes. To do this requires the use of myth comparatively, from several cultures, though always with a view to the specific cultural context in which each myth was told.

Since myth is essentially discursive in its mode of transmission, one can also consider any attempt such as this to study myth as a kind of storytelling, i.e., a myth in itself. As Claude Lévi-Strauss noted in commenting on Freud's use of myth in describing psychological complexes:

> A myth consists of all its variants . . . not only Sophocles, but Freud himself should be included among the recorded versions of the Oedipus myth, on a par with earlier or seemingly more "authentic" versions.[5]

Like the tales of the Arabian Nights, each of the seven key stories in this book contains and connects to other stories, and all of them are furthermore embedded within a frame story. That story, which we shall consider in the first and last chapters, directly concerns the relevance of myth to cultural life in the closing years of the twentieth century. In my opinion, myth is utterly relevant to our society today. If we know how to look, we will see its images and associations playing out in our daily lives and in the lives of those around us, both near and far, small and great. For me, myth represents a great repository of that which is unchanging in the human condition. If we can understand these invariances, we will have a better chance of making wise decisions about our future, decisions which potentially can affect not only our personal lives but the course of our civilization. It is with this prospect in mind that I have written this book.

ACKNOWLEDGMENTS

This work has had a long gestation. It has been twenty years since I first taught the Myth and Culture course from which its core material is drawn at Bridgewater State College. Hundreds of students have been subjected to these stories, and along the way several of them have asked crucial questions that have helped me in refining my presentations and streamlining the story line. I must acknowledge their contribution first, both as listeners and as participants in the process of discovery. Without their input the book could not have been written. Thanks are also due to a succession of department chairs, student advisors, and administrators at Bridgewater State who have supported this course from the outset and have helped me in recruiting students for it

I also want to thank my literary agent, Douglas Storey, for his perseverance in finding the right publisher and negotiating a favorable contract. He believed in the project at a time when I had little hope of its ever seeing the light of day. Frank Darmstadt and the entire team at Insight Books/Plenum have done a remarkable job of guiding the manuscript to the stage of final product in a very short time frame. Their suggestions have been altogether productive.

Also, I wish to thank two anonymous reviewers of the manuscript for their many helpful suggestions and my colleagues who graciously offered endorsements: Jayne Gackenbach, Anita Spencer, Robert Moss, Tyler Volk, Pia Keiding, and Robert Bosnak. Special thanks are due to Edith Gilmore, who on very short notice agreed to write the Foreword.

Permission to republish longer citations was granted by the University of Oklahoma Press (Chapter 1), Crown Publishing (Chapter 2), Princeton University Press (Chapters 3, 9, and 10), Viking Press (Chapters 6 and 10), Lucis Publishing (Chapter 7), HarperCollins (Chapters 7 and 8), Houghton-Mifflin (Chapters 9 and 10), and Simon and Schuster (Chapter 10).

Ulla Kasten and Bill Hallo kindly gave me permission to use photographs of cylinder seals (Figures 10, 13, 16, and 26) and a seal impression (Figure 17) from the Yale Babylonian Collection, as well as the original of the map which appears as Figure 14. Jean-Jacques Rivard, a remarkable artist and scholar who is my co-worker at the Robbins Museum of Archaeology, produced the line drawing for Figure 1 from his own extensive collection of slides of Maya artwork, and also kindly gave me permission to photograph one of his series of paintings on the Iroquois creation myth, which appears as Figure 22. My son Darrel Hoffman photographed this item as well as my image on the dust jacket. He also produced the line drawing which appears as Figure 21. Thanks are also due to the monks of the Namgyal Monastery in Ithaca, New York, who kindly allowed me to photograph the sand mandala they created at the Conference on Education as Transformation: Religious Pluralism, Spirituality and Higher Education held at Wellesley College in September of 1998, and to Gordon Bernstein who took the photograph of the mandala. Jennifer Alden pointed me in the right direction to make contact with the Monastery. Kristine Hook of the Corbis Corporation (formerly Bettmann Photo Archive) and her staff were very helpful in locating the images which appear on the cover and as Figures 4, 6, 7, 8, 9, 11, 15, 18, 19, 23, and 25. Thanks are also due to the Pierpoint Morgan Library for permission to use the image which appears as Figure 12 and to the University Museum of Newcastle-upon-Tyne for permission to use the image which appears as Figure 5.

In conclusion, I wish to acknowledge the support of seven dear friends who inspired me to bring this work out of its long dormancy and who very kindly consented to read and comment on all or parts of it in manuscript form: Joy Gates, Maryanne MacLeod, Dolores Nurss, Victoria Rourke, Patricia Schmieg, Gudrun Weber, and especially my wife, Tobi. Their perseverance and insights have helped to make this a clearer and more salient exploration into the fascinating world of myth.

LIST OF FIGURES

Chapter One

THE BROKEN CIRCLE:

A Dialogue between Myth and Science

This is the first account, the first narrative. There was neither man, nor animal, birds, fishes, crabs, trees, stones, caves, ravines, grasses, nor forests; there was only the sky.

The surface of the earth had not appeared. There was only the calm sea and the great expanse of the sky.

There was nothing brought together, nothing which could make a noise, nor anything which might move, or tremble, or could make noise in the sky.

There was nothing standing; only the calm water, the placid sea, alone and tranquil. Nothing existed.

There was only immobility and silence in the darkness, in the night. Only the Creator, the Maker, Tepeu, Gúcumatz, the Forefathers, were in the water surrounded with light. . . . By nature they were great sages and thinkers. . . .

Then came the word. Tepeu and Gúcumatz came together in the darkness, in the night, and Tepeu and Gúcumatz talked together. They talked then, discussing and deliberating; they agreed, they united their words and their thoughts.

Then while they meditated, it became clear to them that when dawn would break, man must appear. Then they planned the creation, and the growth of the trees and the thickets and the birth of life and the creation of man. . . .

Thus let it be done! Let the emptiness be filled! Let the water recede and make a void, let the earth appear and become solid; let it be done.

Thus they spoke. Let there be light, let there be dawn in the sky and on the earth! There shall be neither glory nor grandeur in our creation and formation until the human being is made, man is formed. So they spoke.

Then the earth was created by them. So it was, in truth, that they created the earth. Earth! they said, and instantly it was made.

Like the mist, like a cloud, and like a cloud of dust was the creation, when the mountains appeared from the water; and instantly the mountains grew.

Only by a miracle, only by magic art were the mountains and valleys formed; and instantly the groves of cypresses and pines put forth shoots together on the surface of the earth.[1]

How Do We Think of Myth?

Most people today, when they read a narrative like the Quiche Maya account of creation above (Figure 1), probably feel that it is strangely out of place. The notion of creation through the word, of a universe created especially for humans, indeed of creative "forefathers" in the first place, may seem old-fashioned or even irrelevant to the modern world, with its scientific explanations of the universe. One cannot dispute the beauty of its poetry, but the most one might ask of the narrator is, "What is the meaning of this to *you* (but certainly not to *me*)?" This is the question asked by the contrary son in the Passover *Haggadah:* four sons react differently to hearing the story of the Exodus, one obedient, one "contrary" ("evil" is the more usual translation), one stupid, and one who does not even know how to ask. The *Haggadah* gives parents advice as to how to answer each one of them. To the contrary son, one is to respond, "This is what the Lord did for *me,*" since such a son would not himself have been favored with the opportunity to participate in the Exodus had he lived at the time.[2]

My position is more lenient: I shall try to show just what the myths might mean to *you,* regardless of which of these four attitudes you may bring to its study. Of course, if you insist on excluding yourself from even the possibility of personal involvement in or transformation through myth, you will necessarily also exclude yourself from the opportunity of achieving much understanding of it.

If we wish to study human behavior, we should certainly attempt to answer this question, but we must first address the popular misconception

Figure 1: Tepeu and Gúcumatz converse about the creation of the world. Original line drawing of a ritual vessel, Maya, 9th century A.D. (Jean-Jacques Rivard)

of myth's irrelevance to us. In the common parlance of civilized people in the twentieth century, the term *myth* has come to describe something which is false, or an outmoded way of knowledge. It is often considered to be the opposite of science, which is expected to provide us with the truth about the nature of the universe, our planet, and ourselves. Even Joseph Campbell, the most well-known apologist for the mythic perspective of our century, says of the cosmological function of myth:

> Today we turn to science for our imagery of the past and of the structure of the world, and what the spinning demons of the atom and the galaxies of the telescope's eye reveal is a wonder that makes the babel of the Bible seem a toyland dream of the dear childhood of our brain.[3]

True believers in science (though not necessarily all scientists) often assert that, while our most primitive ancestors struggled to understand the world by resorting in their ignorance to myth, and our more recent forebears turned to religion for guidance, modern man has freed himself from the shackles of illusion and stands free, embracing the unassailable truths which his reason has wrested from Nature.

By contrast to the purportedly superior truths provided by the scientific method, the explanations given in myths are often considered to be outmoded, silly, or simply irrelevant. Of course we know that the earth revolves around the sun, that creation of the universe did not take place in seven days, and that our ancestors descended from the same stock as the modern apes and were not expelled from a garden. Peoples outside the pale of Western civilization who still value myth highly are considered backward or primitive for this very reason, especially when their myths deter them from adopting Western science, technology, and social and economic forms. For example, many Westerners think of India as a backward nation, in part because it retains its affiliation with Hinduism, a non-Western religion. During the period of the British Raj, many efforts were made to convert Hindus to one brand or another of Christianity, and during the preceding Moghul period, the Muslim rulers attempted to do the same, sometimes by force. This ignores the facts that India's canonical tradition is older than Christianity or Islam and that India has managed to incorporate its traditional perspective into fully "modern" developments, including considerable scientific achievements. Traditionalists in these societies are told that if they wish to keep pace with the rest of the world, they will have to leave their myths behind. Their acceptance of mythic explanations is considered by sophisticated modernists as a sign of cultural immaturity, and as St. Paul said, "When I was a child, I spake as a child, I understood as a child, I thought as a child, but when I became a man, I put away childish things."[4]

Why Myth Can Have a Positive Connotation

The perspective that I adopt in this book is that myth is not necessarily one of the "childish things," that an appreciation of it may actually be necessary for both individuals and societies to maintain balance and attain psychological maturity. The assumption that Western science has all the answers for other cultures, or that we have the right to impose its values on other cultures, is, in strictly anthropological terms, a form of *ethnocentrism,* irrespective of how instrumental those answers have been in transforming our culture. One of the first things introductory anthropology students learn is that anthropologists are expected to refrain from judging the values of other cultures by the standards of their own; it is only our own culture which we have the right to judge. And if we do so judge our culture, we may not necessarily agree that our banishment of myth from the leading edge of speculative thinking has resulted in an unmitigated improvement. We may come to discover that the equation of myth with falsehood is itself a myth—in both positive and negative senses of the word—and moreover a very powerful one, with profound consequences for our society.

In actuality, the word *myth* derives from the Greek *mythos*, which is cognate to the English word "mouth" and simply means a told tale, a piece of the oral tradition that was the chief means of communication prior to the introduction of writing and still remains the most widespread mode of human discourse. A myth might describe creatures or objects that our reason tells us cannot (nor ever could) exist in the domain of the five senses—elves, dragons, talking swords, etc. But the observation that some of a myth's sensory correlates are not present in the field perceptible to the rational waking mind does not mean that they cannot be imagined and talked about. It also says nothing about how accurately the myth may describe the processes of inner reality, the realm of the unconscious mind, where we spend fully a third of our life experience while we sleep. In myths, even descriptions of what appear to be aspects of ordinary physical reality may also be understood in symbolic terms, or as *metaphors* for aspects of either inner or outer reality—or both at once. Mythic thinking contends that these metaphors are absolutely necessary if we are ever to reach an understanding of the world, and of ourselves. The unconscious mind works very largely in terms of metaphor, yet this can also be shown to be true of aspects of our waking consciousness, especially of language. As an experiment in this, the philosopher David Chalmers suggests trying to describe the experience of *redness* in any but metaphorical terms.[5]

Since most physical anthropologists agree that the human psychological constitution (as reflected in both the brain's size and organization and in the manifested products of its ruminations) does not appear to have changed substantially for at least the past 40,000 years,[6] I suggest that in a real sense myths reflect upon that which is *always* true about the human condition and its place in the natural and social world. As numerous mythologists and anthropologists have argued, the same rules which govern the operation of myths at least partially govern our perception of reality. As much as we would like to believe in our ability to view the world objectively, our cultural background places constraints upon our thinking which we take for granted and from which we therefore cannot easily free ourselves. Gregory Bateson presents cogent arguments that this kind of conditioning also characterizes the scientific world-view. In his opinion and that of numerous other cultural anthropologists, the view we have of the world is a social construct which we project onto our observations, whether they be expressed in mythic or scientific terms. By the time individuals become adults, they have often become quite unconscious of this propensity of the mind.[7] But it is in the myths that we find the basis for that cultural background; so our understanding of the world really is conditioned by our understanding of our own myths.

Why Myth Has Acquired a Negative Connotation

Myth as a conveyor of oral tradition first acquired a negative connotation when contrasted with the written canons of the three great religious traditions which sprang from the Near East: Judaism, Christianity, and Islam. However, the historical fact is that these three religions also had their origins in oral traditions. Their written testaments are strongly colored by myth and are the result of a reduction of a corpus of belief which was once much more richly varied. These facts are usually denied vehemently by their orthodoxies, who wish thereby to retain a special status for their particular beliefs, but this does not make them any less true.

With the resurgence of independent thinking in Europe during the Renaissance as an alternative to the dominance of the Catholic Church, there was a revival of interest in myth. Many ancient myths were rewritten in fifteenth or sixteenth century garb (as myths have been reclothed in every age) as a concomitant to the revival of Greek science, but scholars by and large continued to view myth as falsehood. The difference was that now they were willing to include Church doctrine among the falsehoods, and by the early eighteenth century, writers like Voltaire and Bernard Fontenelle reveled in debunking myth as a covert means of discrediting the Church. For example, drawing attention to the prevalence of stories of the virgin birth in Greek mythology, Fontenelle suggested that:

> Some extraordinary happening may have led people to believe that a god had had an affair with a woman. At once all the stories

> will be full only of amorous gods. You already believe the one, why not believe the other as well?[8]

During the Age of Enlightenment (1750–1850), natural science arose to proclaim itself as the successor to both myth and religion, as Sir James Frazer suggested,[9] conveniently forgetting that its roots were in alchemy and astrology, themselves derived from classical myth. Frazer's confidence in the triumph of science over its predecessors was unfettered by any trace of self-doubt about the superiority of modernism. We must recall that he was writing at the dawn of the twentieth century, a time when the British Empire was at its peak, and that he had every expectation that the colonial powers would continue to bring the benefits of civilization to the benighted savages whose myths he was recording. This is one of the reasons why his work seems somewhat ethnocentristic to a post-colonial world.

Science has since become the dominant paradigm of Western civilization. As that civilization has spread its values around the globe, the scientific method has been adopted as the universal standard for expressing truth, even to the point of claiming that science is close to achieving a "Grand Universal Theory" that will explain everything in the universe in terms of elementary particles. It is sometimes forgotten that such a theory would, of necessity, be an explanation in its own terms, which would require decades of study for any individual to understand, and that it would nevertheless remain impossible to fully explain any complex phenomenon on the basis of random quantum electrodynamics at a level which would be meaningful to the average reader. Jack Cohen and Ian Stewart point out that:

> A Theory of Everything is useless for understanding and explanation because it represents the way the universe behaves in such an indirect way that extracting what we want to know requires an inordinate effort. . . . A theory is like a net. It catches what it's designed to catch. . . . If you fish nature with a theory of gravity, you catch elliptical orbits; if you fish with quantum electrodynamics you catch light and electrons. . . . But a Theory of Everything is . . . a net that catches everything in the ocean. . . . if anybody asks you what's in the net you have no idea. It's black, you can't see inside, and even if you could, you can't pick out anything interesting. Yes, it's wonderful to know that the Net for

Everything contains the entire ocean, but it's not much use if you can't get anything out.[10]

Because science is so pervasive, and many scientists (as well as the general public) are so confident in the correctness of its methodology, it would be useful if, at the outset of our exploration of myth, we were to compare the scientific and mythic modes of knowledge. Table 1 will help us in exploring this.

The Way of Science: The Line

Science has classically sought to control phenomena by understanding them, and it strives for understanding under the assumption that the whole is neither greater nor less than the sum of its parts. Thus, any complex manifestation is to be broken down or *reduced* to its parts, which are more amenable to analysis, and the whole is to be reconstructed and is assumed to work as the result of the forces which constituted the parts. For example, mathematics can well describe the properties of straight lines, but in order to study curves, as in calculus, it is necessary to consider them

Table 1: The Dialectic of Science and Myth

Science tends to be:	*Myth* tends to be:
Analytic	Synthetic
Reductionistic	Holistic
Quantitative	Qualitative
Digital	Analogical
Linear	Circular
Detached	Involved
Based on Observation	Based on Participation
Parsimonious	Elaborate
Experimental	Experiential
Progressive	Traditional
Repetitive to Confirm Theories	Repetitive to Enhance Images
Concrete	Abstract
Rational	Transcendent
Left-brained	Right-brained
Masculine	Feminine
Logical	Intuitive
Knowledge-based	Wisdom-based
Seeking Control over the World	Seeking Balance with the World

to be constituted of an infinite number of infinitely small straight line segments, which can then each be analyzed. The total curve is then considered to be the sum of its line segments. It is in this sense that we may describe science as *linear* in its orientation. Even tools as powerful as calculus are insufficient for the analysis of closed figures such as circles; to calculate the slope or area of a circle with it, one must chop off the bottom half and consider the two halves separately. As it turns out, the broken circle is a very powerful mythological image with profound consequences for the fate of Western civilization. We shall return to it in the final chapter of this book.

Science is linear in another way, also. It favors *parsimony,* the reduction of elaboration to the simplest possible expression of terms. This derives from the famous fourteenth century axiom of William, Fourth Earl of Occam: *Essentia non sunt multiplicanda præter necessitam,* "Do not multiply essences beyond the necessary." This principle, called Occam's Razor, suggests that the simplest explanation of a phenomenon is the one most likely to be correct. Oversimplification can at times lead to problems. For example, the old geocentric model of the solar system, with its planetary epicycles (loops), was much less parsimonious than the Copernican heliocentric system, so it was put aside in favor of the simpler explanation, which in turn was refined by Kepler, Galileo, and Newton into more elegant mathematical expressions.[11] Yet an observed perturbation of just four minutes of arc in the orbit of Mercury resulted in the replacement of the Newtonian gravitational model by the more complex Einsteinian model of General Relativity.

Science traditionally represents itself as being the product of cumulative knowledge: in Newton's famous statement, "If I have seen far, it is because I have stood on the shoulders of giants."[12] Each generation is expected to add its bit to the knowledge of the last, gradually refining it until it increasingly approximates truth. However, Thomas Kuhn, in his widely quoted study of the history of scientific revolutions, has shown that this is not really how science progresses at all. Instead, there are waves of ideas which sweep each science from time to time, causing rapid and qualitative shifts in perspective to new models, which Kuhn refers to as *paradigms.*[13] Paradigm shifts are not accomplished easily; there is much struggle involved and if one is on the wrong side of the political fence, one's career can be ruined or at least trivialized. Only between times of paradigm shifts is scientific knowledge cumulative, and in such eras there are strong traditions within each field that tend to suppress the few totally new ideas, and no "giants."

There is furthermore no guarantee that older, or less parsimonious paradigms were discarded because they were inherently false. Cultural factors having little to do with absolute truth may influence which paradigms are "politically correct" in each era. For example, English geologists of the early nineteenth century rejected catastrophism in favor of gradual explanations of earth changes, in large part because England had resisted the wave of political revolutions which swept continental Europe during the period 1789–1849, and also in part as a rejection of the overt emphasis on catastrophes such as the Deluge described in biblical and other mythological texts. Gradualism succeeded in becoming the foundation of modern evolutionary biology through Darwin. But we are coming to understand in the late twentieth century that the biosphere is capable of undergoing rapid, violent environmental perturbations even under relatively slight modifications of "normal" conditions, and evolutionary biologists increasingly see these punctuations, rather than the gradual force of natural selection, as causes of the major changes in earth's biological communities.[14] In short, it begins to look as if Kuhn's model of paradigm shift is descriptive not only of science, but, by analogy, of nature itself, and it is no accident that it gained popularity during the decade of the 1960s, a time of social upheaval throughout the industrialized world.[15] Some Complexity theorists have suggested that this self-similarity may not be accidental, but may be a feature of all complex, self-regulating systems.[16] Ironically, this reevaluation is bringing scientific thinking back into line with the very myths it once sought to overthrow.

Science is inherently theoretical in its approach. It requires the formulation of hypotheses, which are then repeatedly tested under field or laboratory conditions. If the steps in an experiment are followed in the precise order and with the precise quantitative measures prescribed, any competent experimenter should arrive at the same results, regardless of his experience. The observer is required not to interact with the observed, lest he introduce bias. For this reason, the observer presumes to subtract himself from the experiment, and attempts to eliminate any sort of personal feeling he may have about the success or failure of the experiment. All is supposed to proceed from detached logic, and all variables must be computed and explained. For the goal of science is no less than the establishment of human control over all phenomena, through a systematic understanding of the forces which produced them.

As we shall see, this goal is not as divorced from the culture of Western civilization in which it arose as scientists would like to think. Science as practiced in the developed world has until rather recently been an inherently male-oriented drive for power whose roots lie in the predominantly masculine orientation of our society, for which reason I have felt it appropriate to cast the preceding sentences exclusively in the male gender. Even if one has only a passing familiarity with Freud's theories of the psyche, it is not too difficult to see that science's emphasis on straight lines might have phallic connotations!

The Way of Myth: The Circle

The goals of myth are dissimilar to those of science. Rather than seeking to control phenomena for the convenience of humanity from the attitude of the detached observer, myths seek to transform the observers themselves so as to retain or restore the balance between the human population and its physical and spiritual environment. Joseph Campbell has suggested that myth has four basic functions: the *Transcendent,* which relates to that which goes beyond the ability of words to describe; the *Cosmological,* which describes how the natural environment of stars, stones, animals, and plants came to be and establishes their relationship to the human world; the *Sociological,* which describes the correct forms of relationships within the human community; and the *Psychological,* which projects for each individual member of the culture in which the myth is told a model against which they can measure their own personal achievement and maturity. All four of these are, in Campbell's view, necessary to the healthy functioning of any society.[17]

By contrast with science, the mythic perspective on the world views it as a holistic unity, with all its parts bound together in an intricate, interlocking system of relationships. The more complex these relationships, the healthier and more robust the system is; therefore myth revels in what classical science would consider unnecessary elaboration and repetition of detail. Because myth considers the whole to be potentially *greater* than the sum of its parts, it is unconcerned with linearity. As we shall see in the succeeding chapters, the same story can be told with some or even all of its details in reverse order without affecting either the outcome or the essential message the myth is trying to convey. It takes a very different kind of mental training to appreciate myths and to derive the messages embedded at various levels within them, one which concentrates on intuitive perceptions of the recurring symbols and their organic relationship to one another, and to the life of the culture, as parts of a holistic fabric.

Thus, whereas the line is an appropriate symbol for science, the circle is an apt description of myth. For the circle is a feminine symbol, one which emphasizes process rather than result, one which binds together all qualities rather than attempting to dissociate them. The relationship of symbols in a myth is like that of points on the circumference of a circle to one another. They are infinitely capable of interconnection in any order, and each has the same relationship to the center of the circle, which contains and generates the inner meanings of the myth. That center can never quite be reached; as one penetrates, one finds layer upon layer of meaning. The circle is therefore symbolic of the gestation process through which the recipient progressively achieves the myth's (and his/her own) inner potential.

In Jungian psychology, which is the branch of psychoanalysis most receptive to myth, the external personality is but the outer manifestation of what Jung calls the Self, the interior psychological reality, which is characteristically constellated at the center of a circle, with radiating lines moving out from it symmetrically to the periphery. This figure, known in Indian ritual art and dance as a *mandala,* has been discussed in detail by Jung:

> As I have said, mandala means "circle." There are innumerable variants of the motif . . . but they are all based upon the squaring of a circle. Their basic motif is the premonition of a centre of personality, a kind of central point within the psyche, to which everything is related, by which everything is arranged, and which is itself a source of energy. The energy of the central point is manifested in the almost irresistible compulsion and urge to *become what one is,* just as every organism is driven to assume the form that is characteristic of its nature, no matter what the circumstances.[18]

While Jung showed that mandalas appear spontaneously in dreams as symbols of wholeness, they are also products of ritual activity, whether they are painted, drawn, danced, or—as in Figure 2—created as sand figures. The act of producing a mandala requires intense mental concentration, a meditative state which must persist for the entire process, which may take days to complete. Properly understood, the symbolism of a mandala tells a story as it unfolds, much like a myth. Working outwards from the center, the ritual artist creates a picture of the world, complete with its

Figure 2: Lama Tenzin Yingyen explains to the author the symbolism of the sand mandala created by Tibetan monks at the National Gathering on Education as Transformation, Wellesley College, 1998. (Photo by Gordon Bernstein)

centrifugal and centripetal forces. In the Avalokiteshvara Mandala shown above, the lotus in the central circle represents the principle of nonattachment to the impermanence of the outer world. The implements in the four petals are the means of overcoming the sins of jealousy, hatred, pride, and ignorance. The quartering of the periphery of the figure plus the center represents the five elements of space, wind, earth, fire, and water respectively. As a further demonstration of impermanence, the mandala itself is destroyed soon after its completion, and the sand is poured into a body of water as the final act in the ritual.

Thus, the circle expresses a totality which focuses attention on the center but includes the observed world as its periphery. As Nicholas of Cusa, a fifteenth century philosopher wrote, as "God is an intelligible sphere whose center is everywhere and whose circumference is nowhere."[19]

As an apologist for myth-based thinking, it is my experience that the inner meanings of myth, which transcend both time and cultural boundaries, exist at a level transcendent to our normal waking consciousness. They can be grasped only by apprehending all the myth's symbolic motifs as a whole, at once, and following them as pointers toward the center of the mythic universe. This is a participatory process, in which the listener can expect to be transformed rather than remaining outside as a spectator. In myth-based cultures, the myth-maker and the audience are bound together within the circle of myth. In many traditional cultures, the narrator and audience actually sit in a circle when myths are told. This enhances the audience's sense of participation in the myth, in contrast to the linear structures of Western classrooms and church pews. I would encourage the reader to read the myths in this book aloud, preferably surrounded by an audience, for I have found in my own classroom experience that this is empowering for both the speaker and the listeners.

When the Line Meets the Circle: The Confusion of the Opposites

The application of linear, scientific thinking to myth has led to considerable confusion, for the assumption of science is that the periphery, the observable universe, is all that exists. One important school of mythology, *structuralism,* holds that myths are logical constructs devoid of content or meaning, and that their real function is to serve as a kind of structure on which society can hang its subsystems.[20] Its chief proponent, Claude Lévi-Strauss, eschewed the idea that myth could have a psychological explanation or that it could have the function of satisfying people's emotional needs. He argued that "the purpose of myth is to provide a logical model capable of overcoming contradiction,"[21] because he thought that myths, as products of purely conscious mental processes, are designed to direct people's attention toward intellectually satisfying explanations of reality. He even subtitled his four-volume *Mythologiques,* "An Introduction to the *Science* of Mythology." In an extreme, almost nihilistic statement at the end of this work, he asserted:

> We have to resign ourselves to the fact that the myths tell us nothing instructive about the order of the world, the nature of reality, or the origin and destiny of mankind. We cannot expect them to flatter any metaphysical thirst, or to breathe new life into exhausted ideologies.[22]

Science is capable of showing us only the ossified shell of myth, for it denies the significance, or even the very existence of any inner message. Remember that for classical science, based upon mathematical models, a circle is nothing more than the sum of the infinitely small straight line-segments which make up its periphery. The same view pertains to the reductionist examination of the variables in myth, each of which may be explained away as arising from this or that environmental adaptation or historical contingency.

It comes as no surprise to those who still base their lives on mythic and religious ideas that so many people today are turning away from the linearity of the West, seeking solace in dreams, mind-altering drugs, or the ornate and still-intact mythic structures of Oriental or Native American cultures. At times it seems as if science and myth/religion are locked into a bad marriage, in which the feminine partner is consistently abused and mistreated by the masculine, and can only respond (as in the case of fetal tissue research or family planning during the Reagan–Bush administrations) by threatening to cut off science's . . . funding.

If no reconciliation between these two partners is able to materialize, it is not difficult to predict the fate of the children of such parents, for we are all the inheritors of their joint influence upon our culture. All we need to do is to look at the long-term, psychological effects of life in the twentieth century. While we have certainly succeeded in increasing the variety of our experiences through access to the media, its quality has suffered. Alienation is rampant, not only in Western society but wherever in the world it has spread its influence. The sociologist Theodore Roszak views this problem as the primary effect of cultural uprooting caused by the technologization of our environment. Citing the poetry of William Blake, he refers to the scientific perspective as "single vision and Newton's sleep."[23]

While the mythic structures of the past emphasized the harmonization of human interests with the environment, most people today no longer feel that they live in harmony with their surroundings, nor even that this is a desirable goal. Nature is somehow against us, and must be controlled, subdued, reduced to statistically predictable responses lest it cause us economic loss. At the very least, modern Westerners demand insurance coverage against natural disasters! This also applies to our inner lives, but because most of us have never been trained to deal with our own psyches, we rush to quick-fix medications, to psychologists or to more unorthodox purveyors of spiritual truths for answers which can, in the end, only credibly be provided by ourselves. Something in us knows that the type of control over the universe we have childishly demanded is ultimately demeaning to the human spirit, even impossible to achieve, and this has led to a great deal of frustration in Western culture. Anxiety and lack of self-assurance or even of self-awareness lead those who can afford it to the analyst's couch. Those billions who cannot are doomed to "lead lives of quiet desperation,"[24] to use Thoreau's phrase, or, as the lack of self-assurance leads to attempts at self-assertion (in search of external acceptance to compensate for what is lacking within), alienation causes acts of an antisocial nature which constitute serious threats both to their enactors and to us all.

It is not to be thought that these problems do not exist in myth-based cultures, but cultures before the industrial revolution exercised subtle psychological controls upon deviant behavior through myths and rituals, cultural mechanisms which most of us profess to believe we have outgrown and discarded as worthless. The exploration of some of these mechanisms is one of the chief purposes of this book. In fact, some myths (as we shall see in Chapter Ten) accurately predict the social outcomes we are now witnessing. The Medieval alchemists refer to this state as the *massa confusa*, an initial state of chaos which results from the premature union of the opposites, followed by the death of the product of the union and a corresponding putrefaction. But this is followed in turn by purification, intensification, and finally transmutation of the base substance into alchemical gold.[25]

When the Circle Meets the Line: The Reintegration of the Opposites

In fairness to science (and here I must assert that, as an archæologist, I consistently practice it, and enjoy it—in its proper place), in the past few decades there has been a movement within many sciences away from simple, linear explanations. *Chaos Theory* and, more recently, *Complexity Theory*, in which systems are assumed to be complex if they are capable of existence, self-representation, and change,[26] are examples of this paradigm shift. Even such bastions of scientific thinking as the total supervenience of physical forces over complex behaviors of organisms have been subject to challenge within science recently. It is now estimated that the ratio of physical particles (baryons) to light (photons) in the universe is on the order of

1:100,000,000.[27] The mathematician Roger Penrose has suggested that consciousness itself may be governed by the laws of quantum mechanics, in which unpredictability is a necessary feature of the system.[28] And David Chalmers has presented an elegant and detailed proof that consciousness is irreducible to physical phenomena.[29] These new ideas may require a thorough restructuring of the way in which science, and the mathematics which underlie it, are approached. Several writers have noticed that this new way of thinking has significant points of contact with the traditional approaches which are found in myth. As Fritjof Capra has noted:

> For the modern physicists, then, Shiva's dance is the dance of subatomic matter. As in Hindu mythology, it is a continual dance of creation and destruction involving the whole cosmos; the basis of all existence and of all natural phenomena. . . . The bubble-chamber photographs of interacting particles . . . are visual images of the dance of Shiva equalling those of the Indian artists in beauty and profound significance. The metaphor of the cosmic dance thus unifies ancient mythology, religious art, and modern physics. It is, as Coomaraswamy has said, "poetry, but none the less science."[30]

Participants at a recent conference of renowned scientists, as reported in that bastion of orthodoxy, *Scientific American,* are making remarks like, "The inability of science to provide a basis for meaning, purpose, value, and ethics is evidence of the necessity of religion," and, "I have experiences that cannot be expressed in any language other than that of religion. Whether the myths are historically true or false is not so important."[31]

Even in my own field of American archæology, which tends to lag behind the other sciences by at least fifteen years, signs of this restructuring are emerging, for we are increasingly required by Federal legislation to deal fairly with traditional Native cultures over the issue of reburial of human remains, grave goods, and sacred objects. Interaction with peoples whose ideational universe, while seriously impaired by five centuries of contact with European culture, retains a considerable measure of its connectedness with the land, has evoked a surprisingly sympathetic response among many of the supposedly hard-boiled scientists of material culture. As well, the advent of feminism in archaeology has spurred a reexamination of the field's male-dominated theoretical framework, even implying that there is value in reconsidering the hermetic, myth-based philosophies that were rejected by classical science starting in the colonial era.[32] In my opinion, these are hopeful signs. Perhaps our intellectual culture is evolving to a point where both myth and science will be seen as relevant ways of approaching knowledge about both the self and the universe.

Mythic Literacy: An Idea for Our Times

If my only purpose in this study were to decry the loss of myth as the cause of our present deplorable condition, it would have little worth. If myth were really dead in the human soul, there would be no point in trying to resurrect it, and the study of mythology could be relegated to nostalgia. In this book I shall attempt to show you that myth is very much alive, and not only in those corners of the world which have resisted the impact of Western civilization. From my own teaching and experiencing of myth, I must take exception to Lévi–Strauss' nihilism. I have frequently been informed by my students that their dreams have been significantly enriched by the study of myth (as have my own), and not a few have felt, as do I, that it has changed their lives. This is not because of any special ability I personally have to communicate, but because myths, even from cultures other than our own, are still quite potent enough to evoke a response in our psyches. Indeed, I have already suggested that myths can describe our present social condition with chilling accuracy, and some of them can even suggest creative solutions to it. The archetypal symbols of myth pound at our doors and demand recognition, not only in our dreams and visions, but in the events of the world around us, if we know how to read them.

Mythic literacy, therefore, is one of the chief goals of this text. By this I do not mean a familiarity with the plot lines of a few ancient Greek stories (which is what occurs to most people today when they think of myths), either in their bloodless Victorian versions or worse, in the cheap popularizations of characters drawn from these stories fed to us by the cinematic and television media (e.g., *Hercules* or *Xena*). Instead, I mean an ability to understand the processes by which myth weaves its magic spell in all cultures including our own, and to appreciate the contents of which that spell commonly consists across many cultures. We do not need to look to the Greeks for myths (though we certainly shall, especially in Chapter Four), because myths are being played out before our eyes every day upon the stage of history. We shall return to this idea from time to time throughout the book, but especially in Chapter Ten.

To respond to the problem of the decline of myth in Western civilization, comparative mythology offers the following solution. If our own myths have become so fragmented and meaningless that we no longer can follow them reliably to the common human center, we might find that the circle may be reconstructed by placing myths side by side with their correlative myths in other cultures. People never tire of hearing new stories, even though in our jaded modern quest for newness, the old tales tend to pale upon incessant repetition. Yet if the message the myths seek to convey is to strike home, it must be repeated—that is precisely what traditional storytellers do. Therefore, I shall juxtapose several stories from cultures around the world in such a manner that what one culture lacks another by chance or design has maintained, even though it may not be possible to analyze the reasons for this in each case. By repeatedly circling the periphery in this way, we will find that we can gradually get a clearer picture of the circle as a whole, and also achieve some measure of penetration into its core.

An Itinerary of Our Journey

What we shall be doing in the remainder of this book is to explore a series of key myths—seven principal ones, with several related variants for each—which I shall refer to as numbered stories, for easy reference. Each story will first be presented as a text and then analyzed, especially with reference to the cultural context in which it was originally told. At first, the depth of analytical detail may seem daunting, and it may seem to readers that they are going around and around in circles. We *are* going to circle the world on our mythic journey, starting with the Celtic cultures and heading more or less eastwards until we return to our starting point. In fact, our course is more of a spiral in keeping with David Lindsay's image of the tower with its spiral staircase. As we proceed, the circles will become tighter and tighter as certain common threads become apparent. Because I am trying to explore myth through operations isomorphous to its structure, I tend to adopt an acausal approach. Like Lévi–Strauss' four-volume *Mythologiques,* this book *itself* may be regarded, both analytically and synthetically, as a myth.[33]

The seven key myths have been chosen not because they are better, truer, or more representative than any others, but simply because they span the globe yet are closely linked together both in theme and specific imagery. They thus allow a larger story to be told by comparing them, and by weaving into the texture other myths from the same and other cultures. As we proceed forwards, I will weave backwards to the material we have already covered. At times, the texture may become quite dense, but it should be possible for the reader to follow the threads as we proceed gradually from the simple to the more complex. A combination of analytical, mental comprehension with synthetic, intuitional apprehension will enable the reader to most fully appreciate the resulting composite story, which is at once an exploration of the ways myths may be understood and a discourse on the value that myths may still hold for our culture. In the final chapter, I shall return to this overarching theme and attempt to show what role myth may have in steering the future of our civilization. The bibliography and set of endnotes provided at the end of the book are for readers who wish to pursue the issues I have raised further. The glossary defines key terms.

It might be argued that I have loaded the dice by choosing myths that show the correlations I wish to emphasize, or that all of these comparisons only serve to show the train of my own thinking. But the body of recorded world myth is enormously large, and one must make some selections—even Frazer did this for his twelve-volume *The Golden Bough.* I would encourage readers to study myths not covered, or only superficially covered in this text, because I am confident that they will find the burden of world mythic thought to be consistent with what I present here. I continually encounter myths I have not previously read which fit remarkably well into the framework I have constructed. Once you become familiar with the terms, you can share in the thrill of discovering these connections, the sense of wonder this engenders, and the cumulative, transformative effect mythic thinking can have upon your understanding of the world of myth, and of human society in general. That is why, before we embark on our mythic journey through space and time, we will need to spend some time looking at the terms in Chapter Two.

And finally, for the skeptics, I would like to offer a suggestion made by Ursula LeGuin, well-known author of science fiction and daughter of the eminent archæologist Alfred Kroeber, that we may differentiate "reality" into two modes: *factuality* and *truth.* By the former, LeGuin means that which can be discerned about the universe through the senses, abetted by the instruments whose development has been the cornerstone of modern science. By the latter, she means those things which are *permanently* true about the human condition, which are perhaps most clearly addressed via the medium of myth.[34] As another fantasy writer, Orson Scott Card, put it:

> Nothing that is new is ever new twice. While things that are true are still true the next time; truer, in fact, because they have been tested, they have been tasted, and they are always ripe, always ready.[35]

Much of the scientific critique of myth has been based upon the superior ability of science to elucidate the factual world. But the relevance of myth for explaining the operations of psyche and society, both at the individual and the collective level, and for denoting the relationship of these to the transcendent, has not in the least been diminished by the advent of science, which is why it continually reemerges in genres like science fiction. This is also the province of anthropology, for, as Alexander Pope asserted long ago, "the proper study of mankind is Man."[36] As the necessity for the study of myth in its cultural context becomes clearer to science, perhaps these two modes of perception will be able to engage in the kind of respectful dialogue about the universe and our place in it that characterizes the Maya creation myth with which this chapter began.

CHAPTER TWO

APPROACHES TO MYTHOLOGICAL ANALYSIS

Early Attempts to Understand Myth

When sixteenth century European intellectuals received accounts of the myths and rituals of Native peoples in the colonies their nations had established in the New World, Africa, and the western Pacific, they realized they would have to expand their narrow Medieval framework for understanding humanity (Figure 3). For example, the Spanish conquistadors of Mexico were scandalized by the similarity they observed between Aztec human sacrifice and the Catholic Mass. They devised a number of explanations for this similarity, including the idea that the Aztecs were not really human but were demons placed on earth to tempt the faithful.[1] This belief was used by the Spanish as a rationale for their political program of cultural subjugation and genocide, and formed the pattern for the subsequent oppression of Native peoples in the Western Hemisphere and elsewhere.

In 1533 after Pope Leo issued a Bull proclaiming the Native people of the Americas to be human, the Spanish developed an alternative explanation: the Aztecs had been missionized by the wandering apostle Thomas, but had been out of contact with the Mother Church for centuries and their practice of Christianity had degenerated.[2] This revised belief in turn became a rationale for establishing missions to the Indians, to *reconvert* them to what the Spanish were convinced was the True Faith. The main point of Pope Leo's pronouncement was to assert that the Native peoples were endowed with souls, meaning that it was incumbent upon the faithful to convert them to Christianity, by main force if necessary. In practice, the missions were re-

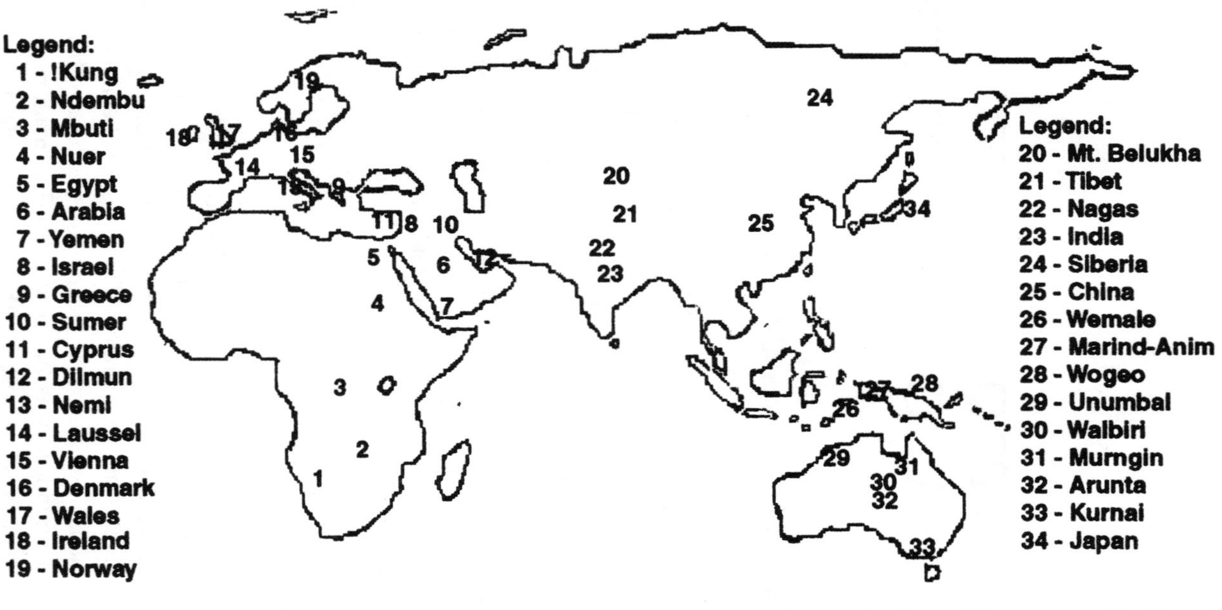

Figure 3: Old World map, showing distribution of cultures mentioned in the text. (Adapted from a map distributed by the National Oceanic and Atmospheric Administration)

ally not much more lenient than the previous program of genocide. In Puritan New England, the same belief in Native recidivism is reflected in statements by several ministers that the local Indians needed to be "reduced" to Christianity, for in seventeenth century English "reduce" did not mean to diminish, but to lead back to a (presumed) previous state of grace.[3]

Some eighteenth century Enlightenment scholars, notably Bernard Fontenelle and Giambattista Vico, suggested that the similarity between the myths of the two hemispheres derived from general cultural or environmental similarities between them. For example, Fontenelle (1657–1757) suggested that the Incas and the Greeks had similar myths about lake spirits because such stories naturally arise in lake environments. He also cynically regarded the chief function of the marvels found in myths was to allow their narrators to enjoy the favor of their audiences: "One is flattered by the surprise and admiration one causes in his audience and is quite happy to augment it further, since something in this seems to please our vanity."[4]

Vico (1668–1744) constructed a whole historical round for cultures outside of the Judæo-Christian dispensation, in which peoples passed through a repetitive four-stage cycle in their search for truth, beginning with a focus on power, then on ethics and the family, then on civilized discourse, and finally, a collapse (*recorso*) leading back to the first stage. He felt that the similarities between distant peoples could be explained according to where along his cycle they were. This is an early example of the idea of creating a myth to explain myths. He was one of the first to acknowledge that "uniform ideas originating among entire peoples unknown to each other must have a common ground of truth."[5] Vico's influence on later generations was great, and his four-age cycle forms the basis of the structure of James Joyce's *Finnegans Wake.*

Some Nineteenth and Twentieth Century Theories about Myth

Later investigators have often attempted to see the commonalities in myth as reflections of their own leading research interests. Some of the more important theories are listed below:

- *Myths reflect important historical processes, such as the establishment of patriarchal social systems over primordial matriarchies.* This idea was championed by Karl Ottfried Müller (1779–1840). His idea was to mine myth for information on the history of religions, and he found "sufficient traces and remnants of a state of the Grecian religion, in which the gods were considered as exhibiting their power chiefly in the operations of outward nature, in the changes of the season, and the phenomena of the year."[6] He was one of the first to document the succession of invading cultures in ancient Greece, which in his view resulted in the replacement of this older, mother-based (Pelasgian) religions by a new, "heroic" faith based upon the worship of a masculine sky god, Zeus.

- *Myths are the textual or oral remnants of the widespread distribution of agricultural fertility rituals.* The "Myth and Ritual School" claimed that myths were the misunderstood relics of religious rituals, many of which had disappeared while the myths lingered on. Sir James Frazer (1854–1941), its most famous exponent, was really the first scholar to compile the accounts of ethnographers on a global scale, and to observe the similarities among the myths of hundreds of cultures, which he felt was a reflection of their grounding in a shared ritual tradition of great antiquity. But he also considered the entirety of myth, ritual, and magic to be "one great disastrous fallacy, a mistaken conception of the association of ideas."[7]

- *Myths derive from a common linguistic heritage, coupled with an interest in astronomical phenomena, but the original forms have become garbled through cultural isolation.* This idea was promoted by Max Müller (1823–1900), a formidable Sanskritist who observed striking similarities between myths throughout the areas occupied by speakers of Indo-European languages. He considered that the differences could be explained on the basis of puns or misunderstandings of words between different linguistic communities; hence his famous statement that "Myth is a disease of language."[8] He also directed the attention of mythologists toward the importance of the names of mythological characters and to their correspondences to astronomical and meteorological phenomena.

- *Myths originate from an underlying instinctive or intuitive substrate common to human consciousness in all cultures.* Sigmund Freud's (1856–1939) view that myths, dreams, and the visions of schizophrenics derive from the same unconscious source is his fundamental contribution to the study of myth. His theory that this source lies in neonatal experience, or that it reflects a prehistoric traumatic event in the life of protohumans, is more questionable; we shall explore this in Chapter Eight.[9] Carl Gustav Jung (1875–1961) began his researches under Freud's direction, but later broke with him over the issue of the primacy of sexuality as the common denominator of myth and dream. His ideas of the collective unconscious as the residuum for all human experience, and of archetypal images as characteristic contents of the unconscious which emerge repeatedly in the psyches of humans everywhere, are his primary contributions to mythology.[10]

- *Myths are adaptive devices for survival or economic success under particular environmental constraints.* The cultural materialist school, of which Marvin Harris (1927–) is a leading exponent, views all human adaptations, myths included, as reflections of the strategies humans need to develop in order to interact with their particular environments. The myths are seen as rationalizations of these strategies, which people would not accept were they not clothed in attractive garb. For example, Harris tries to explain the prohibitions on the eating of pork in Middle Eastern cultures (Jews and Arabs) as a response to the desiccating conditions of the climate of that region during the Holocene epoch, which made it more difficult to raise pigs there.[11]
- *Myths are attempts to work out a structure which logically explains a people's place within the universe.* This is the position of the Structuralist School of anthropology, the chief exponent of which is Claude Lévi-Strauss (1908–). His perspective was that humans always operate on the basis of logic, and that myths are therefore logical products of human minds endeavoring to structure their relationship to one another, and to their environment. In his view, myths are "good to think."[12]

For our purposes, we may consider each of these approaches as having value, but I would strongly contend that *any* unitary approach to myth will be inadequate to cover all situations. In the course of this book, I shall employ all of them, insofar as I consider them appropriate to the particular myths we are studying. There is no reason to assume, as rationalistic science would have us do, that myths may be *reduced* to any one formula or theoretical perspective. The richness of myths derives in large measure from their being inherently *multidimensional:* they are capable of being appreciated and interpreted in many ways at once, without any one perspective being considered the "final" analysis to the exclusion of the others. In some cases, we will be able to determine that one or another of these approaches is preferable to explain *something* about a particular myth, but myths are always open-ended to new interpretations which do not necessarily invalidate older ones.

Cross-Cultural Comparisons: The Origins of Mortality, and the Magic Flute

To explore the similarity that can be observed between distant cultures, let us begin by considering the following Blackfoot Indian tale:

> *As they were standing by the river, the first woman asked Old Man, her creator, "How is it? Shall we always live, shall there be no end to it?" And he said, "I have never thought of that. We must decide. I shall take this chip of dried buffalo dung and throw it into the river. If it floats, people will die but in four days become alive again; they will die for only four days. But if it sinks, there will be an end of them." He tossed the chip into the river and it floated. The woman turned and picked up a stone and said, "No, it is not to be like that. I shall throw this stone into the river, and if it floats we shall live forever, but if it sinks people must die, so that they may feel pity for each other and feel sorrow for each other." The woman threw the stone into the water and it sank. "There!" said Old Man. "You have chosen. And so that is the way it shall be."*[13]

Essentially the same myth is told by the Nuer people of southern Sudan, with the sole substitution of a gourd for the piece of buffalo dung and a potsherd for the stone.[14] Among the Wemale people of the Indonesian island of Ceram, whose myths we shall study in detail in Chapter Six, there is a similar dialogue between a banana tree and a rock; in this case, the tree prevails, and thus arranges for human propagation, but the rock proclaims that man will also have to die.[15] This type of speculation is not limited to so-called "primitive" cultures. Readers familiar with Joyce's *Finnegans Wake* may be reminded of the twilight dialogue between Shaun, the stone, who "points the deathbone and the quick are still," and Shem, the tree, who "lifts the lifewand and the dumb speak."[16]

The Blackfeet live on the eastern slopes of the Rockies in Montana and Alberta, and they once hunted buffalo in the Plains. The Nuer are cattle-breeders and raise gourds for vessels; they live in the Nile floodplain where there is little stone, but they make pottery. The Wemale live on the tropical volcanic island of Ceram, where bananas are a mainstay of their diet. It is not difficult to see how the constraints of their environment could have led each of these peoples to select different items to determine the fate of human beings, but it is harder to see how these constraints would have resulted in the similar idea of a dialogue leading to this choice. Appealing to environmental diversity helps us to explain the differences among these three myths, but not the similarities. It is extremely unlikely that these three cultures on three different continents could ever have been in any kind of direct contact with one another to share myths. But the question of human mortality is a central concern of myth in all cultures, as we shall see.

Another example is a story told by the Mehinaku people of the southern part of the Amazon basin. According to these isolated hunter–gatherers, there was a time when the women had control of the ritual life of the tribe and had in their possession large wooden flutes that they played to mediate between the human and the spirit worlds. The men eventually rebelled against this and took possession of the flutes, forbidding the women to view them under the threat of gang rape or even death. The ritual practice associated with this myth continues to the present day, and involves the initiation of boys into the mystery of the flutes.[17] Essentially the same story is told by the Wogeo people, who live on a small island north of New Guinea, and it is associated there with a very similar ritual practice—except that in their foundation myth it is the women who made the first flutes who debar other women from them, because a young male character disturbed them.[18] Adolescent male Mbuti pygmies of north-central Congo employ enormously long wooden tubes (called *molimo*) as musical instruments, and they informed Colin Turnbull that they forbid women to observe them when they are brought into the village.[19] Turnbull relates, however, that once he became fully familiar with the Mbuti's ritual life he did observe women singing the *molimo* songs which he had been led to suppose they were prohibited from knowing.[20] Thomas Gregor similarly records that the Mehinaku women are well aware of the flutes kept in the men's lodges but choose not to reveal their knowledge, to preserve the appearance of gender separation.[21] Ian Hogbin indicates that the Wogeo women are also well aware of the flutes and the rituals surrounding them, and engage in their own rituals in what he regards as a form of mockery of the men's rites.[22] This kind of story is also not restricted to "primitive" cultures: a similar tale about the transfer of magical power from the female to the male domain, via a wind instrument, is at the heart of Eduard Schickaneder's libretto for Mozart's *The Magic Flute*. Once again, it is difficult to imagine direct contact between these four widely dispersed peoples, yet all four of them share the common element of a long, tubular ritual musical instrument which has become the sole social property of the men, especially the young men.

Freudians, no doubt, would have little difficulty in interpreting this as deriving from the universal need of pubescent males to express their sexuality (the hollow flute as a phallic symbol) and to separate from their maternal attachments; indeed, this is precisely how similar initiatory rites in Australia are interpreted by Géza Róheim.[23] Yet this approach would overlook the specific ritual functions that the flutes serve—especially in Mbuti culture, where sexually active males are not permitted to carry the *molimo* trumpet, whose appearance is used as a corrective to divisive forces within adult society.[24]

Mythologists have long observed these kinds of parallels, and their curiosity about this has led them to struggle to understand what mechanism could account for such a great similarity of detail among myths from such distantly separated cultures. Generally speaking, there have been three solutions proposed to this problem, none of which is necessarily mutually exclusive of any of the others: *diffusion, psychic unity,* and *independent invention.*

The Argument for Diffusion

Diffusionism is the theory that myths, as well as other cultural traits, have been spread from one culture to another over time. Contact between cultures has led to borrowing, in whole or in part, of myths and the beliefs that they reflect. Some researchers, particularly in the late nineteenth and early twentieth century (e.g., Robert Heine-Geldern), were convinced that there were "cultural hearths," centers of "high" civilization from which myths were diffused over a wide area. In the more extreme statements of the theory, cultural advancements diffused from these centers all over the world.[25] This form of hyperdiffusionism was rooted in the political ideology of the time, because it assumed that the distribution of certain myths indicated the social inferiority or superiority of the cultures in which they were found, depending upon their proximity in time and space to the presumed source of the myths. This view was based upon the experience of the past two thousand years of European and Middle Eastern history, which was the time of the rapid spread of militant Christianity and Islam. Diffusionists presumed that the myths of superior cultures could be forced upon peoples who did not already possess them, or whose myths were inferior—almost in a Darwinian sense of competition and survival of the fittest. These "superior" cultures were almost always identified as European in origin or were claimed to stem from the early civilizations of the Near East: Mesopotamia, Egypt, or Syria–Palestine. It is not difficult to see this as thinly veiled ethnocentrism and as a rationalization of colonialism.

In the aftermath of World War II and the collapse of the Nazis' grandiose political schemes of racial superiority, more careful diffusionist researchers have confined their studies to more limited areas. They have found that many mythological ideas are deeply rooted in a particular region's cultural and environmental realities. The idea of superior and inferior cultures which are respectively donors and recipients of myth is now rejected by most anthropologists. Franz Boas, the father of *cultural relativism,* categorically rejected the idea that "the mental character of a primitive tribe is the cause of its low culture." He suggested instead that variability is more a matter of historical contingency: "no large populations of alien races are placed in a position in which they are socially and politically equal to Whites and enjoy the same opportunities for intellectual, economical, and social development."[26] Anthropologists today prefer to consider all cultures as open-ended systems, potentially capable of adopting ideas from other cultures and working them dynamically into their own myths, sometimes without adopting the underlying beliefs.

Mythic Adaptation: The Story of Santo Cristo

Even in situations where a foreign mythic structure like Christianity has been imposed upon a native population, the local inhabitants may retain an impressive ability to recast the new symbols into old forms. The following tale, from the Tzeltal Maya of the highlands of southern Mexico, will illustrate this point:

> *Many, very many years ago, men and women only lived to about thirteen or fourteen years of age. They grew up in two or three weeks and were already old when they reached that age. Those people fought a great*

deal among themselves; they were always killing one another. Much blood was spilt and the foul smell of it reached to heaven and annoyed God very much.

God was already much displeased over it, and Santo Cristo (Christ) began advising him that all the men and women should be killed once and for all, so that they should not continue fighting and infesting heaven with the smell of their blood. God then gave Santo Cristo permission to kill all the people. As this one is a very bad person, he was delighted. With his big cape made of reeds, Cristo fulfilled his mission, making torrents of water flow from the reeds. Thus all the earth was flooded, as if it were one great ocean. Naturally, all the people died. Nothing was left, only water.

But as God is good, he gave life again to all the men and women and, of course, that made Cristo sad. Soon he began to beg God for permission to kill all the people again. When Santo Tómas learned of the plot of Santo Cristo he warned God that what he proposed was very bad. He convinced him that it would be much better to let the poor people live out their lives instead of only thirteen or fourteen years. God agreed with Santo Tómas, but he did not know how to tell Cristo that he would not permit him to drown the people as before, especially since Cristo was so determined to do it. Finally, Santo Tómas and God decided to make a fiesta for Cristo and get him drunk on chicha (their fermented ritual drink), as it would be easier to convince him in that state.

The following day all the saints and their wives gathered. They sat down in a circle to drink chica and to chat, as we do when we have a fiesta. But Cristo did not want to participate, and remained outside, looking on. He would not drink any chica, for he said, "I, no; I'm not going to drink your chica because then I shall get drunk and shall not be able to drown all the people of earth tomorrow with my stream of water."

Cristo resisted all temptation in spite of the fact that God himself, Santo Tómas, and his wife, Santa Maria, explained all the merits of the drink with respect to taste, fragrance, and quality. Cristo paid no attention to them, maintaining himself firm in his plans. But Santo Tómas did not lose hope. He knew that in some way he had to make Santo Cristo drunk, so that he would be unable to carry out his evil intentions. He pondered until finally he found a solution. He made movements like little circles with his right index finger on his other hand and a little cup of aguardiente (a cactus liqueur) or brandy appeared in the palm of his hand. Until then no one had ever tasted that drink. Santo Tómas invented it to be able to make Cristo drunk. As it tastes much better than chica, not even Cristo could resist it.

Now Santo Tómas, armed with his little cup of brandy, returned to Cristo's side and offered it to him. At first he refused it but little by little Santo Tómas broke his resistance by making him smell it and describing it. "Very well, I shall take a little drink but just one, only to taste it," said Cristo. As is natural, after the first drink he wanted more and more. He continued drinking until very late that night when he was so full and so drunk that he could not drink another drop. Santo Tómas and God also drank much aguardiente but they never get drunk.

When Santo Cristo awoke the next morning, he had a terrible hangover. He looked around him and did not know where he was until he recalled the fiesta of the previous night, but now there was no one around. All the saints had returned to their huts, leaving Cristo alone on the ground. Then he looked down at himself and jumped up in surprise because he saw that he was naked. The night before his companions had undressed him, and he was so drunk that he was not even aware of it. Now upon finding himself naked, he began to run in search of the saints to ask them where they had hidden his clothes.

Santo Cristo was not so much worried about the loss of his clothes as of his cape of reeds, which he needed to throw over the earth the water with which to put an end to the lives of the people. By simply shaking the cape, torrents of water burst forth from every reed. For this reason Cristo went about looking for it with great anxiety. He asked every one of the saints where they had hidden his cape but not one of them answered him. Cristo became desperate; he did not know what to do. Finally, Santo Tómas said to him, "I'm going to tell you where your cape is but even then you will not be able to find it. Last night we tore it to pieces and threw the reeds away over all the hills of the earth." Because of this there are so many waterholes on the hills, for everywhere that a piece of Cristo's cape fell, a waterhole appeared.

Upon hearing this, Cristo began to complain bitterly. "Ah," he said, "Now I cannot drown the people because I haven't even a cape." Instead of paying any attention to his complaints, all the saints jumped on him and tied him with ropes to a post. They tied him well, so that he could never escape, because they knew if he succeeded in untying himself from the post and escaping, then he would again insist on killing all the people. After tying him they took him far away, very far, way beyond where

> *the sun sets, and there they left him tied to the post, so that he should never return to do harm.*
>
> *Some years ago a tremor of the earth was felt, as if someone were shaking it. Then all the saints went off to the west where they had left Cristo tied to the post, for they knew that he was trying to escape by breaking his ropes and that because of this the earth shook. Fortunately, Santo Tómas arrived in time to tie him up again with even stronger ropes. They say that roots have sprouted from under the post to hold him more securely. Still the earth continues shaking. Whenever that happens we know that Cristo is trying to free himself from the post.*[27]

This fantastic story recombines elements of biblical tales, particularly the story of Noah and the Flood and Noah's subsequent drunkenness and disrobing, in a creative fashion that would doubtless have given the Catholic priesthood conniption fits, had they been aware of it.[28] But it is true to the structure of mythic imagery, for the motif of drunkenness is often associated with (or is metaphorical for) a flooding of the world. Psychologically, Cristo's unconscious stupor (in which he is deprived of the opportunity to bring about the Flood) is a kind of drowning of his conscious ego. This is similar to Lucien Lévy–Bruhl's description of the primitive mind always living in fear of a "lowering of mental level."[29] The motif of nakedness will be considered in more detail in Chapters Four and Five.

The Tzeltal story also gives a bizarre twist to the New Testament story of the Crucifixion, with the figure of Christ tied to a post. Certainly the references to biblical characters owe something to the imposition of Christianity on the Maya following the Spanish conquest. But in addition the myth reflects, as through a glass darkly, an older, pre-European substrate: the widely distributed Aztec–Toltec myth of Quetzalcoatl (Maya: Kukulcan) (Figure 4). This plumed serpent god of the rain, surnamed *Ce Acatl* (One-Reed), vainly hid himself from the people in his palace. His adversary, Tezcatlipoca (Lord Smoking Mirror), disguising himself as a merchant, magically appeared before Quetzalcoatl and sold him one of his famous obsidian mirrors. Quetzalcoatl became enamored of his reflection, got drunk on *chicha,* slept with his own sister, and was so ashamed of what he had done that he departed for the east on a raft of serpents, resolving to return on his name day (One-Reed, One-Reed in their double calendar system) to visit disaster on all his people. The Mesoamericans believed that the coincidence of specific days in their calendar were omens of potential world destruction, and that the current world would be destroyed by an earthquake.[30]

Figure 4: Quetzalcoatl, the feathered serpent. Relief from Teotihuacan, Mexico, 4th century A.D. (Corbis)

One of the ironies of history is that Good Friday in April, 1519, when Cortés landed at Vera Cruz, was one of the unluckiest days in the Aztec calendar. Cortés was mistaken for the fair, bearded god—his arrival certainly was disastrous for all the Native peoples of Mexico. Yet the influence of the older religion lives on. Tezcatlipoca is the master of earthquakes, and the cathedral of St. Thomas, the patron saint of Mexico, was built directly on top of the ruins of his temple in Mexico City. This cathedral survived the major earthquake of 1984 intact while much of the surrounding city was destroyed. So the old god, under a new name, is still proof against earthquakes! While Lafaye[31] claims that Santo Tómas was more commonly an alias for Quetzalcoatl himself, the two gods also were referred to as White Tezcatlipoca and Black Tezcatlipoca and were, as we shall later see, close allies in the Aztec creation of the universe. We shall explore the motif of sibling incest in Chapters Eight and Nine.

Another myth probably reflected in the Tzeltal Maya tale is the Quiche Maya story of the third race of men, who were puppets made of wood and were unable to converse with one another or to worship the gods. The gods resolved to destroy them and sent a flood. Only after this did Tepeu and Gúcumatz create the fourth, modern race of men.[32] The number thirteen (the age the people had reached when Santo Cristo would flood them) is a significant symbol in Maya numerology and chronology; it refers to the levels of the heavenly realm, as well as to their calendar. From what we can now read of the Maya writing, internecine warfare was indeed endemic to this area prior to the arrival of the Spanish and their "new" god. The Spanish also introduced hard liquor (*agua ardiente*), whereas *chica* is an indigenous drink. Notice that the "sin" which led to the destruction of the third race is their failure to participate in conversation, which as we saw in Chapter One was the fundamental basis of the Maya creation.

This myth demonstrates clearly that even under circumstances of political and religious oppression, people are perfectly capable of taking the myths of the conquerors and realigning them to their own purposes, even blending them with their own. The distinctly negative role assigned to Christ in the myth, and his peculiar crucifixion by the saints themselves, may be a way in which the native people can thumb their noses at the Church while retaining the elements of their pre-Christian polytheistic beliefs. The names have been changed, as they say, to protect the innocent! While we know that diffusion has taken place here, any attempt to allege that it is the main mechanism at work must account for the way in which the myth has been incorporated into the existing mythic structure of the culture that borrowed it, rather than simply assuming that the transmission will be direct and unaltered. Sometimes the character of a people is retained in spite of or even by means of diffusion. This should suggest to us that myth is hardy enough to survive even under the most repressive of political conditions—or even that it *must* survive if the people for whom it has meaning are to escape extinction themselves. It is almost impossible to conceive of displaced peoples like the Jews, the Gypsies, the Cherokees, or (in the latter half of the twentieth century) the Tibetans surviving long without the strong traditions provided by a living corpus of myth to support them.

The Argument for Psychic Unity

Psychic unity is the view that there is somehow an underlying connection among all peoples of the world that does not depend upon physical contact between cultures for transmission of ideas. In this view, all cultures share a common heritage that is maintained as central to the culture and which consciously or unconsciously generates similar mythological images and ideas independent of cultural contact. Variants of this theory suggest that the common ground derives from prehistoric common experience that has somehow become socially, or even genetically encoded. The Swiss psychologist C.G. Jung concluded that the mythological images reside in a *collective unconscious,* from which they continually rise to the surface of consciousness.[33] This collective unconscious differs from Freud's concept of the Id in that Jung viewed it as a source of wisdom, rather than merely the seat of animal instincts. His conclusions, based upon a lifetime of psychoanalytic research, clinical practice, and self-study, are slowly gaining ground over the more reductionist Freudian interpretations, especially among "New Age" adherents. Some of the latter have extended the theory to suggest that the core concepts around which the myths form are maintained at a superconscious or telepathic level by a network of psychically gifted individuals: supershamans or adepts who have been initiated into the Mysteries.[34] These approaches all have in common the idea that mythic imagery is inherent within the human constitution, and its meaning is potentially accessible to people in every culture in the same way, through dreams, rituals, and the retelling of myths.

A serious drawback of this approach is that in its quest for universality, it tends to overlook the sociocultural fabric from which the myths arise. In anthropology, we must always be careful to work from the ethnographic particulars toward generalizations, rather than the reverse. Thus, we shall have to establish the cultural context for each of the myths before we can begin to allege cross-cultural psychic connections between them. Nor is there yet any good genetic basis for assuming that *specific* mythic structures are hard-wired into our brains. Jung was writing at a time when the belief in a heritable racial consciousness was prevalent. This idea has since fallen out of favor, especially because of its association with Nazi racial propaganda. In his defense, Jung did not actively embrace the extremes of racial theory. He abhorred Nazism, and he professed not to know the ultimate origin of the contents of the collective unconscious.

However, there is some new biochemical evidence that suggests that the *capacity* for mythic imagination is indeed heritable and resides in the deep structures of the brain. Anthony Stevens argues that instinctive reactions may be responsible for certain deeply ingrained symbols: for example, the well-documented aversion of primates to snakes may condition the frequent appearance of ophidian symbols in myths and dreams.[35] Researchers investigating the development of neuronal connections within the brain have also found evidence of consistent "packets" or "modules" of neurons that may turn out to be the physical correlate to the archetypes.[36] Whether this provides any evidence for psychic contact between adepts of different cultures is far from being proven, yet at the very least it would provide a common framework for cross-cultural understanding if individuals of different traditions happened to meet and share one another's stories.

Similarities perceived under this explanation, either within or between myths, are referred to as *isomorphisms*. Isomorphism is a device that compares things that appear alike in form, even though very different in scale. Certainly the easiest way for us to first grasp difficult concepts is to form analogies to that which we already know. Isomorphism is often used to teach popular science: for example, the structure of the Niels Bohr model of the atom, with its electrons orbiting a central nucleus, is isomorphous to the structure of the solar system. Despite the fact that physicists now conceive of electrons as probability states rather than particles, the image is still a useful model. The anthropologist Clifford Geertz has suggested that mythological structures function for cultures in two ways, as *models of* and as *models for* reality. In the first case, the myth describes the way the universe factually *appears* to be; in the second, it models the way in which a universe peopled by humans of that culture *ought* to be.[37] Isomorphisms can be used for both functions, but it is with the second function that we are most concerned, for this book is an anthropological approach to myth, not a text in astrophysics. Isomorphisms used in this way do not necessarily imply causality, but rather posit a set of perceived relationships which are useful in establishing cultural values.

This acausal kind of connection, referred to as *synchronicity* in the writings of C.G. Jung,[38] was common in late Medieval European natural philosophy, where it was called the "Doctrine of Signatures." The rationalistic science of the Enlightenment made much of its ability to debunk the factual claims of the Doctrine of Signatures as a *model of* the universe, since it was often possible to disprove the validity of its associations on the basis of cause and effect reasoning. For example, astrology, which appears to posit a geocentric universe, was (and still is) the target of scientific derision. But this should not prevent us from exploring cultural contexts in which astrological symbols are active components in the life of the imagination. As Jung points out:

> I do not hesitate to take the synchronistic phenomena that underlie astrology seriously. Just as there is an eminently psychological reason for the existence of alchemy, so too in the case of astrology. Nowadays it is no longer interesting to know how far these two fields are aberrations; we should rather investigate the psychological foundations on which they rest.[39]

But only in the most superficial, mechanistic sense was the Doctrine of Signatures ever intended to imply linear causality. Instead, it functioned as a gigantic metaphor, a *model for,* whose real purpose was to structure human behavior within the context of the perceptible universe. Science has not succeeded in replacing that function of the older system; it tells us what we might do in the universe but not why we should or should not do it.

The Argument for Independent Invention

Independent invention is the concept that different cultures are likely to devise similar structures, whether in myth or in other aspects of social life, not because they have borrowed them from each other or because they are in psychic or unconscious contact, but simply because the number of possible solutions to the perennial questions of human existence are rather few. Consequently, alert minds in any culture will have hit upon very similar conclusions in the course of time, because these conclusions work well to explain, and ultimately to control, observed phenomena. In some cases, the similarities may be attributed to peoples living in similar environments in different parts of the world, as Fontenelle and Vico suggested. For example, both the Blackfeet and the Nuer live in plains environments with large herd animals, while the Mbuti, the Wogeo, and the Mehinaku (but certainly not late eighteenth century Austrians!) live in tropical rainforests. This view assumes that myth operates at a fully conscious level, and that it involves mental facilities identical to those which have produced science in our culture. Of course, modern science is much more effective at controlling nature than is myth—or at least it seems to be so in the material world. Myth, in the view of this theory, is simply to be regarded, as Frazer regarded magic, as "failed science."[40] It is therefore irrelevant to the present and the future, except as a historical curiosity; it shows how clever ancient men were, as a rationalization of how clever *we* are!

One of the chief proponents of this idea in anthropology has been Claude Lévi–Strauss. He based his conclusions upon his own fieldwork in Amazonia and British Columbia, as well as extensive research into the myths of Native peoples in both North and South America. He considered it essential to recognize that peoples living in technologically uncomplicated societies are every bit as capable of intellectualization and logical reasoning as philosophers in Western civilization.[41] Lévi–Strauss hastens to add that, though the logical abilities of "savages" are equivalent to our own, the premises upon which their logic is based are often factually incorrect. This view has gone a long way to dispel the earlier notions of cultural superiority and inferiority, for there is no doubt that in every culture there are at least some individuals who possess formidable intellectual strengths. However, it is unlikely that this has ever been the case for the majority of people in any culture, including our own. Lévi–Strauss has been justly criticized for overemphasizing the intellectual aspect of myths at the expense of their emotionally evocative qualities. He favors structure over affect.[42] This makes his explanations of mythic similarities intellectually interesting, but often they are rather dry. Myths are not only good to *think;* they are also good to *feel!*

While there is no doubt that similar circumstances have conditioned similar behaviors among peoples in many parts of the world, one of the chief problems with independent invention is the degree of fine-grained detail that can be observed between myths in separate cultures. There is no obvious rational reason why, for example, flutes should be associated with the emergence of male sovereignty, or why the onset of human mortality should be initiated by a dialogue, in the myths of so many different cultures. Independent inventionists tend to attribute these similarities to pure chance, but the more comparative evidence that emerges, the harder it becomes to maintain chance as the sole explanation for mythic analogues between cultures.

At this point in our study, I would advise the reader not to attempt to choose among these alternatives as an overall approach to myth. Each of them has its strengths and weaknesses, and sometimes one of them may be more useful than the others in explaining a particular myth or a segment of a myth. Sometimes this will not be possible, and it must be used in combination with the others. I would instead ask the reader to keep an open mind and to become familiar with each of these theories as potential tools for understanding myths. At the very least, you should suspend judgment on this question until we have considered all the evidence. Above all, what you need is an ability to pay attention to the details, and a willingness to try to understand each myth within its cultural context as well as within the larger picture of world myth. Your skills in these areas may be small in scope at first, but by the end of our mythic journey you should be well equipped to use them whenever you encounter new myths, and also when the events around you take on a mythic resonance—as they surely will!

CHAPTER THREE

THE PURSUIT OF THE WHITE STAG

As we saw in Chapter One, myths are circular rather than linear in their structure and internal logic. Therefore, our study of myth may begin anywhere. Any point on the periphery of a circle is just as good a starting place as any other, because all are equidistant from the center, and one can reach any other point simply by traveling around or across the circle or even repeatedly return to the same point for further elaboration. Using this metaphor, I would suggest the possibility that every myth is connected to every other myth, though the connections may be distant. Claude Lévi–Strauss made just such an argument for all the myths of the Americas considered in the *Mythologiques*. He suggested that the exchange of myth among all these nonliterate cultures was maintained by intercultural interactions he referred to as "weak" (metaphorically, in the sense that physicists refer to the "weak" force within the atom):

> The constant activation of the social surface means that weak, low-powered, local vibrations gradually extend to the limits of the field, independently of demographic, political or economic changes, which occur less often, and produce their effects more slowly and at a deeper level.[1]

We shall begin our exploration of myth in cross-cultural context with a tale from northwestern Europe. The Celtic peoples, whose myths were first recorded by the Romans in the first century A.D., were one of the formative influences upon our own culture. As the direction of our journey will for the most part be from west to east, it makes sense to begin in the westernmost portion of the European continent, in Ireland. I have another personal reason for starting here, for it was my discovery of Story One that first led me to consider writing this book. I was familiar from childhood with the Greek myth at the center of Chapter Four, and my study of Mesopotamian literature in college brought me into direct contact with the central myth in Chapter Five in the original cuneiform text. But in 1975, when I found the story I present below, it brought home to me the power of cross-cultural mythological comparison, the method we are exploring in this book. This story was collected by Lady Francesca Wilde and published in 1887 in her study, *Ancient Legends, Mystic Charms, and Superstitions of Ireland*.

Story One: Fionn and Bran

> *The great Irish hero, Fionn MacCumhaill* (pronounced Finn MacCool) *was a great hunter, and in his youth he possessed a famous bitch hound named Bran whom he had raised since childhood. She was said to have been whelped by a goddess who had taken on bitch form. She and Fionn had shared many adventures together and were closely bonded to one another. One day the pack was out hunting, and they spied a white stag. They gave chase, but the stag was so swift and tireless that one by one all of the hounds dropped behind—all except Bran. The stag came to the edge of a precipice, with Bran at his heels; he jumped off the precipice into a pool of water, and Bran followed. But as soon as the stag was submerged in the water he was transformed into an old woman, the guardian spirit of the pool, who grabbed Bran by the scruff of her neck and dragged her down to her death. Fionn was so upset by the death of his favorite hound that he ordered the pool to be drained; but it proved to be bottomless. In despair, he jumped into the pool himself, and when he emerged he had become prematurely old, and his hair had turned completely white. It took the spells of all of his wisest druids to restore him to his youth and vigor.*[2]

In reality, this story stands on the margins of the Leinster Cycle of Irish mythology. Its main human character, Fionn MacCumhaill, was the king of the Fianna, the chieftains of the Tuatha de Danaan, warriors whose fantastic exploits dominate southern Irish myth. While Bran appears in stories of Fionn's earlier adventures, this particular episode is not part of the canonical editions of the cycle, and was collected by Lady Wilde from surviving oral tradition. At this stage of his career, Fionn was a young man who would have just assumed the kingship of Ireland after overcoming obstacles and defeating various ogres. Bran, his childhood protector, vanishes thereafter from the scene, and this myth attempts to explain why.

The chase scene is one of the most characteristic motifs of our series. We shall encounter it again and again, for it is nearly as obligatory in myths as it is in Hollywood movies. It is possible that hunting scenes like this refer to a time when our ancestors had not yet developed agriculture and relied upon hunting and gathering for their subsistence. By the seventeenth century, when the Leinster Cycle was first written down, hunting had long ceased to be necessary for survival for all but the poorest Irish peasants. It had degenerated into a sport for gentlemen of the upper class as a way of demonstrating their superiority over Nature. It is in this social context that the turning of the tables, with the hunters becoming the hunted, assumes a most powerful irony, much as in César Franck's tone-poem *Le Chásseur Maudit,* in which the Count of the Rhine defies religious taboos by hunting on Sunday, for which he is condemned to flee a horde of demons who pursue him day and night without respite.[3]

The figure of the mysterious old woman who brings about Bran's death is a familiar one in Celtic myth. Fionn, and later his youngest son Oisin, encounter her in several guises. Usually she is among the ancient powers the Fianna must conquer in order to establish their rule in the land, but Oisin discovered that she is capable of granting great favors as well. The ugly, boar-tusked woman whom he meets is transformed by his kiss into a beautiful maiden, who takes him off to the land of eternal youth across the sea, *Tir-na-n'og*. Here he loses all sense of time and only returns centuries later to relate to St. Patrick the saga of the Fianna, who have long since vanished from the land.[4] Oisin's relationship to Story One is much closer than this. His mother, Sadb, was enchanted by a dark druid into a doe, and while she lay with Fionn in mortal form she bore Oisin as a deer. On his return journey from Tir-na-n'og, Oisin is shown a vision of a hornless fawn pursued by the red-eared white hounds of Hell over the ocean.[5]

Oisin's encounter with the goddess recalls the story of the five sons of the Leinster king Eochaid. Each set forth on adventure, and each came to a crossroads where there was a well guarded by an ugly, boar-tusked crone, who invited them, each in turn, to give her a kiss. Only Niall, the youngest, was uncritical enough to accept her offer; she was instantly transformed into a beautiful young maiden, who announced that she was Royal Rule personified and granted Niall the boon of succeeding to the kingship at Tara. She explained that the effort needed to obtain Royal Rule seems repulsive to those who lack it, but attractive to those who succeed in gaining it.[6]

Royal Rule

The question of rulership occurs in many of the myths we shall consider, especially in those cultures where centralized authority is permanently vested in a small class of hereditary leaders (called by anthropologists *chiefdoms* and *states*). In such societies the leaders are almost always males, and leadership is usually inherited by the eldest son (the principle of *primogeniture*). Younger sons, in the feudal Western European societies where these myths first were told, were usually shunted off into the military or the priesthood, and did not normally have the opportunity to assume their fathers' crowns. Perhaps in part as a compensation, European folklore is full of stories about youngest sons who, after a period of obscurity, emerge as the true and just rulers of their lands—often, with the supernatural aid of animals (like Bran). The idea behind these and many other hero myths is that, when the power system has become too corrupt to function with a modicum of justice, the balance can only be restored by one who has retained his innocence and found wholeness often by remaining outside the system or by having been rejected by it. This theme has been explored exhaustively by Joseph Campbell in *The Hero with a Thousand Faces*.[7] We shall return to it in our final chapter. Jung adds a psychological dimension to the manifestation of the child-hero archetype, claiming that:

> especially in affinity with the symbolic animal, [it] personifies the collective unconscious which is not yet integrated into a human being, the hero's supernaturalness includes human nature and thus represents a synthesis of the ("divine," i.e., not yet humanized) unconscious and human consciousness. Consequently he signifies the potential anticipation of an individuation process which is approaching wholeness.[8]

We shall consider what Jung meant by *individuation* later in this chapter. In the case of Eochaid's sons, as in many folktales, the *structure* of the myth is simply a series: a set of wrong examples followed by a right one. We shall observe many such series in our exploration of myth. However, unlike mainland Europe and England, Ireland never passed through a feudal period; until it was conquered by the English in the seventeenth century, it was still divided into chiefdoms, whose leadership could be contested at the death of a chief by any candidate, male or female, however obscure. Fionn was an orphan, and his childhood was definitely a period of obscurity.

Royal Rule is personified in the tale of Niall as feminine, and the necessary requirement for a man to become king is that he put aside his immediate sensory impressions and see through to the essence of that which confronts him. This is a major theme that will recur repeatedly in our exploration of myth. As well, it could be said to characterize our method of studying myths. Robert Graves uses the motif of the pursuit of the roebuck to symbolize his method of chasing myths to their deeper levels of meaning, using a combination of respect for their mystery, the use of penetrating logic, and a willingness to follow chains of free association to see where they lead.[9]

We shall find that gender appearances in particular can be deceiving. Several mythologists have understood these images of feminine power in myth to be sociological evidence of a time when political authority itself was delegated by women, if not entirely under their control, and that the king was once subject to a female authority. For example, Johann Jakob Bachofen posited that the rule of "Mother-Right" dominated Europe prior to the invasion of the Dorian Greeks.[10] While Bachofen's conclusions were dismissed by anthropologists earlier in this century, they have been revived as a result of feminist scholarship, and some recent archæological investigations in Europe and Asia Minor have tended to reinforce the conclusion that before the Late Bronze Age female deities tended to dominate the religious scene, if not also the political structure of the region.[11] Pagan Ireland may have harbored a late survival of these Bronze Age customs, for it was renowned for its formidable war goddesses and female political leaders. Some of the former, like Brigid, were retained as saints once the island was converted to Christianity by Patrick. There is actually some historical evidence of the late survival of this relationship between the king and the goddess in Ireland. Citing Giraldus Cambrensis, Robert

Graves describes the crowning of a petty king at Tyrconnell in the twelfth century, A.D.:

> a preliminary to which was his symbolic rebirth from a white mare. He crawled naked towards her on all fours as if he were her foal; she was then slaughtered, and her pieces boiled in a cauldron. He himself entered the cauldron and began sucking up the broth and eating the flesh. Afterwards he stood on an inauguration stone, was presented with a straight white wand, and turned about three times from left to right, and then three times from right to left—"in honour of the Trinity." Originally no doubt in honour of the Triple White Goddess.[12]

We shall return to this particular perspective in later chapters, but for the moment we may note Graves' endorsement of the idea that:

> the coronation ceremony throughout the ancient world typified the marriage of the Sun King to the Earth Queen, his death as a member of his former tribe and his rebirth with a new name into that of his Queen, then the ritual on which all these myths are based must have included a mock-assassination of the king in the course of the bath-ceremony. [13]

This may help us to understand why the young king Fionn plunged into the hag-haunted pool, and why he thereby underwent a symbolic death and rebirth.

Readers familiar with Sir James Frazer's *The Golden Bough* may also note a suspicious, but inverted similarity to the central ritual in that work. A priest-king once ruled at the grove of Nemi in Italy, sacred to the Moon Goddess Diana. He was dedicated to her service and (though she is usually depicted as a virgin goddess in myth) she had granted him her favors in return for his devotion. But there was a limit to his rule. He awaited his slaughter at the hands of a younger man who would pluck a golden bough from the tree in the center of the grove, thereby earning the goddess' favor.[14] The entire twelve volumes of *The Golden Bough* are an attempt by Frazer to explain why anyone would *wish* to be priest–king at Nemi. Although Royal Rule sometimes appears in the enticing form of the young goddess, the man who wins her places himself in a situation where he is subject to her transformations, for she is the mistress of change through time. Once he grows old (as Fionn does briefly in our story) he inevitably loses her favor and she betrays him to his death.

The Triune Goddess

In all three of these Irish myths, the feminine figure possesses impressive power over men by her ability to transform herself from one guise to another—even across the lines of gender and species in the story of Bran. In Celtic myth, she appears in three familiar forms: Maiden, Matron, and Crone. Known therefore as the *Triune Goddess,* she rules the three modalities of time: past, present, and future. The feminine is a natural symbol for this, because women's lives are biologically divided into premenstrual, fertile, and postmenopausal phases, each accompanied by obvious physiological and behavioral transformations. In Figure 5, a second century A.D. lintel from High Rochester in Northumbria, the Crone is at the center, with her typical frown. The peculiar running position of her legs as she stands upon the water is one which we will encounter again in connection with

Figure 5: The Celtic Triune Goddess. Bas relief, High Rochester, Northumbria, 2nd century A.D., England. (University and Society of Antiquaries of Newcastle upon Tyne Museum of Antiquities)

Story Three. To the left is the pregnant Matron, accompanied by a wheat staff and holding a horn of plenty over her womb, while to the right is the Maiden with a jug of water.

Joseph Campbell says of her:

> The goddess is red with the fire of life; the earth, the solar system, the galaxies of far-extending space, all swell within her womb. For she is the world creatrix, ever mother, ever virgin. She encompasses the encompassing, nourishes the nourishing, and is the life of everything that lives.
>
> She is also the death of everything that dies. The whole round of existence is accomplished within her sway, from birth, through adolescence, maturity, and senescence, to the grave. She is the womb and the tomb, the sow that eats her farrow. Thus she unites the "good" and "bad," exhibiting two modes of the remembered mother, not as personal only, but as universal. The devotee is expected to contemplate the two with equal equanimity. Through this exercise his spirit is purged of its infantile, inappropriate sentimentalities and resentments, and his mind opened to the inscrutable presence which exists, not primarily as "good" and "bad" with respect to his childlike human convenience, his weal and woe, but as the law and image of the nature of being.[15]

The white color of the stag (and of Fionn's hair after his bath) is a deliberate symbol. White is the color of the Moon, whose prominent phases (waxing crescent, full, and new) correspond to the three guises of the Triune Goddess. Her male consort is *Cernunnos,* the stag-horned god, which is the reason she can transform herself into the white stag. Figure 6, from the famous silver Gundestrupp Bowl, shows him controlling a serpent, another key image which we shall encounter again. In later Medieval Christian symbolism, the stag was considered a figure of Christ, while in contemporary alchemical treatises, as *cervus fugitivus,* the elusive hart, it symbolized Mercurius, the completion of the Great Work.[16] The white horse of the Irish coronation ceremony may be a similar figure, for in both Wales and Celtic Gaul the goddess was worshipped in horse form as Epona.[17] We shall explore this substitution of one animal symbol for another in more detail in Chapter Five. However, the goddess is not mastered by this male figure. In Welsh mythology he is known only as Mabon

Figure 6: The Celtic Horned God, Cernunnos. Gundestrupp Bowl, 1st century A.D., Denmark. (Corbis)

ap Modron, "Son, son of Mother"[18]—a mysterious royal figure whose identity Arthur and his court are required to guess. Similarly, one of the titles of the Egyptian pharaoh was *Ka Mut-ef*, "The Bull of his mother."[19] Niall, Oisin, and Fionn each meet the goddess in her Crone aspect; but Fionn's determination to attack the pool with his engineers displays immature irascibility, like Eochaid's older sons, and he is punished, while Niall and Oisin respect her for what she is and are granted her favor as a consequence.

Fionn's Plunge as a Quest for Individuation

One of the most productive tools for exploring the psychological dimensions of this myth is the perspective of Jungian psychology. For Jung, hunting assumes an inner meaning: a quest for one's real self. That self is divided into conscious and unconscious portions, and the unconscious is characteristically symbolized (both in myth and dream) by water.[20] For the conscious portion to become aware of the inner Self at its core, it must first look downwards into the unconscious, to endure whatever trials that process entails. Thus it is hardly surprising that the pool turns out to be bottomless: Fionn is attempting in effect to drain his own unconscious, which is never a fruitful quest. The archetypal images which rise to the surface of the unconscious have a numinous power, which can drag the conscious mind into the depths, resulting, if undertaken prematurely, in insanity and biological deterioration. However, when the time is ripe, the encounter with this figure, which Jung has termed the "archetype of life," leads inevitably to a further, more deeply buried archetype, named by Jung the "Wise Old Man"—the archetype of *meaning*. He asserts that "in all cases of dissociation it is therefore necessary to integrate the unconscious into consciousness. This is a synthetic process which I have termed the 'individuation process.'"[21] For males especially, the figure of the *anima,* the archetype of feminine gender, has this power. Coming to terms with the contrasexual aspects of one's personality is exceedingly difficult work, but it does have its rewards if one approaches the process with the kind of humility exhibited by Oisin and Niall. The same process, as we shall see in Chapters Six, Seven, and Eight, applies to the exploration of the corresponding male *animus* archetype within the female psyche.

Fionn's plunge represents what anthropologist Victor Turner terms a *liminal event:* a critical moment or phase which defines a change in one's life or status.[22] Such events take place outside of the normal flow of time, and are often used by cultures to mark the attainment of puberty or the achievement of adult status, and that is the time of life at which we find Fionn. From this point forward, he must leave behind the protective feminine figure of his youth and venture forth alone. A Jungian might say that Fionn, who grew up without parents, was too closely bonded to the mothering aspect of the feminine and had projected his *anima* onto his dog, who had herself acquired too much of the pursuing, domineering quality of the male psyche. To give Fionn the opportunity to develop a new, less dependent relationship with his feminine side, his faithful dog must return to the depths of the unconscious whence (as the offspring of a goddess) she originally came. Fionn must be thrown back upon his own conscious resources to function as a mature adult. His temper tantrum at the pool is a clear indication of his resistance to this necessity.

On the personal level, the question of proper behavior is central to the myth. Bran is marked out by her excellence, and Fionn himself is usually depicted as a giant. In these ways, both exhibit the overweening pride which the ancient Greeks called *hybris:* the overestimation by mortals of their personal qualities which leads to their downfall. For both Bran and Fionn, the myth depicts this fall by a downward motion: off the cliff and into the pool. The result is death for Bran and something very close to death for Fionn. He is restored to youth only by the intercession of his druids, who, as old men, know how to deal with the mysterious forces of the world which lies outside of time and civilization.

Robert Graves has explored the Druidic religion in considerable detail in *The White Goddess.* From his studies, it is apparent that the training of druids involved an integrated knowledge of the stars, the trees, the animal powers, and the human psyche, each having its own set of correspondences to the letters of the Ogham alphabet.[23] Their practices are closely related to the nearly universal human institution of shamanism, the ancient wisdom teachings which still characterize the belief systems of peoples in marginal parts of the world today such as Australia, Siberia, the high Arctic, and Amazonia. We shall encounter many survivals of shamanic practice in the later chapters of this book. The lower orders of the druidic hierarchy, the bards, were also the storytellers, the communicators of myth. They were attached to royal courts but really operated independently of them, as if to suggest that Royal Rule is all very well and good in its place but that druidic wisdom lies beyond it. In this way, Story One is self-referential in that it attributes to storytellers a power greater than that of kings.

Though he was an orphan, Fionn's mother was the daughter of the Archdruid, and in his childhood he was raised by a druidic priestess, which perhaps explains the willingness of the druids to assist him in his plight.[24] Fionn is far too young at this stage of his life to have acquired druidic powers, but even later in the Leinster cycle as a mature man, he shows himself full of bluster in the face of forces beyond his control, which eventually results in the death of his beloved Grianne and her lover, Diarmuid (whom Fionn, in the guise of a boar, kills), and eventually of himself and all the Fianna. It is necessary to the logic of the Leinster Cycle that Fionn *not* perish or become an old man at this early point in his career—at least not before he fathers his sons!

The Prospect of Resurrection: Fionn, Again

The motif of restoration is also linked to the image of the Moon, which grows full, declines, and reappears each month as a waxing crescent after three days of darkness and is therefore sacred to the Triune Goddess. It symbolizes the cyclic power of growth, death, and rebirth. This has a special relevance in the case of Fionn, since as a national hero he is expected to return from death to save Ireland, much as King Arthur is expected to return from Avalon to save England. Fionn's giant body is buried under the city of Dublin, his head under Howth Castle, pointed toward the Irish Sea, and his feet under Phoenix Park, which by its name is associated with resurrection or, as James Joyce described it in *Finnegans Wake:*

> *The humptyhillhead of humself prumptly sends an unquiring one well to the west in quest of his tumptytumtoes, and their upturnpikepointandplace is at the knock out in the park where oranges have been laid to rust upon the green since Devlins first loved Livvy.*[25]

In this respect, the revenant Fionn is similar to his Welsh counterpart, the giant Bran the Blessed, the king in the second branch of the *Mabinogion,* the Welsh national epic:

> *Bran set out with his army to rescue his sister Branwen, who was being mistreated by her husband, the king of Ireland. Though Bran succeeded in defeating the Irish, he received a poisoned wound in his foot, and begged his brother to cut off his head and bring it back to Britain. For many years, Bran's oracular head continued to converse with his people, but finally it gave them instructions to bury it under a hill in London, where it would protect Britain from invaders.*[26]

Although Bran's head was said to have been exhumed by King Arthur, who subsequently assumed the role of protector for Britain, the Tower of London, the location of its burial, continues to be associated with decapitation, for the White Tower is famous as the scene of many a royal execution and is still said to be haunted by the ghost of Anne Boleyn, who walks its halls "with 'er 'ead tucked underneath 'er arm."[27]

The identity of names between the Irish hero's dog and the Welsh king is probably no accident. In Gaelic, *Bran* means the alder tree, whose wood is used in Ireland to make milk pails (thereby linking it to the cow, another symbol of the White Goddess). The alder is one of the trees associated with resurrection.[28] Bran is also the Norman French word for the husk of the grain (usually wheat), and it still has this meaning in English today. As Frazer has shown, many of these myths of dying and resurrected heroes in agriculturally-based economies relate to the grain, which grows, is harvested, and then is replanted to grow again, providing for the life of the population.[29] There is no doubt that this is reflected in the Christian *mythos* as well, both in the substance of the Host and in Christ's parable about the grain of wheat.[30] We shall return to this idea in subsequent chapters.

Decapitation in Celtic Myth

The myths of the Celtic sphere contain an alarming number of decapitation scenes. For example, we might consider the Medieval legend of Sir Gawaine and the Green Knight:

> *On New Year's Day, the darkest point in the annual cycle, the bizarre figure of Bertilak de Haute Desert, a very unjolly green giant armed with an axe, appears before King Arthur's court to offer a challenge: to decapitate him with his axe, and then to suffer decapitation at his hands a year later. Only Sir Gawaine, Arthur's nephew, is brave or foolhardy enough to accept the challenge, after which the Green Knight calmly picks up his head and retrieves his axe, reminding Gawaine not to fail in his part of the bargain. Gawaine sets out around Halloween, Celtic Samhain, and arrives in the vicinity of the Green Chapel just after Christmas. He is invited to lodge with a huntsman and his wife for three days, and the two men agree to share whatever bounty comes their way. The huntsman returns with game; Gawaine is tempted by the Knight's wife but (more or less) successfully resists three times, the two exchanging only kisses. He exchanges these with the lord, who has hunted, in succession, deer, boar, and a fox. It later transpires that his host is none other than the Green Knight, who was testing Gawain's chivalry, and who spares his head as a reward.*[31]

The Green Knight, with his archaic bronze axe and his peculiarly powerful consort, is clearly a fertility figure of great antiquity. The axe or *labrys* was a symbol of the goddess throughout the Bronze Age Mediterranean before it was replaced by the swords of Iron Age patriarchy. The timing of the quest, related to the dark part of the year initiated by the Celtic death-festival of Samhain, is important, and we shall return to calendrical symbolism in Chapter Five. This story is likely derived from an older one in the first branch of the *Mabinogion*, in which King Pwyll of Dyfed is rewarded for his resistance to the temptations of his patron Arawn's wife—or perhaps mother. Pwyll later pursues a white stag into an ancient burial mound and thereby wins his bride.[32]

Gawaine's quest, and his courteousness to the Green Knight's woman, is related to a much earlier story in the Arthurian cycle:

> *At the inauguration of the Round Table, the wedding breakfast of Arthur and Guinevere is interrupted by the following tableau: a white hart pursued by a white hound pursued by thirty black hounds. One knight is knocked over by the hart and seizes the hound and makes off with it. At this point, Nimue, the Lady of the Lake, arrives on a white horse and demands the return of the hound. A strange knight enters and abducts her. Arthur dispatches three of his knights: one to find the hound, one to find the lady, and Gawain to find the hart. Gawain's quest leads him to a castle where he slays the hart, but the lord of the castle grieves for it since it was a gift to him from the goddess and kills two of Gawain's dogs. Gawain overcomes him in battle and is about to behead him when a lady of the castle casts herself in the way of his sword and is beheaded instead. Though Gawain returns with the hart's head as a trophy, he is forced to wear the head of the lady he killed around his neck. Upon his return to Camelot Guinevere forces upon him an oath that he will ever after be courteous to ladies.*[33]

Here the chase scene seems like a tableau, a set piece on the threshold of adventure. But coming as it does at the very outset of Arthur's rule over the Round Table, and his marriage to the White Goddess (Guinevere's name means something like "White Shadow") which sanctifies Royal Rule, we should not ignore the symbolism. In both stories, Gawain, Arthur's brash young nephew, undertakes the quest as a substitute for the king. I shall have more to say about substitute kings in Chapter Five, but the point here is that Gawain, whose character is much more like Fionn's than Arthur's, may function as the questor while the king remains at home to govern—much as Arthur does also during the Grail quest. Gawain's popularity with women derives in part from the *geas* (ritual obligation) Guinevere places on him after this incident. Unlike Fionn, who never gets over his machismo, Gawain is at least required to treat women with respect after his accidental act of decapitation.

The Cult of the Well

Oracular heads will be with us throughout our exploration, and the practice of preserving heads is of the greatest antiquity. In the grotto of Monte Circeo in Italy, a Neanderthal skull was found in the center of a circle of quartz pebbles; whereas in early Neolithic Jericho the skulls of ancestors were coated with plaster and placed in niches in the homes of their descendants.[34] In the Celtic sphere, the decapitated skull is specifically related to the adoration of wells and deep pools, for wells were considered to be the eyes of a primordial giant and their waters his/her tears. Nigel Pennick relates that "the most famous Welsh holy well of them all, that at Holywell, is said to have sprung fourth when St. Gwenfrewi (Winefride) was beheaded. When her head touched the ground, the waters burst forth."[35] Deep pools like the one in our story are still visited by women throughout the Celtic world, especially at key times of the year like the winter solstice and the spring equinox, and are considered sacred places. Women leave votive offerings in the form of small artifacts, flowers, or dairy products. The pools have been taken over by Christian saints in name only and are often associated with healing and youth-restorative powers. But they can also be dangerous: the Irish rivers Boyne and Shannon are each said to have come into being when a goddess profaned a holy well, which overflowed and pursued the goddess to her death.[36]

The well cults are closely related to those surrounding sacred lakes, which in the Celtic sphere are likewise dedicated to the goddess. Nimue, who appears for the first time in the story of the Quest of the White Hart, was a member of a college of oracular priestesses and healers who traveled under the generic name "Lady of the Lake."[37] These wise women appear to offer advice and prophecy at crucial turns of the Arthurian legends. It is to their realm, Avalon (a timeless place like Tir-na-n'og, itself a lake name), that Arthur goes at the end of his reign to be healed of his wounds. Nimue is the daughter of a huntsman, who in turn is the "godson" of the goddess

Diana, who grants her powers of prophecy and power over Merlin.[38] Lakes, especially those with islands in them, are centers of pilgrimage and mystery throughout the Celtic world. I have no doubt that, within a generation, the lake isle on which Princess Diana is buried will take on this character, for it is already a place of pilgrimage, and Diana is already being spoken of as the Lady of the Lake.

In conclusion, what might have appeared superficially to be a charming folktale on the margins of Irish myth turns out to possess unexpected depths, very much like the pool it describes. We should be prepared for this to be the case for all of the myths we will consider, though as we progress through the cycle we shall find that the myths assume an increasingly central place in the cultural systems which created them.

Chapter Four

AT THE WATER'S EDGE

Our second story brings us into the more familiar domain of Græco-Roman mythology. The tale appears in its fullest version in the Roman poet Ovid's *Metamorphoses*, but it is based upon Greek originals of which only brief fragments have survived.[1] It is one of a long series of stories compiled by Ovid about mortals transformed into animals and plants, usually as the result of a dangerous encounter with a god or goddess.

Story Two: The Transformation of Actæon

Actæon was a prince of the royal house of Thebes, a young hunter who delighted in the chase. One day, he was hunting with his dogs, and became separated from them. At noontime, he chanced into a forest grove in which the goddess Diana was bathing in a pool, surrounded by her maidens. The lusty young hunter did not avert his gaze from the naked form of the goddess; she turned red with shame as her maidens attempted to shield her with their own bodies, but she stood much taller than they and thus remained exposed. Normally the goddess would have slain the offending mortal outright with her bow and arrows, but these lay out of her reach on the bank of the pool. She therefore dipped her hand into the water and splashed Actæon in the face, saying, "Now you are free to tell others that you have spied on the goddess unrobed—if you can tell." Immediately, Actæon's head began to sprout horns; his arms and legs turned to hooves; his body sprouted hair; and his voice was silenced. When the transformation was complete, he had become a great stag. His own dogs caught his scent and pursued him to his death. Unable to hear his cries for mercy, they tore him apart. Only when other hunters discovered his body was the truth known.[2]

Superficially, this story, like many of Ovid's other tales, appears to contain a warning about appropriate conduct, especially for young people. The concept of *hybris* is central to all of them. In the Greek view of proportion, there is a proper place for Man in the universal scheme of things, distinctly subordinate to the gods. But humans are inclined to forget this and to appropriate to themselves a higher status than that which has been allotted to them. For this fault, the gods punish them with transformation and/or death. *Hybris* is especially a problem for the members of the Theban royal house! We shall encounter many errant members of this family in our exploration of myth. In Greek folklore, the region of Thebes, Bœotia, was renowned for the stupidity of its inhabitants.

Actæon's *hybris* lies in his failure to avert his gaze from the naked form of the goddess. He regards her as if she were his inferior, a mortal woman subject to the domination of his patriarchal lust. Because of his misappropriation of higher status than the goddess, he is downgraded in status to an animal (Figure 7), and ironically is pursued to the death by his

Figure 7: The Transformation of Actaeon. French engraving, 17th century A.D. (Corbis)

own hunting pack. A feminist interpretation might say that she simply transforms him into a lusty young buck—the actual form for which his behavior is a metaphor—much as Circe transforms Odysseus' crew into (male chauvinist) pigs.[3]

The Power of the Goddess

However, there is much more to the story than this. First, we must consider the nature of the goddess whom Actæon affronted, and then ask what she was doing out in the woods in a pool with her maidens. Diana (Greek Artemis) is, as we have already seen, the goddess of the Moon. She is also a huntress. She is the daughter of Zeus and Leto. Upon her birth, she assisted her mother in the birthing of her twin brother Apollo, the god of the Sun. Hence, she is the patroness of midwifery, and women call upon her in childbirth.[4] Her close association with the female reproductive cycle is essential to an understanding of the myth.

Many cultures have observed the apparent synchrony between the lunar month and the female menstrual cycle. In many hunting and gathering societies, menstruation is considered women's essential power, because it signifies the negation of the birth of a new member of the society. For example, among the Cheyenne, menstruating women are required to spend a period of four days away from the lodges (of which they are in fact the owners), to keep them away from their male relatives, lest their blood "contaminate" the men's hunting equipment.[5] Among the Wogeo, woman is believed to possess the ultimate power in the battle of the sexes; all she need do is to touch her husband's food while menstruating to cause his death by illness forthwith.[6] In these societies, men's magic consists of their ability to hunt (and, in some societies like the Cheyenne, to engage in warfare), to take life *culturally* by shedding other creatures' blood, while women's magic consists of their ability to control the reproductive process, to give or take life by shedding their *own* blood *naturally*. Hunter–gatherers often conceptualize their relationship with the hunted animals as a kind of a covenant in which the animals agree to "give away" their lives as individuals to the people, if the people agree not to overhunt them as a species. But refraining from overhunting implies that people must take control of their population growth, a decision considered to be women's responsibility in these societies. Thus, it is not illogical for people in many societies to have conceptualized these two forms of power—hunting and menstruation—as being of equal *strength* but of opposite *charge*. Hence the need to keep men and women separate when the power of each is at its respective peak, lest they "discharge" one another. This rationale is used in many hunter–gatherer societies to restrict or even forbid women from hunting: it is believed that the odor of their menstrual blood will drive the game away.[7] While hunting had long ceased to have the economic importance among the ancient Greek farmers and city-dwellers that it has for hunter–gatherers, the Greeks appear to have retained many of their old menstrual taboos, and some of these are still present in industrialized societies today. We will return to this issue in Chapters Seven and Eight.

Diana and her band of hunting women are quite unusual as a social phenomenon in the context of Iron Age Greece, and certainly they are the last thing that a hunter such as Actæon would expect. However, there is another layer of meaning in this scene. Throughout the Mediterranean basin, ritual bathing has been prescribed for women at the conclusion of menstruation, and it is still required in orthodox Judaism and Islam.[8] What Actæon has stumbled upon is a ritual cleansing, a means by which women at the close of their menstrual periods could reenter ordinary society, removing or canceling their "charge" by contact with the element of water, which, as we have already seen, often symbolizes the feminine. Such ceremonies are absolutely forbidden to males—especially hunters. In many hunter–gatherer societies, men about to embark on hunting or warfare expeditions are even expected to refrain from sexual intercourse, lest they "discharge" themselves. Among the !Kung San Bushmen of the Kalahari, one man earned the nickname of "Wildebeest" because on the day after he consummated his marriage he killed five of these large animals, which was considered to be an impossible feat under the circumstances.[9] The same belief in the need for ritual abstinence is perpetuated among male athletes in our society today.

The apparent synchrony between the lunar and menstrual cycles has been observed for at least twenty thousand years. Stone figurines and bas-reliefs of the Upper Paleolithic period from Europe and central Asia depict females with grossly exaggerated breasts, buttocks, and genitals. One of the most famous of these, the "Venus of Laussel," a bas-relief some 46 cm high from the Dordogne region of France, was once painted red with ochre, perhaps to simulate blood (Figure 8). She faces right and holds in her right hand a crescent-shaped object that bears thirteen marks.[10] Some scholars have interpreted the marks as representing days, comprising half of the lunar/menstrual cycle. The object she holds may represent the Moon, but it may also be an animal horn, like the one held by the Matron

Figure 8: The "Venus" of Laussel. Bas-relief, Dordogne region, France, Upper Paleolithic period. (Corbis)

in Figure 5. Alexander Marshack has published several examples of Upper Paleolithic lunar calendars engraved on ivory or horn, especially on deer antlers.[11] Perhaps it would have been more appropriate to name this figure the "Diana of Laussel"? Andre Leroi-Gourhan, one of the foremost authorities on Paleolithic art, cautions that we know so little of the minds of these people that the figure might as well have been a Juno or a Persephone as a Venus.[12]

In fact, there are not one but four "Venuses" in the Laussel grotto. A second faces left and holds a similar object in her left hand, while a third faces forward and a fourth appears to be giving birth to a mirror image of herself—or are we merely seeing her reflection as in a pool of water? Also present is a bas-relief of a male hunter carrying a bow or spear, and several deeply engraved images of horned animals. Unfortunately, each of the figures was found on a separate block of stone on the floor of the Laussel grotto, to which it had fallen from an original vertical frieze, so we cannot be certain of their relationship. However, LePorte has freely reconstructed the three single female figures as a triptych, with the hunter and his prey below them.[13] Such a triptych also appears at the slightly later grotto of Angles-sur-l'Anglin.[14] It appears that we are on familiar ground, in the domain of the Triune Goddess of the waxing, full, and waning Moon, the mistress of midwifery, under whose domination both the hunter and his prey fall. It is remarkable to consider that these traditions may have survived for twenty millennia in this part of the world!

The Goddess of Wild Beasts

Horned animals are perennial consorts of the goddess Artemis, as they are for the Celtic Triune Goddess. The stag and the boar are her particular favorites (Figure 9). She is consistently depicted as a huntress, equipped with bow and arrows that always hit their mark. Despite her reputation (outside of Nemi, anyway) as a virgin (or lesbian) goddess, she is said to have consorted with Pan, the goat-footed, horned fertility god. Her festival day of August 13 (very close to the date in the Christian calendar of the Feast of the Assumption of the Virgin!) is exactly six months from the festival day for the god Pan on February 13.[15] The latter is very close to St. Valentine's Day, the iconography of which includes hearts pierced by arrows.

Figure 9: Diana and her animals. Bas-relief from Germany, 2nd century A.D.? (Corbis)

Thus, the choice of animal for Actæon's transformation is by no means accidental. While I referred earlier to this change as downgrading, it is in a sense an exaltation, too, because the goddess converts him into her own familiar animal. The antlers of the stag are lunar symbols and are also used to make the goddess' bow, with which she normally slays wrong-doers. (Freudians would no doubt hasten to add that they are phallic symbols, too!) The boar, her other favorite animal, is frequently depicted in Greek myth as the slayer of heroes. Its tusks are lunar symbols because of their curved shape and whiteness. We have already encountered the boar-tusked goddess in conjunction with Oisin and Niall in our exploration of Story One.

Diana is also frequently accompanied by hunting dogs and wolves, whose snapping canine teeth can also be considered lunar symbols. Perhaps this is the reason why vampires are depicted in folklore as nocturnal creatures with projecting canine teeth and an affinity for blood. Certainly they are "children of the night" who shun the light of the Sun. Both projecting canines and nocturnal behavior are archaic evolutionary features in hominid lines. Our canines are much shorter than those of any other primate, scarcely projecting above the jawline.

The name Artemis in Greek is related to the word for another carnivore, the she-bear, *arctos*. Hymns praise her as *Artemis Kallistene,* "Bear-goddess most beautiful," which brings us to another of Ovid's stories. Zeus had seduced one of Diana's female entourage, Kallisto (surely revealed by her name as a reduplication of the goddess herself), by disguising himself as the goddess. In order to protect her and her newborn child from the goddess' wrath, Zeus transformed her into the constellation Ursa Major and the child into Ursa Minor.[16]

Throughout the northern part of the northern hemisphere, the bear is the power animal *par excellence,* because it is a bipedal omnivore—like ourselves—but is endowed with strength far greater than that of a human. Bears were subject to veneration and ritual decapitation as early as Neanderthal times. Several Middle Paleolithic cave sites high in the Alps have yielded stone enclosures containing bear skulls ritually arranged. Some, like the human skull at Monte Circeo, are surrounded with pebbles, while others have their thigh bones thrust through their zygomatic (cheek) arches.[17]

The Greater and Lesser Bear constellations are northern circumpolar stars; at the latitude of Greece they never sink below the horizon. In the Kallisto myth this detail is explained by saying that she thereby avoids contact with Poseidon, the god of the sea. But her removal to the zenith of the sky is a further symbol of the goddess' inviolability. We shall observe several other myths in this book in which the placement of a human figure high in the sky is symbolically significant.

We must also consider the nature of the transformative agent: in this case, as in Bran's pool, water. Water is obviously associated with the Moon through the tides, and we are beginning to understand that the human psyche, as well as the body, is affected by the lunar pull. The flow of water is further associated with menstrual flow. According to Ovid, the pool in which the goddess stood was enclosed in a grotto, which is obviously a symbol for the womb. As we saw in the last chapter, grottoes have been used as shrines since Middle Paleolithic times. In a real sense, the pool represents the goddess herself, since she is the apotheosis of the power of women to give or to take life. The water she splashes in Actæon's face is no ordinary water; it is water charged with the feminine power at a point when it is most dangerous and most antithetical to the male.

The Subjugation of Machismo

The scene into which Actæon has blundered is the domain of the feminine: the goddess, her reduplication in the form of her maidens, the pool, the grotto, the lunar bow, the water itself, and the animal forms—even Actæon's own dogs—are all indicators of the liminal entry of an adolescent male into the mysterious and powerful world of sexuality, particularly a sexuality opposite to his own yet, surprisingly to him, just as powerful or even more so. In this sense, Actæon's initiation experience is a universal one. (There are corresponding puberty experiences for females as well, as we shall shortly see.) Actæon's name means "shore-dweller"—one who lives at the edge between the earth and the water. This clearly indicates his liminality. In the myth, he stands transfixed at the point of high noon, the apex of the solar day from which the light subsequently declines, at the shore of the pool which he dares not enter but from which he also lacks the good sense to turn aside. Nor does he possess Fionn's courage (foolhardy though it may have been) to plunge into the pool headlong. Instead, he remains perpetually on the edge as a concealed observer until Diana takes notice of him and forcibly drags him into the action.

From this perspective, Actæon's failure and subsequent death arise from his inability to interpret his world in any way other than adolescent male terms. In his immaturity, he derogates the goddess to the status of a *Playboy* centerfold. As numerous feminist authors have pointed out, pornography is more about power than sexuality, because it disempowers the personhood of its object by demystifying the female body. It is quite different from eroticism, in which the mystery of gender difference is celebrated and empowered. Fixating the libido of adolescent males (and older men who have never outgrown their adolescent attitudes) upon the demystified female body grants them power over that which they fear, all too frequently resulting in abusive behavior.

Actæon's impulse upon discovering his error is to flee, not at all an uncharacteristic psychological response when one is confronted for the first time with powerful unknown forces, but never a very successful strategy. Mythological figures around the world succeed in escaping the dreaded powers only if they possess strong magical aids. For example, in the Japanese saga *Kojiki*, the young god Izanagi descends into the netherworld to seek out his sister Izanami who has died after giving birth to their child. When he sees her, she is a rotting corpse, who pursues him in anger; only by discarding various items of apparel for her to devour is he able to escape.[18]

But Actæon has no such resources at his disposal, so he flees, is caught, and is dismembered. His fate resembles that of the Greek bard Orpheus, who, like Izanagi, descended to the underworld to retrieve his deceased wife Eurydice. He was warned not to look upon her as he led her out but disobeyed this rule, and had to flee from the underworld without her. Later, he was dismembered by a group of *mænads*, ecstatic female devotees of the god Dionysius. Like the Welsh Bran, Orpheus' decapitated head continued to issue prophecies, until Apollo asked it to stop.[19]

Both Izanagi and Orpheus looked upon the nakedness of the goddess in its extreme. They saw her unclothed not merely of her garments, but even of her flesh—a horrific vision which is likely to evoke fear and flight. The relation of Actæon's dismemberment to that of Orpheus is probably not accidental: Eurydice died as the result of being bitten in the foot by a serpent while fleeing the amorous embrace of Actæon's father, Aristeus.[20] We may be justified in reading a message about the patriarchy into this scene. Eurydice's name means "wide justice," and may refer to the prevailing feminine-based justice of the Bronze Age which was forced underground by the emergence of male-dominated Iron Age aristocracies.

The Lamed King

Dionysius was actually Actæon's first cousin once removed; both were grandsons of Kadmos, the founder of the Theban dynasty, whom we will encounter again. Orpheus was not the only character in Greek myth dismembered by the *maenads*. Pentheus, another Theban king of the line of Kadmos, once attempted to imprison Dionysius and to stamp out his worship. While spying upon the *maenads'* ritual from a tree, he was discovered and torn to pieces, and his own mother Agave wrenched off his head in her frenzy.[21]

As a child, Dionysius himself had been dismembered by axe-wielding Titans, but was reconstituted and resurrected by his grandmother Rhea. Raised in female disguise by the king and queen of Orchomenos, he was discovered by Zeus' jealous wife Hera, who struck the king with madness, so that he killed his own son, mistaking him for a stag.[21] According to Ovid, Actæon's encounter with Diana took place near Orchomenos.

Robert Graves considers the frequent scenes of pursuit and dismemberment in Greek mythology to represent a Bronze Age custom of *ritual regicide,* in which the king was originally killed, later emasculated and lamed, and ultimately merely required to simper about on high heels. He comments:

> in ancient times the sacred king of the mystery drama who appeared in response to the invocation of the Three Graces really had a bull-foot. That is to say, the dislocation of his thigh made one of his feet resemble that of a bull, with the heel as the fetlock, and he hurried among them with a rush and clatter of buskins.[22]

As we shall see in Chapter Ten, the laming of the king by the goddess can be applied metaphorically to contemporary political situations. The transformation of Actæon's legs into deer legs could be a parallel to laming as it enables him to be caught by his pursuing hounds and killed. The wounded foot, as we saw in the Welsh story of Bran, is linked to the oracular head. We shall see that this is frequently the case in other myths. For example, Oedipus, another member of the Theban royal house, had his feet pierced at birth; his name literally means "swell-foot." Later on, he wounded himself in the eyes, and became a renowned oracle. Graves suggests that Dionysius' name, also, means "Lame God of Light" and likens him to both the lame forge-god Hæphestos and the biblical patriarch Jacob, whose thigh was dislocated in his wrestling bout with the angel.[23]

Dismemberment as an Initiatory Ordeal

In Story Two, Actæon's dismemberment and death is the end of the myth, but in many traditions dismemberment precedes some sort of resurrection. For example, among the Arunta aborigines of Australia, a candidate for *shaman* (sacred specialist) presents himself at the mouth of a cave inhabited by spirit beings, who cast one spear that passes through his head from ear to ear, and another spear that enters through his mouth and exits through the back of the head, and he falls down dead. The spirits then dismember him, rearrange his internal organs, and replace some of them with quartz crystals. Then they sew him up, bring him back to life, and send him back to his camp, where he behaves (quite justifiably, under the circumstances!) as an insane person. After a year of apprenticeship to an older shaman, if the wound in the candidate's tongue has not healed, he is considered eligible to practice as a shaman.[25] Similar stories of death, dismemberment, and reanimation are told of shamanic initiations all over the world, and they seem to relate to a profound experience of psychological dissolution common to all cultures in which the individual feels that he or she has died and been reborn in a new and impervious form.[26] We shall explore the institution of shamanism in greater detail in Chapter Seven.

No such rebirth is afforded to Actæon, but perhaps this is because he is just not the type of material of which shamans are made. The psychologist William James has suggested that in every culture there are two types of personalities: the *tough-minded,* who are mainly preoccupied with survival and wealth and who need religion only to carry them through the liminal experiences in their lives, and the *tender-minded,* who are alienated from the usual goals of their societies and who are led to explore beyond the ordinary; they assume a permanently liminal state.[27] For example, Michele Stephen describes the career and personality of a "Man of Sorrow" among the Mekeo people of New Guinea, a shaman who is permanently marginalized by his community because they fear his powers yet need his services.[28] She contrasts this with the career of the "Man of Kindness," the political leader who lives in the center of the community and whom everyone is supposed to like.[29] It is only the tender-minded who become shamans; Actæon is too preoccupied with his own budding masculinity to be anything other than tough-minded.

A Comparison of the Stories of Fionn and Actæon

It is interesting to observe how many motifs Stories One and Two share in common: the young male, the dogs, the stag, the goddess, water, transformation, death, hybris, irony, the chase, the Moon (by implication via the white color in Story One, and by reference to the Moon Goddess in Story Two), and punishment. Yet they are not presented in the same order. In Story One, the stag transforms himself into human form after being pursued by the dogs; in Story Two, the human is transformed into a stag and then pursued by the dogs. The result of both chases is death, for Bran in Story One and for Actæon in Story Two. Fionn expresses anger at the bottomless pool and its goddess; for Actæon the goddess is the unattainable object of his desire, and she expresses her anger with him. One might imagine that the tellers of both tales were each equipped with a little box containing the same set of counters, one for each of the motifs. They could shake the box to scramble the counters, toss several of them out, and tell a story (the same story, in its ultimate import) along the lines suggested by the random placement of the counters.[30] The *order* of the motifs is apparently less central to the story than their simple *presence* together. We shall see many other permutations of the same motifs in the other myths in this book.

In this case, we have a backwards transformation between the two myths, which is referred to by mythologists as an *inversion*. Within myths, inversion is a device for achieving a particular emphasis—for example, the inversion of Actæon's assumption of higher status into a lower status, or the gender inversion of the typical hunting party, or, in Story One, the age inversion of the young Fionn into an old man. Inversion also can be observed between myths, as in this case. Lévi–Strauss has suggested that this may be a way in which members of one culture may appropriate a myth from another culture and deliberately make it their own.[31] But this does not account for the popularity of inversion as a device within myths or between myths of the same culture.

As will be the case throughout the cycle of key myths in this book, it is difficult to explain the many similarities between these two myths. Ireland and Greece are close enough to one another that Bronze Age trade contact and exchange of ideas between the two is likely. In Irish mythology itself there are descriptions of waves of invaders, among them the Tuatha de Danaan themselves, who are represented as being of Greek origin.[32] It is difficult to identify any of the pre-Celtic peoples of Ireland with archæological cultures, but the existence of the tradition may point to some form of contact with the Mediterranean world. Later, the Romans conquered Britain and imported their literature there, and Romano-British clerics like Patrick brought it from England to Ireland in the early Middle Ages. During the Middle Ages, Irish monasteries preserved much of the learning of classical antiquity at a time when it had all but vanished from the European continent. So it is possible that direct or indirect contact between Ireland and the Græco-Roman cultural sphere could have led to the transmission of mythological ideas through diffusion. However, the many inversions between the two myths cannot so easily be explained by this process, unless we assume that they are the necessary products of translation between the cultures, the means by which the Irish made the Actæon story their own. Because Story One is deeply rooted in a specifically Celtic context, this is rather unlikely. Fionn, unlike Actæon, enjoys a long career after his encounter with the goddess. Moreover, the Celtic world was not simply a passive recipient of ideas from the Mediterranean Basin, as the early diffusionists thought. Archæologists have discovered that sophisticated astronomical monuments such as Stonehenge actually preceded the construction of the Egyptian pyramids.[33]

As for psychic unity, Greek, Latin, and Gaelic are all Indo-European languages. The speakers of the proto-Indo-European language which is hypothesized to underlie them might have possessed some form of this myth that developed in different directions as the peoples became separated in much the same way that biological species diverge. This hypothesis would require the absence of similar imagery from non-Indo-European speakers' myths, which as we shall shortly see is far from being the case. We might also argue for a common human ground in the collective unconscious, which is itself symbolized by water and which therefore could have inspired both myths. As we have seen, images of the Triune Goddess in European grottoes are very ancient, indeed. However, this would still not explain the impressive congruity of detail.

Adherents of independent invention might point out that the function of both stories is to delineate a similar societal problem: the propensity for adolescent males to commit *hybris* when confronted with the feminine. This argument suggests that every culture will need to develop myths like these as a means of regulating male behavior, which would certainly account for the similarity of theme between Stories One and Two. We must grant that this is a common problem, one which many males in our own society never outgrow. This might cause us to wonder whether the rates of abuse of women are so high (a recent study found that one in five American girls in grades nine through twelve has been physically or sexually abused[34]) because we lack such a myth. But once again, this hypothesis fails to account for the similarity of the details. As we shall see in Chapters Six and Seven, many of the same motifs are associated with adolescent females in some cultures. Perhaps we can only account for the similarities by using all three hypotheses!

Once again, what appeared superficially to be an admonitory tale for young men turns out to contain a wealth of symbolism concentrated within an extremely compact form, which connects the story to universal human concerns about life, death, sexuality, and selfhood. These deeper meanings do not detract from the primary moral directive of the story. They reinforce it in a way that appeals, not only to the intellect, but to the emotions as well. Myth has the peculiar talent of affecting us on many levels at once. Undoubtedly this is one of the reasons that it has endured as a feature of human culture. Simply using reason and intellect to tell young people how they are expected to behave is unlikely to be very effective at a time when they are trying to discover their individuality separate from their parents and social group. Because the story of Actæon rests within a complex context of symbolic references well known to everyone in Græco-Roman culture, it speaks more directly and potently to its audience than any moral prescription ever could.

Chapter Five

THE MEASURE OF ALL THINGS

The next story is by far the earliest of our entire set to have been recorded in written form. It derives from the Sumerian culture of ancient Mesopotamia. The Sumerians appear to have been the first people in the world to create an urban civilization, economically based upon the vast surplus of wheat and barley which could be grown in the fertile floodplain of the Tigris and Euphrates valleys in what is today southern Iraq. To establish the timing of the planting cycle, and the apportionment of land tracts in this flat, featureless plain, they developed techniques of measuring time by the stars (astrology/astronomy), and land by geometry. These two sciences were so important that they elevated them to the status of gods: Anshar (sky-measure) and Kishar (earth-measure).

The Sumerians also invented cuneiform, a system of writing produced by inscribing with a stylus on a wet clay tablet, by around 3100 B.C. At first it was chiefly used to record economic transactions, but by about 2400 B.C. they had begun to record highly literary, canonical forms of their myths on this medium. The Sumerian scribes learned their craft by rote so many copies were made of the more important texts. Unfortunately, unbaked clay is rather breakable, and while scholars can collate copies to obtain a more or less complete version of a text, there are often gaps which no extant copy fills. The cuneiform literary tradition spans more than two thousand years, for it was handed down by the Sumerians to their Babylonian and Assyrian successors, who wrote in Akkadian, an entirely different language. During this span of time, the myths changed—though remarkably little, given the time and the cultural differences involved. Because we have so many texts, as well as pictorial representations, the level of analysis which will be applied in this chapter is much deeper than that which we used in the last two chapters.

The story of Inanna and Dumuzi (also known as the Descent of Ishtar, Inanna's later Babylonian counterpart) presented here is a composite version, which hews more closely to the older texts—not because, being older, they necessarily carry more authenticity, but because the earlier Sumerian poets gave freer rein to expression than did the later Babylonian redactors. But much of the detail from the third millennium B.C. Sumerian originals survived in the first millennium B.C. Akkadian texts.

Story Three: Inanna and Dumuzi

The goddess Inanna, Queen of Heaven, decided to depart from the "Great Above" to visit the Underworld, the "Great Below," to attend the funeral ceremonies for Gugalanna, the husband of Ereshkigal, Queen of the Underworld. Because she knew that this was a dangerous venture, she ordered her chief minister, Ninshubur, to wait three days and, if she had not returned, to seek the aid of the great gods. Then she set her face toward the "Land of No Return." When she approached the main gate, the gatekeeper attempted to bar her entry. She threatened that if he did not let her in, she would break down the other gate, which has never been opened, allowing the dead to ascend to the upper world and consume the living. The gatekeeper ordered her to wait until he obtained instructions from Ereshkigal, who ordered the gatekeeper to admit her, but only in accord with the laws of the Underworld.

As Inanna passed the gate, the gatekeeper removed her crown. When she questioned this, he explained that the laws of the Underworld are inflexible. She then approached the second gate, and the scene was repeated, except that this time the gatekeeper removed her earrings. At the third gate, she was required to relinquish her necklace; at the fourth gate, her breastplate; at the fifth gate, her bracelets; at the sixth gate, her "birth-stones" (some type of pubic ornament); and at the seventh gate, her loincloth; so that when she appeared before Ereshkigal she was stark naked—and powerless. Upon encountering one another, Ereshkigal and Inanna flew into a rage, and Ereshkigal ordered her servants to direct the sixty miseries against Inanna: miseries of the sides against her sides, miseries of the front against her front, miseries of the back against her back. She then ordered them to hang Inanna's corpse on a stake like a slab of rotting meat.

Meanwhile, in the upper world, the departure and death of Inanna caused the withdrawal of the earth's fertility. The animals would not copulate, nor would the people. Ninshubur viewed all this with alarm, and after three days she sought the aid of the great gods: first Enlil, the king of the gods; then Nannar, the moon god and Inanna's father; and finally Enki, the god of the subterranean sweet waters. The first two could not help, but Enki, who is also the god of wisdom, devised a plan. Out of clay, he created two sexless beings, whom he dispatched to the Underworld to beg of Ereshkigal the Bread of Life and the Water of Life. When Ereshkigal saw them, she became remorseful and granted their request. They sprinkled Inanna's corpse with the Water of Life and fed her the Bread of Life; she was revived, and returned to the upper world. And as she passed each gate, she was given back the items of apparel she had relinquished on her downward journey.

But the laws of the Underworld are inflexible. Until this time, no one had ever returned from death. Ereshkigal agreed to release Inanna only on the condition that she designate someone to take her place, and a crowd of galla-demons accompanied her on her return to carry off the one whom she would select. So she traveled to the cities of Sumer, where the kings, her lovers, were reigning. At each city, the king observed the approach of the demons from the city walls, and he put on coarse clothing and groveled in the dust before the city gate. At each city, Inanna honored the humility of the king and ordered the demons to pass on—until she came to Uruk, where the young king Dumuzi was the ruler. When he heard of her approach, instead of abasing himself he threw a party and got drunk. That night, he had a dream in which he saw himself being carried off from a reed enclosure by an eagle. He saw the sheep and goats in his fields weeping for him, his milk churn overturned, and his cup broken. The next morning, he asked his sister, Geshtin-anna, to interpret the dream for him. She saw all these images as premonitions of death and urged him to flee the town. She and a male companion took an oath not to reveal his hiding place; if they should, they asked that Dumuzi's dogs pursue and eat them.

When Inanna learned of Dumuzi's effrontery, she was enraged, and directed the demons to carry him off to the Underworld. Geshtin-anna's companion betrayed his hiding place, and the chase was on. Seeing that he could not outrun the galla-demons, he appealed to Utu, the sun god, to transform him into a gazelle. In this form, he was able to outrun his captors, but the transformation only held during the daylight hours when

Utu was in the sky. Each night, he was forced to seek shelter in his human form while the demons regained lost ground. Each morning, he appealed to Utu to transform him again and the chase resumed. On the third night, he sought shelter at the house of Belili, an old woman. But Belili betrayed him, and on the next morning he returned to his sister's sheepfold, where he was surrounded by the seven demons, who smote him on the cheek and carried him off to the Underworld.

This is not quite the end of the story. Inanna loved Dumuzi, and she therefore repented of her anger and wept for him. The salt tears of the goddess are a magical substance; and after she and Geshtin-anna located Dumuzi's corpse with the help of a fly, he was brought back to life. The laws of the Underworld still required a substitute, so a compromise was effected, whereby Dumuzi would have to spend six months of each year in the Underworld, but his sister offered to replace him for the other six months.[1]

Story Three lies at the very core of Sumerian religious beliefs. The myth is clearly part of a literary tradition of considerable sophistication, and it branches out in numerous directions different from those I have discussed in the last two chapters. The first half of the myth, in particular, belongs to another cycle involving death and resurrection. This feature of myth is known as *recombination:* different tales can be grafted together, or split apart and rejoined at another point, much as geneticists are learning to do with the DNA molecule. The noted physicist Murray Gell–Mann refers metaphorically to these recombining elements of myth as "cultural DNA."[2] This type of flexibility is built into the structure of myth, and it allows portions of myths to be transmitted from culture to culture and to be reinterpreted according to the needs of different groups of people, a process which we have already observed in Chapter Two.

To understand the many ramifications of Story Three, I propose to examine its relationship to a number of cultural subsystems, some of which will recall the different theories of myth presented in Chapter Two: the ritual, economic, political, psychological, zoological, cosmological, and somatic contexts. In a way, the analysis of these seven contexts might be considered analogous to the seven stages of Inanna's descent, for we shall be stripping off layer after layer of meaning. We will also examine the roles of the three chief characters in the story, consider the importance of numbers, compare the story with the others we have so far studied, and conclude (as we did with Stories One and Two) with a section on the relevance of its message for our society today.

The Ritual Context: The New Year's Festival

For at least two and a half millennia, the Mesopotamians—the Sumerians as well as their successors, the Akkadians, the Amorites, the Babylonians, the Kassites, and the Assyrians—celebrated the death and burial of Dumuzi every year at the spring equinox, while the celebration of his resurrection was held every fall equinox. The timing of the death and resurrection of Dumuzi is crucial. Like the opposition of Pan and Diana's chief festival days, these events are six months apart. The equinoxes are the only times of year when day and night are of equal length. These are also the only times when the sun rises and sets directly to the east and west. Many peoples celebrate the beginning of the agricultural year at one or the other of these times, and the Sumerians were no exception to this rule. The spring equinox was the time of the New Year's Festival, a liminal period of particular risk, for the survival of their large urban populations depended upon the amount of grain that could be harvested at this time.

The traditional weeping and wailing of the women for Dumuzi (Tammuz) was customary throughout the ancient Middle East, so popular even in Israel that the biblical prophets inveighed against it.[3] The ritual has actually survived to the present in altered form in southern Iraq among Muslims of the Shi'a sect. There, it has been translated into the ritual mourning for the martyr Hussein, who was supposedly killed at the battle of Karbala during the war of succession following the death of Muhammed, but who, according to some sects, was mysteriously spirited away from the battlefield. Like Fionn, he will one day return with a flaming sword as the Imam Mahdi to avenge the wicked and restore righteousness.[4] The mourning ceremony for Hussein at Karbala, vividly recounted by Elizabeth Warnock Fernea in her *Guests of the Sheikh,* is unmistakably a survival of the ancient pagan rite for Dumuzi:

> Each *taaziya* group performed the prescribed ceremony before the tomb of the martyr and then marched out . . . repeating the ritual, in religious ecstasy, before the thousands of pilgrims . . . Mourning for the lost martyr was exalted into a great drama of sorrow and became the individual sorrow of every pilgrim . . .

> "Ohhhhhh—Hussein, our beloved martyr, we grieve for thee," cried the leader.
>
> Tears streamed down the faces of sobbing men standing near me, and the piercing wailing cries of the women spoke of loss and pain and grief and lamentation. [5]

Nor is this the only ritual survival from Sumerian times. The descent of Inanna, and her progressive disrobing, was still celebrated as late as the beginning of the Christian era, for this is what Salome's Dance of the Seven Veils is all about—and Salome's request as a reward was the decapitated head of John the Baptist on a silver platter.[6] Once again we have the motif of the severed head associated with the goddess. John was born at the summer solstice, at the beginning of the lunar-ruled zodiacal sign of Cancer, just as his cousin Jesus' birthday is celebrated at the winter solstice, so his rite is a lunar rite, a transformation (baptism) by water. The timing of their birthdays in the church calendar is once again six months apart.

Because of its white color, silver is the metal assigned to the moon in Near Eastern, and subsequent Græco-Roman culture; it was also the medium of monetary exchange. It is associated with the death of Jesus, too, for Judas is given thirty silver coins as a reward for betraying his master.[7] Thirty is a lunar number, an approximation of the lunar month in days. In Mesopotamia, it symbolizes the Moon God Nannar, Inanna's father. In Oscar Wilde's play *Salomé,* the moon plays an even more significant role; as the deluded king Herod Antipas exclaims: "She is like a mad woman, who is seeking everywhere for lovers. She is naked, too. . . . She reels through the clouds like a drunken woman. . . ." To which his tough-minded wife Herodias replies, "No; the moon is like the moon—that is all."[8]

It is not surprising to find additional parallels to the New Testament in the story of Inanna and Dumuzi. The three days spent by Inanna in the Underworld, hanging on a stake, and her revival using the Bread and Water of Life, are clearly isomorphous to the crucifixion of Christ, the three days of his sojourn in Hell, and the communion sacraments of bread and wine at the Last Supper. The order of these motifs is inverted, as between Stories One and Two. Another obvious ritual parallel is the Good Friday mourning for the crucified and buried Jesus in the Eastern Orthodox Church. We have already seen in the Tzeltal Maya story that the figure of Christ on the cross may be reinterpreted as a figure tied to a stake, and the crowd of saints who gang up on Santo Cristo in that myth sounds suspiciously akin to the crowd of *galla*-demons in Story Three. As Geshtin-anna's oath suggests, the *galla* are also isomorphous to the packs of dogs in Stories One and Two.

The idea that the fertility of the earth is dependent upon the goddess is an important one to which we shall shortly return. For the moment, we may observe another direct parallel, to the Greek myth of Demeter and Persephone:

> *The maiden Persephone had been abducted by Hades to his dark underworld kingdom. Demeter, her mother, embarked on a search for her whereabouts with the aid of Hecate, the goddess of the dark of the moon. When she discovered the truth, Demeter pronounced a curse on the earth's fertility until her daughter should be yielded up to her. Zeus interceded with his brother Hades, and they effected a compromise: Persephone is permitted to live in the upper world for six months of the year—the spring and summer seasons—while she must spend the remaining six months in the underworld, because she inadvertantly consumed six pomegranate seeds while in the underworld.*[9]

The three female figures represent, once again, the Triune Goddess: Persephone the Maiden, Demeter the Matron, and Hecate the Crone. The story of Persephone's descent and ascent is also embedded in a ritual context, for it formed the basis of the Eleusinian Mysteries, in which the initiate discovered his or her own death and resurrection. The compromise at the end is very similar to the one at the conclusion of Story Three, with the main character alternating between the Great Above and the Great Below according to the seasons.

The Economic Context: Harvests of Barley and Dates

There is however an inversion between the Greek myth of Persephone and Story Three, since the six months spent by Persephone in the underworld are the six months spent by Dumuzi in the upper world. The reason for this is closely related to the idea of agricultural fertility. Greek farmers living at 40 degrees north latitude, like farmers in the temperate zone of North America and Western Europe, plant in the spring and harvest in the fall. The new shoots appearing above the ground in the spring are likened to the tender maiden Persephone, whose mother Demeter is the goddess of the wheat. In Latin, Demeter's counterpart Ceres is the origin of our word "cereal." The cutting down of the harvest and its winter storage in underground silos is likened to the descent of Persephone into Hades.

Iraqi farmers, living around 30 degrees north latitude, plant wheat and barley in the fall, since it is too hot to grow grain in the summer, and they harvest in the spring. Here, the warm-season storage of the grain is in the darkness of the granary, which in artistic representations is dominated by Inanna's symbol.[10] This is likened to Dumuzi's sojourn in the Underworld, and his resurrection, keyed to the time that the remaining seeds are taken from the granary for planting, is likened to a rebirth from the warm, dark womb of the goddess. The iconography of Inanna's symbol, which was the origin of the cuneiform sign for both the goddess and the number fifteen (half a month in days, like the marks on the Laussel Venus' horn), is unclear. It may represent a long-haired female figure, or perhaps a rolled-up rattan screen such as may have been used to cover the door of the storehouse. However, the symbol is often shown elevated on a post outside the granary, like a standard. It may also appear associated with shrines, like the one carried on the back of the bull in Figure 10. The same symbol is found, sometimes doubled, at the top of a reed hut from which baby animals emerge (Figure 10), indicating the relationship of the goddess to animal as well as vegetal fertility, as in the myth.

Figure 10: Bull with Inanna symbols. Mesopotamian stamp seal, Jemdet Nasr Period. (Yale Babylonian Collection)

The date harvest is on the opposite schedule from barley: dates ripen in the fall and are planted in the spring. Therefore, it should not surprise us to learn that Dumuzi, in addition to being a shepherd, is a god of the grain, and that Geshtin-anna's name literally means "Date-wine of Heaven." Food staples of great economic importance are often mythologized, as we saw with Bran in Story One. For the Sumerians, who did not have hard liquor, the principal alcoholic beverages were barley-beer and date-wine. That each of these should be personified by a divinity is not surprising, given their power to intensify emotional expression—as we saw with Dionysius, who is the god of the grape. We still refer to alcoholic beverages as "spirits," and the transsubstantiation of the wine and wheat into the blood and body of the risen Christ is the central mystery of the Christian Mass.

The Political Context: Kings and Priests

The Sumerian civilization was the first, as far as we know, to depend upon a centralized political and religious authority. Judging from the large size of the early temples and the ornate architectural decoration lavished upon them, the priesthood appears to have been dominant in the early Mesopotamian cities, but its authority was gradually superseded by that of the wealthy landowners or "real men" (*lú*), the most wealthy of whom, the "big man" (*lugal*), eventually became the hereditary city ruler or king, and his large private house became the palace. Over the three millennia of Mesopotamian kingship during which this myth was told, the size of palaces gradually increased while that of temples decreased.[11] Dumuzi's name appears in the Sumerian King List just before that of Gilgamesh, who is thought to have reigned around 2500 B.C.,[12] a time when the ascendency of the *lugal* had just begun.

This change was not accomplished without considerable social tension, at least at the upper echelons of the highly stratified Sumerian society. One of the ways in which the older priesthood sought to retain control over the emerging institution of kingship was to oblige the king (originally only at the outset of his reign but eventually every year at the time of the New Year's Festival) to participate in a ceremony the Greeks called the *hieros gamos* or Sacred Marriage. In this five-day ritual, he impersonated Dumuzi, while a priestess of Inanna impersonated the goddess.[13] Unlike Dumuzi but like the other kings in the myth, the king was expected to behave with humility toward the goddess, to abase himself before her in order to obtain her favor. If she approved of his behavior, she would reward him with the symbols of kingship, the Ring and the Rod.[12] Like the Inanna symbol, the Ring and Rod combination (German, *Bügelschaft*) appears in early artwork on poles outside the granary, or on top of it. Later, it is characteristically offered to a royal figure by a god or goddess, most often by Inanna herself but sometimes by her grandfather Enlil (the king of the gods), her father Sîn/Nannar, the Moon God, or her brother Utu, the Sun God. This composite symbol, when we see it represented in close detail as in Figure 11, appears to have derived from the surveyor's line and measuring stick, the essential tools for dividing property in a flat, featureless landscape such as the southern Mesopotamian plain.

Although the behavior expected of the king in the Sacred Marriage is a complete inversion of Dumuzi's role in the myth, he is called Dumuzi in the Sacred Marriage texts.[15] The goddess, through her priestess, could potentially refuse the king. For example, in the Kutha legend of Sargon of Agade,

Figure 11: King Ur-Nammu receives the Ring and Rod from the Moon God, Nannar. Mesopotamian stela, Ur III Period. (Corbis)

the young Sargon was a court official of the king of Kish, who committed a cultic offense and lost the favor of the goddess. She subsequently favored Sargon, who left Kish to found a new city and dynasty which soon claimed hegemony, not only over Kish but over all of Mesopotamia.[16] Another anticipated consequence of the goddess' rejection was even more severe: famine for the land. Actual famines and other disasters were interpreted as being the result of the goddess having withdrawn her favor from the king. Wensinck has suggested that "the humiliation of the king means also that chaos swamps society for a moment to such an extent that even its very summit is submerged,"[17] and suggests a relationship between the motif of royal derogation and the story of the Flood. And Jacobsen has noted,

> The ability of humans to incarnate gods and powers is momentous, implying that they can act as these powers and so commit them; in the rite of the sacred marriage the commitment is one of the love and bonds of marriage: to have and to hold forever the power that provides and maintains, Dumuzi.[18]

There is some tenuous evidence that the early Sumerians, like the devotees of Diana at Nemi, may have engaged in ritual regicide for a time during the course of the historical evolution of kingship. This practice was widespread throughout southern Asia and adjacent Africa and Europe,[19] and it appears in most cases to relate to a period of conflict between church and state. By the early second millennium B.C. in Sumer, it had apparently become the practice in certain cases to appoint a substitute king (often a commoner or a criminal) for the five-day duration of the New Year's Festival. This person would be dressed in the king's regalia, paraded around the city, and ritually sacrificed at sundown on the last day of the festival, and the king's regalia destroyed. Following the sacrifice, the presiding priest was required to manufacture a series of pairs of clay images, one to represent evil departing, the other, justice entering. These images are reminiscent of Enki's clay creations, and we shall see that all of them are of particular interest for our story: wild dogs, divine bulls, dragons, goat-fish, and lion-men.[20] We know about this custom largely through an ironic accident. A substitute king appointed in the city of Isin, a gardener named Erra-imitti, was preparing for his fate while the real king and his relatives were partying in the palace. The real king died as a result of drinking boiling soup, and the priesthood had no logical choice other than to appoint the gardener to be the new king.[21] One can almost hear their reasoning across the millennia: after all, look what happened to Dumuzi when *he* threw a party!

In later times the ritual for the substitute king was reserved for times of eclipses of the Sun, Moon, or planets.[22] But some echoes of the old custom of ritual regicide may have survived into the first millennium B.C. In Assyria, it was the practice for the king at the spring equinox to name each year after an important official, starting with himself in his first year of reign and followed by the crown prince, the army commander, and on down the ranks of officials and provincial governors. But apparently the king's reign was not expected to last for as long as thirty years, for when Shalmaneser III approached his thirtieth year of reign and declared that the year would again be given his own name the following spring, the result was a bloody civil war with his elder sons, which nearly tore the Assyrian empire apart.[23]

One political interpretation of this custom is similar to that which we have already seen in Stories One and Two: that the female representatives of the goddess Inanna used the Sacred Marriage to maintain some measure of power over the male political leaders. This may hark back to a time when the women actually chose the rulers and determined the length of their reigns. In the earliest phase of Mesopotamian civilization, there are depictions of tribute being brought before a huge figure of the goddess, who is attended by the much smaller figure of the city ruler.[24] Whether or not this means that the goddess' priestesses *factually* wielded political power at one time, it is probably more important to observe that, at the time the story of Inanna and Dumuzi was first transcribed, the Sumerians apparently *believed* that they had. In later times, the New Year's Festival celebrated the triumph of order over chaos, symbolized by the conflict between the storm-god Marduk, a son of Enki, and the mother-goddess Tiamat, a great sea serpent. This may indicate a change toward a more patriarchal, solar mythology, as Marduk's name appears to mean "Son of the Sun" while Tiamat's name means "Mother of Life."

The Psychological Context: Dumuzi's Dream

An important part of the later creation epic is Marduk's establishment of the courses of the stars and planets—the orderly sky—out of the dismembered body of the primordial mother-goddess.[25] The practice of Sky-Measure (as astronomy), while it was primarily used to establish the agricultural calendar, also came to be used as a means of foretelling the future (as astrology), in particular, that of the king. It was not until the Hellenistic Greeks borrowed the trappings of Mesopotamian star-lore that horoscopes were cast for ordinary individuals. Mesopotamian astrology was less systematic than its Greek counterpart. Most predictions consisted of long lists of observations associated with corresponding events which took place at or near the time of their previous occurrence, which astrologer–priests could consult when the particular planetary configuration recurred. We shall return to the study of the heavens later, but astrological prediction was only one of many methods of divination used by specialists among the Mesopotamian priesthood. Others included the reading of the entrails of sheep, the shapes taken by water poured over the threshold of a new building, the landing positions of spears thrown into the air, and, most important for Story Three, the interpretation of dreams. As Joseph Campbell has noted, "dream is the personalized myth, myth the depersonalized dream; both myth and dream are symbolic in the same general way of the dynamics of the psyche."[26] So when we find a dream embedded within a myth, we should pay particular attention to what it has to tell us.

Dumuzi's dream would appear to be one of the earliest ever recorded, and Geshtin-anna's professional role (like that of Joseph in the Old Testament) indicates that even as early as the middle of the third millennium B.C. dreams (especially those of monarchs) were taken seriously and acted upon. Like Dumuzi's dream, the dream of pharaoh which Joseph interprets is closely related to the themes of animal fertility and famine, and its symbolism emphasizes the number seven.[27] We learn from later Akkadian texts about the Flood that a ruler who wished to obtain guidance from dreams would go sleep in a special incubation hut made of reeds. The walls of the hut were permeable so as to receive messages from the gods.[28] These huts may be analogous to the reed enclosure from which Dumuzi dreamt he was abducted. Reed huts, which are still built by the Marsh Arabs in the Tigris-Euphrates estuary, are thought to have been the oldest structures of the Sumerians. Once they mastered the art of making houses of mudbrick, they still retained reed shrines, like the dream huts and Inanna's granaries and birthing huts—an example of a deliberate archaizing tendency.[29]

Several cylinder seals from the Akkadian Period (ca. 2350–2250 B.C.) seem to depict the events of Dumuzi's dream: a man is carried aloft by an eagle while his sheep and goats watch from below, and a reed structure, a churn, and a milk cup are present. Just beneath the eagle are two dogs

Figure 12: The ascent of "Etana." Mesopotamian cylinder seal, Akkadian Period. (Pierpont Morgan Library)

(Figure 12). In some versions, a supplicating female figure (Geshtin-anna?) is placed between the dogs. This scene has usually been interpreted to depict the flight of Etana to heaven on the back of an eagle. We shall meet Etana again in Chapter Seven, but that myth does not include any of the detailed motifs present in both Dumuzi's dream and the seal designs. Etana's flight takes place during the day, while the consistent presence of the crescent moon on the seals indicates that this is a night scene, perhaps a reference to the time of the original dream.

For the psychoanalytical school of mythology, dreams are of great importance, because they are avenues used by the unconscious to touch waking consciousness. In the hands of a capable interpreter, they can elucidate much about the developmental process through which a person is passing. How might a modern Jungian interpreter read Dumuzi's dream, and how accurate was Geshtin-anna's interpretation? The dream carries a clear warning of danger. Dumuzi's protected herd animals, representing his instinctual nature, have lost the guidance of his ego and are in mourning. The broken cup and overturned milk churn are feminine symbols. That they are in an inverted or broken state may suggest that there is something inappropriate about Dumuzi's relationship to the feminine (though not so much that he is unwilling to listen to his sister's advice), and that, like Inanna at the beginning of the story, he is about to be broken and to undergo a downward journey into the land of death. In the Royal Tombs of Ur, thought to date a century or so later than the time at which Story Three is set, sixteen monarchs were buried in splendor in underground chambers surrounded by large numbers of sacrificed servants, mostly women, and an inverted pot was placed over the top of each tomb.[30] We shall shortly see that the eagle flight can be viewed as a premonition of death even though the direction is just the opposite of a descent to the Underworld. Perhaps it implies Dumuzi's eventual resurrection.

Geshtin-anna clearly sees all of this as representing a danger to her brother, coming from the feminine side. But, as was the case with Actæon, flight is not a very useful option, especially when Geshtin-anna's male companion (Dumuzi's *Shadow,* in Jungian psychology: the negative side of his personality) is ready to betray him. Perhaps a modern Jungian psychoanalyst would advise the analysand to stand his ground and accept the transformation which is inevitably going to overtake him, with the understanding that it is an opportunity for the expansion of consciousness in a new, and greatly needed direction, even though it is at first fraught with terror.[31]

The Zoological Context: A Mesopotamian Taxonomic System

The subsequent chase scene and animal transformation should by now sound quite familiar. Notice the oblique association of the *galla*-demons with Dumuzi's dogs, who are present only in Geshtin-anna's oath. The transformation this time is requested, rather than being involuntary, by the male figure and is into a gazelle rather than a stag. This allows us to examine another principle of mythic structure which is very common, that of *free substitution.* Under certain conditions, symbols may be freely exchanged for one another without changing the structure or meaning of a myth. The conditions are determined by the culture's view of its world, and a careful study of the variants can reveal a great deal about their rules of classification.

In Mesopotamian artwork, of which we have far more examples than texts, there are many representations of animals. Persons of property (even those who owned only small plots of land but who were forced by economic circumstances to sell what little they had) were required to witness financial documents by rolling their personal cylindrical seal over the moist clay of the tablet. While each stone cylinder seal was handmade and more or less unique, one of the most popular scenes depicted on the seals shows pairs of lions attacking pairs of herbivorous animals, which are in turn protected by male human figures. The animals under attack may be bulls, goats, sheep, human-headed bulls, stags, gazelles, or donkeys, and the pair need not be identical with each other on the same seal, but they can never be any other type of animal. It was also permissible to substitute leopards or leonine monsters (winged lions, lion-headed men, etc.) for one or both of the lions, but again, never any others. The human figures may appear in various guises, and may have some animal parts—wings, hooves, horns, tail—but they always have at least a human torso. At times, there are small "filler motifs" inserted in open spaces in the frieze; these are usually oviparous (egg-laying) animals, such as birds, fish, reptiles, or scorpions, none of which appear in other positions in the design.

These variances and invariances, all of which appear in Figure 13, suggest strongly that the Mesopotamians categorized the faunal life around them into four classes: carnivores, oviparous animals, humans, and herbivores. These classes were epitomized by their most frequently appearing members, which were also the ones most often combined in monstrous forms (called *Mischwesen*, or "mixed creatures" in German): the lion, the eagle, the man, and the bull. Within these classes, in the seals, free substitution of one member of a class for another was permissible, but not between classes.[32] The substitution of a gazelle for a stag would be perfectly acceptable in this system. Within Story Three, we actually have such a substitution: sheep and goats appear in Dumuzi's dream, while the gazelle is the animal of transformation later on. In fact, the same free substitutions occur often in literary texts, for the Mesopotamians were fond of

Figure 13: Animals and humans in combat. Mesopotamian cylinder seal, Early Dynastic III Period. (Yale Babylonian Collection)

hendiadys, a literary device in which a pair of adjacent lines of text contain similar content but different phrasing.

The same device is also very common in the Old Testament, where a similar categorization of four classes of animals, as represented by their epitomes, is the foundation for the Chariot of God in the visions of both Ezekiel and the Apostle John.[33] When considering the possibility of free substitution between myths of *different* cultures, it is essential first to establish the classification system each of them has developed, to see if it allows for the substitution. Otherwise this would be tantamount to an assumption of diffusion or cultural contact between the cultures, which should properly be demonstrated on external grounds instead of being inferred solely from the myths. The case of Ezekiel is very likely one of direct diffusion, since the prophet was wandering just outside of Babylon when he had his famous vision of the wheels. The second case is almost certainly borrowed from the first. But in either case, the four-fold animal symbolism already had deep roots in all the ancient cultures of the Eastern Mediterranean.[34] We have also seen that there is permissible substitution between stag and horse in Celtic myth, and between stag and boar as favorites of the goddess in Greece. Beyond this it is not possible to go at the present state of our knowledge, though we shall later see that there is some evidence for diffusion among these cultures.

The Cosmological Context: The Origins of the Zodiac

The four most common animal symbols on the seals are also related to important markers in the calendrical cycle: the zodiacal signs of Leo (the lion), Scorpio (the scorpion, but also the eagle), Aquarius (the man), and Taurus (the bull). The names of the modern zodiacal constellations, for the most part, derive from Mesopotamian astrology. The constellations of Leo, Scorpio, and Taurus are among the few that actually look like the animals they are supposed to represent, and each contains a bright first magnitude star (the case of Aquarius is different, and will be discussed below). All three have the same names in Sumerian as they do in later Græco-Roman astrology. The positions of these stars in conjunction with the rising sun were used to determine the dates of the equinoxes, which are rather difficult to fix in any other way.

During the period of the early Sumerian city-states (ca. 4300–2300 B.C.), at dawn on the day of the spring equinox—the day of the New Year's

Festival and of Dumuzi's death—the sun would have risen in the constellation Taurus, while Leo was at the zenith and Scorpio was setting in the west. Aquarius would have been invisible, below the horizon. This symbol grouping was carried over into succeeding ages without change, even though the astronomical observations no longer accorded with it because of the *precession of the equinoxes:* due to the wobble of the earth's axis, every seventy-two years the position of the zodiac at the time of the spring equinox appears to slip backwards by one degree. The first magnitude stars in Taurus, Leo, and Scorpio are close to 90° apart, forming a right-angled T-cross.[35] The angle between Aldebaran in Taurus and Antares in Scorpio (both first magnitude red giants) is so close to 180° that a Mesopotamian astronomical text states, "The Bull and the Scorpion are one,"[36] a paradoxical statement to which we shall return.

Aquarius lies in a region of the zodiacal band that has no bright stars. However, the ancients recognized such dim portions of the zodiac by their association with better defined constellations on either side of the band of the ecliptic, called by the Greeks *paranatellonta*. The most obvious *paranatellon* of Aquarius is the familiar square of Pegasus, called by the Sumerians *1–iku*, the "One-Acre Field."[37] This brings us back to the symbolism of the Ring and Rod, from Sky-Measure to Earth-Measure, for it was the responsibility of the Sumerian king to determine the boundaries between fields, thereby assuring the reliability of land ownership. In the flat, mostly treeless landscape of the Tigris-Euphrates floodplain, it was easy to lay out rectilinear fields with these simple surveyor's tools. Since annual flooding would eradicate field markers, the artificial boundaries continually had to be renewed. This was considered to be a crucial part of the king's dispensation of righteousness; for this reason, Dumuzi's name means "right son." (Also for this reason, the device we most commonly use to measure linear distance today is called a "ruler.") For the Sumerians as for us, the word "right" had triple connotations: justice, handedness, and angles of 90° such as appear in both the Pegasus square and Mesopotamian field corners.

The Mesopotamians conceptualized the compass directions, the "world's four quarters" forming a right-angled cross, which was visualized in terms of the human body: as you stand in the central sacred city of Nippur and face east toward the rising sun, your left hand is to the north and your right hand to the south. For this reason, the name of the nation of Yemen, at the southern tip of the Arabian peninsula, literally means "right hand," while in ancient times the area to the northwest of Sumer, in modern southern Turkey, was called Sam'al, "left hand." From Sumer, the south is the domain of Enki, the land of Dilmun, simultaneously equivalent to both the underworld and the earthly paradise, where old age and decay are unknown. The winter season, the time of the Sun's movement from its extreme southerly position at the solstice and the time of Dumuzi's ascendency, is dominated by zodiacal signs associated with water: Capricorn, the sea-goat, Aquarius, the water-bearer, and Pisces, the fish. These constellations are all of Mesopotamian origin, and it appears that, unlike Ptolemaic astrology, in which the four elements of fire, earth, air, and water are rotated through the seasons starting with Aries, the Mesopotamians assigned one element to each season: spring for earth, summer for fire, autumn for air, and winter for water.[38]

Enki, like the Græco-Roman god Hermes/Mercurius, is a god of the mind and a Trickster figure. He is the old god of the southern priesthood of Eridu, and it is from him that Inanna originally obtained the right to confer Royal Rule (*nam.lugal*), in a southward quest and return isomorphous to her descent to the underworld. She departed from the city of Uruk down the Euphrates in her boat for the Abzu in Eridu. Enki, like Ereshkigal, had his vizier admit her to his presence, but by contrast the vizier was told to treat her as an equal and offer her food and drink (the water of life and the bread of life?). After getting Enki drunk (after fourteen toasts), Inanna stole from him the fifty *mes,* the gifts of civilization. *Nam.lugal,* kingship, stands nearly at the head of the list of *mes,* preceded only by priesthood (*nam.en*) and divinity (*nam.dingir*). After the inevitable chase scene up the river, Enki reluctantly agreed to cede his powers to the young goddess.[39]

The direction of Inanna's journey is significant, for the Mesopotamians were the first to make maps with north oriented up and south down, creating a correspondence between Earth-measure (geography) to Sky-measure (astronomy). The northern circumpolar constellations, as we saw in the Kallisto myth, never touch the earth; therefore, they are associated with the god of the Above, An. During the third and second millennia B.C., when Story Three was formed, the central point of the northern sky was not Polaris as it is today. Probably the first magnitude star Alpha Draconis was the best approximation to true north. The bright second magnitude stars of the Big Dipper, called in Sumerian *mar.gid.da,* the Chariot, would still have been an important directional marker. This constellation was associated in their system with the city of Nippur, in the north of Sumer, and very probably its seven bright stars were isomorphous to the seven levels of the Underworld, as Geoffrey Ashe has recently suggested.[40] The Heaven of An also includes the northern third of the zodiacal band, including the constellation of Leo, Inanna's chief symbol. The central third, containing the equinoctial zodiacal constellations, is the Heaven of Enlil, the king of the gods. The southern third of the zodiacal band and the stars visible to the south of it are part of the Heaven of Enki, including the river constellation Eridanus, "of Eridu," with its bright first magnitude star Fomalhaut, "the head of the fish."[41] Once Inanna appropriated Royal Rule from Eridu to Uruk, it seemed thereafter to proceed to the north, at first to Nippur, Enlil's city, and later to the "capital district" of central Mesopotamia that includes Agade, Babylon, Hellenistic Seleucia, Parthian Ctesiphon, and the modern Baghdad, while the south remained a center of priestly activity (Figure 14). Both Inanna and Dumuzi were worshipped at Nippur, which city had to be controlled by any ruler with pretense of being "King of the World's Four Quarters."[42] This dichotomy between the south and the north has been a source of social and religious tension in the Tigris-Euphrates Valley for millennia. As the opposition between the Sunni central

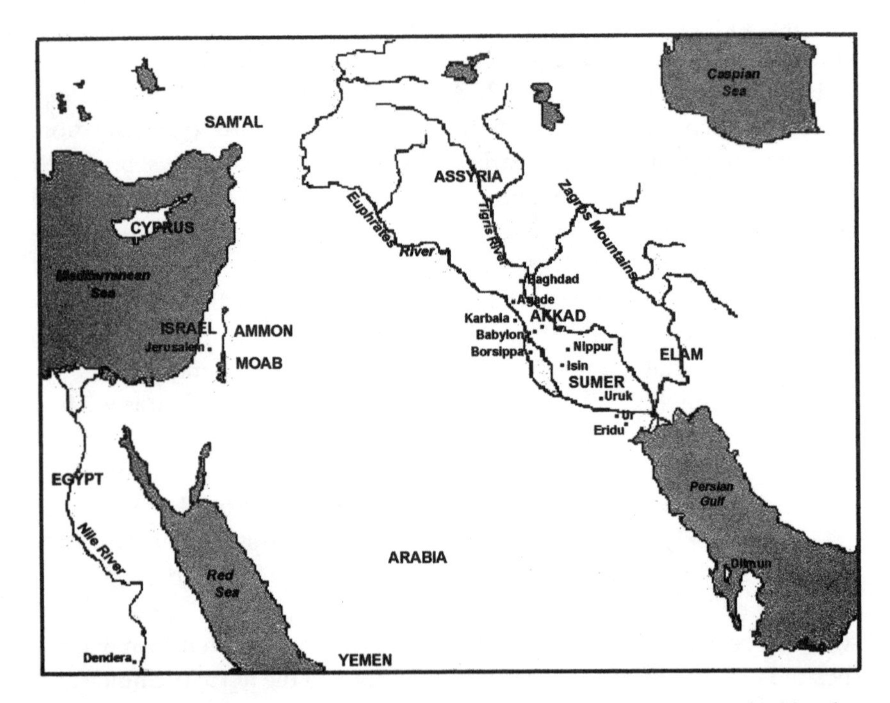

Figure 14: Map of the Ancient Near East. (Adapted from a map supplied by the Yale Babylonian Collection)

authority in Baghdad and the Shi'a Muslims in Karbala and Basra shows, it remains a problem to the present day.

The Role of Dumuzi

Before we proceed to the seventh and final context for Story Three, we need to digress in order to consider the roles of the key figures in the myth: Dumuzi, Geshtin-anna, and Inanna. Though he is the king of Uruk, Dumuzi certainly does not demonstrate the quality of dispensing justice in Story Three. He behaves in a cavalier manner toward the goddess and then flees from her wrath—most likely a case of inversion, for kings often liked to portray themselves as instruments of divine vengeance upon their enemies. However, in numerous hymns he is depicted as the protector of the fields and sheepfolds. If we ask whose "right son" he is, the answer both the texts and artistic representations give us is Enki. Elizabeth Douglas Van Buren has demonstrated the association of Dumuzi-abzu, "Dumuzi of the Deep," with the common iconographic figure of a nude man with a flowing vase (later the standard icon for Aquarius) who provides water to herd animals.[43] Many representations show him kneeling with his legs forming 90° angles, which is also characteristic of the Aquarius icon (Figure 15). We have already seen this position, associated with the water and the jug, in Figure 5. Some cylinder seals depict the nude bearded man carrying a catch of fish, and fish are also sometimes shown

Figure 15: Dumuzi, lord of Right Rule. Mesopotamian cylinder seal, Akkadian Period. (Corbis)

in the streams of water that flow from the vase held by the nude bearded man. In the Sumerian King List, Dumuzi is actually referred to as a fisherman, and while he is listed among the kings of Uruk his city is given as "Kua," which simply means fish.[44] The flowing waters of the rivers are essential for the fertility of the grain fields of which Dumuzi is also the protector. Enki himself is often depicted with the same streams of water flowing from his shoulders. In one of the creation myths, he ejaculates into the empty beds of the Tigris and Euphrates rivers, thus directly giving life to the land.[45] In Sumerian, the word *A* denotes both "water" and "semen." In later times, Enki was known by the name Ea, which means "Temple of Water," and his temple at Eridu contained a large subterranean room lined with bitumen, a waterproof material. Presumably it was a pool associated with his worship.

And there is more than this. In Sumerian historical texts, the king was often referred to as *nita kalaga,* "virile bull" much like his Egyptian counterpart. One of the most common words for lion, *ur-Gula,* means "dog of Aquarius," the sign directly opposite Leo. Gula is a daughter of Enki and a goddess of healing. Inanna is usually represented riding or standing on the head of a lion when she is approached by the king, accompanied by Nin-shubur (Figure 16), and is addressed in hymns as "lioness" or even "lion."[46] The first magnitude star in Leo which we call Regulus, "the little king," was called *^mul^lugal*, the king-star, in Sumerian, and was held to gov-

Figure 16: The Goddess Inanna on her lion. Mesopotamian cylinder seal, Old Babylonian Period. (Yale Babylonian Collection)

ern the destiny of the king.[47] The traditional astrological attributes of Leo—prideful, domineering, dramatic, self-centered behavior—are certainly excellent descriptions of Inanna! We should note that Diana's feast day on August 13 falls within this astrological sign. Scorpio, the traditional sign of sex and death in modern astrology, was also associated in Mesopotamia with sexuality: Ishhara, the scorpion goddess, is often depicted under the bed in scenes of the Sacred Marriage.[48]

The symbolism of all this is not difficult to read: the king, like a bull or gazelle, arises in power until the Sun reaches the sign of Taurus, but at the spring equinox the goddess is rampant at the zenith in Leo, and their whole relationship is colored at the opposite horizon by sex/death in Scorpio.[49] The message is clear when we consider the conditions under which Royal Rule was obtained in Mesopotamia: the goddess is dangerous, capable of granting or withholding her favors from the king and from the land, and of cutting him down like a stalk of ripe grain at the height of his powers. In order to keep his throne, the king must treat her with proper respect. Any other attitude would be punished as *hybris*, as was the case with Dumuzi.

The Role of Geshtin-anna

An important figure who appears for the first time in our series of myths is the faithful sister Geshtin-anna, who agrees to take her brother's place in the underworld. Like the Greek Antigone, "the most sisterly of souls," as Goethe called her,[50] she seeks out the body of her brother for decent burial. Antigone, too, submits voluntarily to burial underground on the principle that while a husband or child can be replaced, once the parents have died a brother never can be. Her threnody in Sophocles' play also suggests a deeper relationship, founded upon the Sacred Marriage and death of Dumuzi: "Woe! Woe! My brother! You, fallen into a disastrous marriage! I, whom you left behind, you now drag after you in death."[51]

We shall encounter the motif of the sister again in Stories Six and Seven. There, the brother–sister relationship is colored by incest, of which there is no apparent trace either in Story Three or Sophocles' *Antigone.* However, Kramer has translated a Sumerian Sacred Marriage text in which Dumuzi sexually initiates Geshtin-anna in the sheepfold.[52] Of course, Antigone and her brother Polyneices are the *products* of an incestuous union between Oedipus and Jocasta—yet another generation of aberrant Theban royalty!

Antigone's act of resistance to the state is further evidence of the tension which exists between inflexible patriarchal political structures and the imperatives of the family which have been the concerns of women throughout the ages—a tension which also permeated Sumerian society. The *galla*-demons in Story Three behave much like abusive police, in a manner all too familiar to us in the late twentieth century from Third World dictatorships (and poorly run departments in U.S. cities—e.g., the Rodney King incident). In one text, in their zeal to discover Dumuzi's hiding place they first try to bribe Geshtin-anna, then torture her by stripping her naked and pouring pitch into her vagina, to no avail. They complain: "who since the beginning of time has ever known a sister to reveal a brother's hiding place?"[53] This certainly suggests that harsh interrogatory methods such as these were not unknown to Sumerian city rulers.

The Role of the Goddess

Innana's role in this story, as well as elsewhere in Mesopotamian literature, is extraordinarily complex. She impulsively seeks to enter the Great Below, against all its rules; but on her return she is the enforcer of the same rules. In the *Exaltation of Inanna* text, she is described as a bird of prey who swoops down upon the lands to punish the wicked.[54] In the final section of the myth, we see the goddess in a different role as the lamenting figure whose salty tears revive the slain Dumuzi. She appears in this role frequently in cuneiform literature, most notably in the Flood story, where she weeps for drowned humankind.[55] In so doing, she raises her necklace, which is made of flies—this may relate to the fly which enabled her and Geshtin-anna to find Dumuzi's corpse. In later times, particularly, Ishtar became a goddess of battle, delighting in carrion, and had the epithet Belet-zumbi (Lady of the Flies). In early Christian times, this title was masculinized into Beelzebub and also demonized.

The significance of salt water in the Mesopotamian context should not be overlooked. Agricultural fertility depended upon the continued deposit of alluvial soils by the annual flooding of the Tigris and Euphrates, but it also depended on keeping the brackish waters of the Persian Gulf from backing up the estuary into the canal systems. If the central political authority did not keep the canals dredged, the fields could become sterile as a result of salinization, resulting in famine. This situation is depicted graphically in the *Atra-hasis* myth as one of the plagues afflicting Mesopotamia, where it is blamed upon the propensity of humans to overpopulate.[56] Thus, the dredging of canals by the city ruler was considered a sacred duty. At the opening of *Atra-hasis,* the great gods direct the lesser gods in this task, and the canals they dredge are the Tigris and Euphrates Rivers. In the late creation epic *Enuma Elish,* the salty waters of the Gulf were associated with Tiamat, the great Mother Goddess, as the sweet waters were originally the domain of her consort, Abzu, and the creation of the universe was attributed to the mingling of their waters.[58] This is an obvious metaphor for sexual intercourse. Enki eventually took over the sweet waters by murdering Abzu, his great-grandfather. As we have seen, the victory of his son Marduk over the sea-serpent Tiamat was the focus of later celebrations of the New Year's Festival.[57] The salt tears of the goddess are a powerful magical substance, indeed!

In *Enuma Elish,* Marduk splits Tiamat like an oyster and places her upper half in the sky; her lower half forms the earth. This is a situation obviously echoed in the biblical creation,[59] where the "deep" over which the spirit of God hovers (Hebrew *tehom*) is actually cognate to Sumerian Tiamat. In the Neo-Babylonian New Year's texts, a bird is split in half and one-half is thrown upward; this represents the splitting of the primordial sea-serpent goddess. Once again, we have the two aspects of the Scorpio symbol: serpent and bird. Oysters are old fertility symbols because of their resemblance to the female genitalia; it is for this reason that they are consumed around the Mediterranean today as an aphrodisiac.

Mythological characters' names are often significant, as Max Müller noted.[60] If we can understand the meaning of their names, we will also understand something about the underlying meaning of their presence in the myth. For example, we saw that Geshtin-anna's name revealed something about the agricultural significance of the substitution between her and her brother. Ereshkigal's name means "The Harvest of the Great Earth," the harvest, of course, being the dead. As we have already seen, the harvest of the grain is under the supervision of Inanna herself, and the grain is Dumuzi. This suggests most strongly that Inanna, the Queen of the "Great Above," and her elder sister Ereshkigal, the Queen of the "Great Below," are in some sense one and the same goddess. This is further suggested by the reason given for Inanna's descent in the first place: to witness the funeral of Ereshkigal's husband, Gugalanna. Gugalanna's name means "The Great Bull of Heaven," which is none other than the constellation Taurus, with which, as we have seen, Dumuzi may be associated. In the Akkadian version of the Gilgamesh Epic, the hero rebuffs Ishtar's advances by reminding her of the dire fate which each of her lovers (including Dumuzi) have met. Outraged, she appeals to her father An to release the Bull of Heaven to attack Gilgamesh. When Gilgamesh and his companion Enkidu kill the bull and throw its thigh in Ishtar's face, she and her priestesses set up the traditional Dumuzi lament over it.[61] As in Story Two, we have the association of the herbivore's leg with the goddess. It might be noted that in the Roman period Egyptian zodiac of Dendera, heavily influenced by Mesopotamian astrology, the central position in the northern sky is occupied by the severed leg of a bull.[62] So what could it possibly mean that the consort of the Queen of the Underworld has died and is being buried? If the king is the "virile bull," then is it not Dumuzi himself who is being memorialized?

Thus, the brilliant goddess of the morning and evening star, the "Lady of the Resplendent *Mes*,"[63] is *also* the Queen of the Underworld, the Lady of Darkness. The name of Ereshkigal's mortal counterpart in the myth, Belili, means "The White Lady"—appropriately, because as the betrayer of the hero she plays a role similar to that of the Celtic White Goddess, who is also the hag of Story One. Once again, we have the Triune Goddess: Maid (Geshtin-anna), Matron (Inanna), and Crone (Ereshkigal/Belili).

We may expect that the identity of these goddesses had very different meanings for Sumerian men and women. The message for men, as in Stories One and Two, is that the goddess is not to be trifled with: she is the epitome of change, and one must take care (especially if one is a king!) not to buck her flow. For women, the message is much deeper, since Inanna's descent, like that of Fionn, is into her own unconscious. There she must deal with terrifyingly numinous powers which are ultimately hers to wield once she has passed through the initiatory ordeal of death and resurrection. Prior to this event, Inanna is clearly unable to revive even herself without the aid of Enki; after it, she holds the keys of life and death and can resurrect Dumuzi—or condemn him to death again, if need be. Women who have undergone this transformation of consciousness and learned to relate to the goddess in all of her aspects, to allow the energy of Maiden, Matron, and Crone to be expressed in their own lives, are strongly empowered by the experience. The myth acts as a confirmation of this process, especially in a social context overwhelmingly dominated by patriarchal values.

The Significance of Numbers

Numbers are of great importance in myth, because they represent encapsulations of ideas in coded form. Especially for the Sumerians, whose economy depended upon accurate measurement of land, property, and the night sky, the concept of number was crucial. In most cultures, the numbers from one to ten (corresponding to the fingers) are assigned particular symbolic meanings, but there are remarkable cross-cultural parallels for these most elementary of symbols. For example, one almost always represents spirit, unity, divinity, and the masculine. Two almost always denotes matter, duality, the feminine, and separation into the pairs of opposites. The reasons for this universality are matters of dispute among the three theoretical schools described in Chapter Two, but it seems difficult to imagine how any human group could get along without at least *some* concept of number. The structural properties of number are somewhat invariant, so diffusion is a less likely explanation for these similarities than the other two theories. Complexity theorists suggest that the prime integers are essential features of the universe, which are likely to be comprehended in similar ways by any sentient species.[64]

In Story Three, the numbers two, three, and seven have the greatest importance. Two appears in the contrast between the "Great Above" and the "Great Below," in the opposed pair of queens of these realms, Inanna and Ereshkigal, in the two exits from the underworld, in the two neuter beings made by Enki, in the two sacraments administered to revive Inanna, and in the brother–sister pair. Three appears in the number of days Inanna spends in the underworld, in the number of great gods consulted by Ninshubur, in the triad of goddesses, and in the number of days of Dumuzi's flight.

The number seven is the most interesting of all, represented by the number of gates of the underworld, by the items of clothing removed and retrieved by Inanna, and by the number of demons who pursue Dumuzi. It is obviously related to the title of this book, thus some further commentary on it is necessary. Seven is a number often associated with adeptship and skill, because there is no mathematical construction for a regular heptagon. It is the sum of the triad and the quaternary, representative of spirit and matter combined. To the ancients, there were seven visible heavenly bodies whose position changed against the "fixed" stars: Sun, Moon, Mercury, Venus, Mars, Jupiter, and Saturn. These correspond to the seven great (*Anunna*) gods in Sumerian mythology: Utu, Nannar/Sîn, Enki,

Inanna, Enlil, An, and the many-named Mother Goddess (Ninhursag, Nintu, Ki, Mami, or Ereshkigal) respectively. It formed the basis of the quartering of the twenty-eight-day lunar cycle into seven-day weeks, each day named for a planetary god. This system, which we still use, was invented by the Sumerians. So the number seven is important to Sky-Measure.

The *ziggurat* (stepped temple tower) in the city of Borsippa actually had seven levels—a *literal* seven-story tower—each dedicated to a planetary god, and its name, *Etemenanki,* means "the house of the bond between Heaven and Earth." The *ziggurat* also is related to the Sacred Marriage, for it was believed that while the king and priestess engaged in sexual union in a temple at its base, the god and goddess did likewise in the temple at its summit, thereby assuring by sympathetic magic the fertility of the land.[65] The Hebrews, spending time in captivity in Babylonia, looked upon such rituals, as well as the towers themselves, with great disdain. This—plus the cosmopolitan, multilingual character of the cities there—may have given rise to the negative story of the Tower of Babel, and the scattering of tongues which followed its collapse.[66] In Chapters Six and Seven we shall see that the idea of the division of an originally united humanity is an important mythological theme.

The Somatic Context: The Measure of Man

And so we reach the seventh and final context of this myth. The association of the number seven with Inanna's sequential disrobing has a special significance, for another of the coding systems with which myth concerns itself is the human body. As Lévi-Strauss has shown, these coding systems are often interlinked on many levels, and it is essential to explore them all if one wishes to achieve an understanding of the cultural system which produced a myth. He states:

> [The] cosmographic code is no truer than any other; and it is no better, except from the methodological point of view, as far as its operations can be checked from without. But it is not impossible that advances in biochemistry may one day provide objective references of the same degree of accuracy as a check on the precision and coherence of the codes formulated in the language of the senses. Myths are constructed on the basis of a certain logicality of

tangible qualities which makes no clear-cut distinction between subjective states and the properties of the cosmos.[67]

In studying any repeated sequence in myth, it is helpful to observe its *direction*. In this case, it is clearly vertical. Inanna's status is reduced as she descends from that of a crowned queen to that of a naked slave—much in the same way that Actæon, in his prurient immaturity, would reduce Diana's divinity. In Story Three, the reduction is depicted as being due to the implacable laws of the underworld. It is interesting to consider that the Sumerians, who invented patriarchal bureaucracy, conceptualized Hell as an inflexible bureaucracy. This speaks volumes about their attitudes toward their own political system! As the goddess descends, she sheds power along the axis of her spinal column (note that the sequence ends at the loincloth and not lower), and, as she moves in the opposite direction, she regains power. We should recall that when Santo Cristo was stripped of his reed cloak by the saints, he was rendered powerless to flood the world. The vertical axis of the body of Inanna is also isomorphous to the vertical or north–south axis of the world, for as we have seen she travels from south to north carrying the precious *mes* to Uruk, and that political power subsequently moved yet further north to Nippur, the central city.

The next question that should be asked is, are there any mythological systems in which an increase in power is associated with rising along the vertical axis of the body? There are at least four well-documented examples of this: the ritual *!kia* trances of the !Kung San Bushmen of Namibia and Botswana, in which men "heat" themselves by drawing an energy called *n/um* up their spines in order to heal the sick;[68] the doctrine of the vibratory centers of the Hopi people of Arizona, by which healers are able to diagnose illness by observing the quality of vibration in each center, and in which the crown center at the top of the head, the *kopawvi,* is a means by which people communicate with the Creator;[69] the Tree of Life of the Jewish Qabbalah; and the Kundalini system of India. One reason for the emphasis in all these systems upon the vertical axis of the body and its relationship to the Great Above and the Great Below is that humans, unlike other mammals (except, at times, bears!), are bipeds, with our spines oriented up and down rather than parallel to the earth.

The first two of these cases are probably too distant to be useful parallels, except they confirm that there exists in many cultures a knowledge of the body's energy centers that can be tapped for certain sacred purposes by healers or shamans. The other two cases are closer to the geographical domain of Story Three and may be related to it by diffusion, so we will consider them in more detail. As well, both of these systems, as practices and as philosophies, have become popularized in New Age circles during the past thirty years—that is how I familiarized myself with them.

The Tree of Life refers to the scene in the Garden of Eden in which the human pair eat of the fruit of the Tree of Knowledge of Good and Evil (the pairs of opposites) and immediately become aware of their gender duality. Adam and his wife are banished from the Garden "lest he put forth his hand, and take also of the fruit of the Tree of Life and eat, and live forever."[70] In the Qabbalistic tradition, the Fall of Man into duality is counterbalanced by a prospective redemption, achieved by ascending the branches of the Tree of Life until, eventually, divinity is attained. The tree is divided into ten spheres or *Sephiroth,* and these are arranged into seven levels through which the adept must ascend. Each of the Sephiroth corresponds to a part of the human body, beginning with the feet and ending with the crown of the head.[71] The higher levels of this system are only rarely attained, and it is suggested that only the prophet Moses achieved the highest level, where, after his bodily disappearance from the summit of Mount Horeb, he was transformed into Metatron, the Archangel associated with the highest of the Sephiroth, *Kether* (the Crown), and with brilliant white light. It is for this reason that many depictions of Moses (including Michelangelo's famous statue) show him with horns on his head, since horns are symbols of the divine power of *Kether.*

In Mesopotamia, the crowns worn by gods and goddesses (including Inanna's) also display sets of horns. Alexander the Great was also depicted as being horned, and in Islamic tradition he is referred to as *Dhul-Qarnein,* the Horned One. The Qur'an contains a mysterious story of a journey undertaken by Moses and Joshua to visit Bahrein, the shrine of Dhul-Qarnein, whose minister, el-Khidr ("The Green Man") had a shrine at Karbala, where Hussein was martyred.[72] Bahrein, "the two seas," an island where the fresh water springs (Abzu) mingle with the salty Persian Gulf waters (Tiamat), is the site of the god Enki's legendary paradise, Dilmun, where sickness, old age, and death are unknown (like Tir-na-n'og).[73] Since Enki is often depicted as a horned god, we should have little difficulty in associating him with Dhul-Qarnein, in which case el-Khidr is likely to be his eldest son, who is none other than Dumuzi, the "right son," the god of the fertile (green) grain. So Moses, whose name means "drawn from the water," and Joshua, "he saves," have a veiled association with the old Sumerian water god via the Islamic tradition. It is possible that Bahrein is also related to the Old Testament location of Eden, which is at the junction of four rivers: the Tigris, the Euphrates, the Pishon, which flows around Havilah (Arabia), and the Gihon, which flows around "Ethiopia" (an ancient name for both east Africa and India).[74]

The Kundalini system is a part of the discipline of yoga in India. Here, the vital force within the human body is likened to a pair of intertwined serpents coiled at the base of the spinal column. The adept learns to awaken this energy in the form of heat and light and to raise it from this lowest center or *chakra* through six successive vortices corresponding to the genitals, the solar plexus, the heart, the throat, the brow, and finally the crown of the head, at which point one achieves *nirvana* or release from earthly bondage.[75] There is some evidence that this form of yoga was known in ancient Mesopotamia: Figure 17, a cylinder seal impression from the early second millennium B.C., depicts a goddess whose lower torso consists of intertwined serpents, accompanied by a winged

Figure 17: Snake-footed Goddess and winged yogic figure. Mesopotamian cylinder seal impression, Old Babylonian Period. (Yale Babylonian Collection)

human figure whose body is bent in a position peculiar to the Moon Salute (*Chandrasana*), a series of Indian yoga postures.[76] Yoga is apparently older in India than the Indo-Aryan invasions of the mid-second millennium B.C., since figures in yoga positions, accompanied by deer, are attested in Indus Valley stamp seals, contemporary with this Mesopotamian seal impression.[77] There are also several Mesopotamian cylinder seals from the late third millenium B.C. that depict worshippers approaching a god whose lower portion is a coiled serpent. So we might next ask the question, are any of the characters in Story Three ever depicted as snake-footed? The answer, surprisingly, is yes: in a variant of the chase scene, Dumuzi asks Utu to transform his hands and feet into snake hands and snake feet![78] This might seem to violate the rule I suggested above against free substitution between animal classes. However, remember that "the Bull and the Scorpion are one." In a hymn to Inanna, the goddess is called "falcon" and "wild cow" in successive lines, by hendiadys;[79] the bird of prey and the serpent being free substitutions for the scorpion as we have seen.

In the Kundalini system, the serpent power is normally coiled at the base of the spinal column; liberation from earthly bondage (wings) comes when it is raised to the head centers; but the middle *chakra* of the system, the heart center, is symbolically represented by the deer. In another Sumerian myth concerning Inanna, the *huluppu*, a cosmic tree with its root in the underworld and its crown in heaven, is infested by a serpent and an eagle. She desires the wood for her throne and marriage bed—the two seats of her power—and seeks the aid of various gods to drive off the pests. There follows a series like that in which Ninshubur seeks the aid of the great gods for Inanna—until she obtains help from the hero Gilgamesh, another king of Uruk.[80] We shall return to this story in more detail in later chapters.

Did the Sumerians have such a system of bodily centers? There are no texts which are absolutely explicit about this, though the inferences of the seal designs and the myths are certainly suggestive that the ideas which later manifested as Qabbalah and Kundalini Yoga were already present in Mesopotamia in the second millennium. The absence of direct references is not entirely surprising, because in both of the later systems there were often restrictions on who could have access to esoteric knowledge. The teachings were frequently veiled in obscure language, and many were never committed to writing until the late twentieth century. The Mesopotamians also had their secret texts, whose contents were practically labeled "Classified":

The initiate shall show it to the initiate;
They shall not show it to the uninitiated.
It is a secret of the great gods.[81]

They also had a guild of professional physicians called *a.zu* ("knower of the waters"), and there are several medical treatises extant from later Mesopotamian cultures that indicate a fairly comprehensive knowledge of the body and its parts. This included a system of associations between various organs (and their dysfunctions) and specific divinities and emotions.[82] The fact that systems of this sort are also documented among peoples like the !Kung and the Hopi, who are unlikely to have been influenced by diffusion from Mesopotamia, further suggests that the systems are all tapping into something which is common to the human condition—and recall Vico's statement that "uniform ideas originating among entire peoples unknown to each other must have a common ground of truth."[83]

A Comparison of Story Three with Stories One and Two

Story Three, as we have observed, is the first of our set to have been recorded in canonical form. It is therefore important to explore the possibility that it was diffused from Sumer to the other cultures we have been studying. We have already seen that rituals for Dumuzi (Tammuz) existed in various forms on the eastern Mediterranean coast. In fact, there is good reason to believe that ideas from Mesopotamian culture were also diffused to Greece. In the third century B.C., a Babylonian priest named Berossus established a school of astrology on the Ionian island of Kos. Several documents from this school survive that are clearly copies of Mesopotamian originals. There is the possibility of a much earlier contact, too: archæologists excavating at the site of Thebes recovered a Mesopotamian cylinder seal of the fourteenth century B.C. bearing the name of Kidin-Marduk.[84] This is suspiciously close to the name of Kadmos, the founder of the Theban dynasty, whom Greek myth depicts as a Phoenician prince who crossed the Bosporus in pursuit of his sister, Europa, who had been abducted to Crete by Zeus in the guise of a white bull.[85] M.B. Sakalleriou notes that the worship of Dionysius at Thebes included a pole surmounted by a human head called *Dionysius kadmos* or *Dionysius orthos.*[86] While we are not informed whether the head was thought to be oracular, it should be noted that Orpheus' decapitation at the hands of Dionysius' *mænads* was in revenge for his rejection of the worship of the ecstatic god, Kadmos' grandson. The name of Dionysius, a god who came from the east, might be a corruption of Dumuzi.

Another possible echo of Story Three in Greece is the myth of Adonis (whose name might also derive from Dumuzi), the young hero beloved of the Cypriote goddess Aphrodite/Venus; as we have seen, Inanna is the goddess of the planet Venus. Like Actæon, Adonis is a hunter, but to match his passion for venery (which means both hunting and love-making![87]), Venus adopts the dress and hound-pack of her sister Artemis, as a prototype of the Jungian *anima woman* (or *hætera*) who takes on her male consort's attributes as his reflection. The Mesopotamians did not separate these two aspects of the goddess; Inanna combines sexuality and hunting, and her later Babylonian counterpart, Ishtar, a renowned archer, is frequently depicted with weapons springing from her shoulders, as in Figure 16. A standard list of astrological omens states that "the Bow-star is the Ishtar of Elam, daughter of Enlil."[88] This constellation consists of stars from Argo and Canis Major, the bright star Sirius (with which Ishtar was also associated) forming the arrow. Perhaps this is the origin of the association of Aphrodite/Venus with the notorious archer Eros/Cupid.

Nevertheless, Venus retains an aversion to the animals of the hunt—lions, bears, wolves, and boars—and warns Adonis about encountering them. He is killed by a boar during a hunt, and the goddess weeps for him and beats her breasts[89]—as the Mesopotamian women wept for Dumuzi, or as the Judaean women wept for Tammuz, or as the modern Shi'a Muslim women of southern Iraq weep for Hussein. The location of Adonis' death on Cyprus is a glen known as Idalion, "I see the Sun," located between two suspiciously breast-shaped hills, between which the equinoctial sunrise can be seen. Only on this date (and on the corresponding equinox six months away) will the sun reappear at exactly this position. That this method of determining the date of the equinox was known to the Sumerians is suggested by the fact that the cuneiform sign for the sun was originally an ideogram of the celestial orb rising between two hills.[90] This suggests that the Cypriote ritual for the death of Adonis, like that of Dumuzi, was also centered on the equinox. The island of Cyprus itself is said to be the phallus of the emasculated sky-god Uranos, which engendered the goddess Aphrodite, "foam-born" when it fell into the sea. A glance at a map will show why they thought so! After his death, Adonis, like Dumuzi, spent the winter part of the annual cycle in Hades as the lover of Persephone, and the summer months in the upper world with Aphrodite.[91]

Such dying and resurrected gods were extremely popular throughout the eastern Mediterranean, and at least during the first millennium B.C. there was a great deal of free borrowing between the cults of this region. Christianity became popular here early largely because of its ability to syncretize these beliefs and weld them into a single canonical version. The motif of the hero killed by the boar also extends far beyond the Mediterranean world: Diarmuid, the lover of Grianne, Fionn MacCumhaill's wife, is killed by Fionn disguised as a boar. We have seen how, in the *Odyssey*, Circe has the power to transform men into boars, from which fate only Hermes/Mercury can rescue Odysseus.[92]

As for connections to Ireland, there is a folk-belief that Fionn MacCumhaill himself, at one point in his career, traveled to Palestine to study wisdom teachings.[93] The main body of the Leinster cycle relates an incident in Fionn's childhood in which he accidentally partook of the salmon of wisdom and obtained the gift of tongues. This salmon lived in another of Ireland's sacred pools.[94] The Latin *Salmo* is similar in sound to Hebrew *Shlomo,* Solomon, whose reputation for wisdom was widespread in Medieval Europe. He was also renowned as the author of the richly erotic poetry of the Song of Songs, which celebrates the Sacred Marriage with his feminine counterpart, *Shulamit*.[95] Furthermore, the ritual coronation scene at Tyrconell we observed in Chapter Three is very likely akin to the Sacred Marriage, especially since in Mesopotamia this rite was originally performed only at the accession of a ruler and only afterward became an annual event.

The Relevance of Story Three Today: The Cult of Personality

Diffusion, though it certainly took place, fails to explain why these beliefs should have been so popular over such a wide area. To explore this, it may be useful to consider why Stories One and Three concentrate on the figure of the king; why, indeed, so many myths and folktales have princes, princesses, kings, and queens as their chief characters; why, even in nonmonarchist America, there is so much interest in the foibles of the British Royal Family. There are several reasons why this may be the case. First, in all societies with populations of more than about ten thousand, there is felt to be a need for permanent political authority to be vested in distinctive leaders. These individuals are the focus of public attention, and the more power they wield, the more attention is directed to them. This, of course, is very gratifying to their egos, but it also serves a useful purpose for the society at large. It allows people's collective fears and aspirations to be projected onto a single individual who receives both credit and blame for what happens to the society. The Bronze Age societies of the Near East, starting with the Sumerians, greatly expanded the institution of kingship, so it is natural for Story Three and myths like it to focus on the person of the ruler. This is true even in societies which have done away with hereditary royalty; a similar and inescapable glamour surrounds the figure of a president, a premier, or a prime minister. In Marxist doctrine, this is referred to as the "cult of personality" and, especially in the People's Republic of China, is officially eschewed, but has never been entirely eradicated. The students who defaced the giant picture of Mao in Tienanmen Square in 1989 were singled out for particularly severe punishment.

In American society, a glance at the periodical shelves at supermarket checkout counters will reveal the depth of popular interest about the personal lives of politicians, stars in the movie, television, sports, and popular music industries, the wealthy, and such royalty as survives into the late twentieth century. The mythological imagination seizes upon these figures precisely because they call forth our attention and projection, and, as Fontenelle pointed out long ago,[96] myth-makers will use every device possible to keep us listening in the interest of pursuing their occupation. In the most mercenary terms, the scandals of kings and presidents help the sale of tabloids.

In a deeper psychological sense, the figure of the ruler represents a highly marked and empowered version of the inner core of personality, which Jung refers to in his writings as the Self.[97] In our dreams, we may see ourselves in royal roles, and this should not be dismissed as simply wish-fulfillment. In a sense, each of us, if we are able to function from the Self, has both the authority and the responsibility to rule over our own psyche, and within this inner domain we may function as royalty. Images of kings and queens thus represent our own innate right to personal empowerment and offer us opportunities to take advantage of it. However, such *lése ma-*

jesté carries with it the danger of mythic inflation or *hybris* if we attempt to dominate the psyche as the conscious ego, and even more so if we project our domination outwards onto others. Not every gardener would make as good a king as Erra-imitti!

There is another, even more profound reason for this concentration on royalty, however, one which is suggested directly by the ritual context of Story Three. The fertility of the land is held to depend upon the appropriate behavior of the ruler. This is made even more clear by a speech of Ninshubur to Inanna in one of the Sacred Marriage texts:

> *Give him a favorable and glorious reign. Grant him the king's throne, firm in its foundations . . . As the farmer, let him make the fields fertile; as the shepherd, let him make the sheepfolds multiply. Under his reign let there be vegetation; under his reign, let there be rich grain.*[98]

Under normal circumstances, as celebrated in the richly erotic imagery of these texts, the relationship between the goddess and her king is harmonious and loving, and the land prospers. However, if the ruler commits *hybris,* the land will go waste. This is a powerful idea, a peculiar but widespread notion that is deeply embedded in human consciousness, one that is not nearly as illogical as it might seem at first to our modern minds. It is a consistent motif in much of the world's mythology, and it brings the myth home to our modern situation, where the massive pollution of the earth's ecosystems threatens the survival of our civilization. If we ask who is responsible for this, the natural reaction is to blame it on our political leaders, who have indeed often colluded with private industry to encourage short-term profits at the expense of environmental sustainability. Yet this would be to cede our own personal responsibility in this vital matter. Our leaders are a projection of our individual will, and though it is true that a corrupt leader stimulates the Shadow archetype in each of us (as a *model of* reality), it is also true that our projection of our personal Shadows onto our leaders empowers them to embody the corrupt qualities which we possess within ourselves (as a *model for* reality). In this sense, Story Three has an important message for each of us, one to which we shall return in the final chapter of this book.

In summary, with Story Three we have come a long way from Fionn's pool and Diana's grotto. The myth encompasses the agricultural cycle, the nature of kingship, the alternation of the seasons, the structure of the heavens and the earth, the powers of the body, and the idea of resurrection. It would certainly be difficult to say which, if any, of these dimensions is the "real" meaning of the myth; clearly it is capable of meaning all of them at once without being contradictory. All this is done by incorporating the same set of symbols we have observed in Stories One and Two into a larger set, with isomorphous branches in many directions within the eastern Mediterranean world—and beyond.

CHAPTER SIX

WORTHY IS THE YAM THAT WAS SLAIN

Story Three took us on a long journey through both space and time, but we have much farther to go. Story Four is told by the Wemale people, who live in the western interior portion of Ceram, a large island in the eastern part of Indonesia. In it, we have a myth which is even more central to its culture than the story of Inanna and Dumuzi, for it relates the origin of everything the people know in their world.

Story Four: The Sacrifice of Hainuwele

After the original nine families emerged from clusters of bananas on Mount Nunusaku, there lived an unmarried hunter named Ameta who went out hunting with his dog. They spied a great boar and gave chase; the boar plunged into a pool of water and eventually drowned there while the dog and the man remained on the bank. On its tusk, Ameta found a coconut, which a voice in his dream instructed him to plant. From it grew in three days a great cocopalm tree. In three more days it was bearing blossoms, and Ameta climbed it to cut off a blossom. He accidentally cut his finger, allowing a little blood to fall on a leaf and mingle with the sap of the cut blossom. Three days later, he returned to the tree to find a human face on the leaf. In three more days, the torso of a person was visible. In three more days, he found that the leaf had been transformed into a young girl, whom he named Hainuwele. He took her home wrapped in a bark cloth with a snake design on it, and raised her as his daughter.

In three days, Hainuwele reached puberty, and there was a great Maro dance in the village. The men danced for nine nights in great spirals, while the women remained in the center and handed betel nut to them. On each night of the Maro dance, Hainuwele took part, and from the center of the spiral gave to each of the dancers a present she had produced from her own excrement. On the first night, she gave them the usual betel nuts; but on the second she gave them coral; on the third, Chinese porcelain dishes; on the fourth, larger dishes; on the fifth, bush knives; on the sixth, copper betel boxes; on the seventh, golden earrings; and on the eighth, gongs.

By the ninth night, the people had become jealous of Hainuwele because she gave them so many gifts, and they resolved to kill her. They dug a hole in the center of the dance ground, and when the dancers converged on the center of the circle, they surrounded her and forced her into the hole, where they buried her, raising a great shout to drown out her cries. The next morning, when she had not returned, Ameta became suspicious. He visited the dance ground, determined where she had been buried by divination, and exhumed her body. Then he cut her body into nine parts, and buried each part under one of the nine circles of the Maro dance, saving her arms only. After he did this, the buried parts of Hainuwele sprouted into tuberous plants: the yam, the taro, etc.

Ameta cursed mankind and called upon the Dema-goddess Satene to avenge the death of Hainuwele. Satene was born from an unripe banana, whereas all the other people were born from ripe bananas, and she was the ruler of them all. Satene took the two arms of Hainuwele and set up a gate through which she told the people to approach her one by one. Some were unable to do this; these were instantly transformed into animals: pigs, deer, birds, fish, etc., and fled. Some she struck with Hainuwele's left arm; others she struck with Hainuwele's right arm. These remained people, but were divided into two tribes, the Fivers and the Niners. Finally, she told them that as punishment for murdering Hainuwele, she was going to depart from them. They could only come to see her if they died and then crossed nine mountains.[1]

This remarkable myth was collected by Dr. Adolf Jensen during his 1946 expedition to Ceram. A similar story was recounted to Lyall Watson during a visit to an anonymous Indonesian island (for which Nus Tarian is his pseudonym) in 1963, somewhat modernized, and documented in his book *Gifts of Unknown Things.*[2] Interestingly, his version substitutes a stag for the boar at the beginning of the story. Apparently this is a free substitution within the local classificatory system, since, in the list of animals at the end of the story, pigs and deer appear as a pair together, followed by a pair of oviparous animals. Due to the presence of a snake tapestry in the early part of the myth, which Ameta was instructed to place over the coconut before planting it and again over the newly retrieved Hainuwele, Joseph Campbell has suggested that the boar must have been a substitution for an original serpent which came out of the pool[3]—we may recall that Dumuzi may have either serpent or gazelle feet. The serpent motif is found in numerous other Pacific myths, and the Wemale themselves relate that in the distant past the Dema wandered around as serpents, creating the landscape.[4] We shall have occasion to use both versions of the story.

The Economy of Ceram: Swidden Agriculture

The Wemale are *swidden horticulturalists:* they clear areas of the forest using fire and then plant root vegetables, especially yams, among the ashes. They also practice a form of *sylviculture,* planting various types of trees and harvesting their fruit, chief among these being bananas and coconuts. They also hunt for wild boar and other animals, as the myth suggests, and raise domesticated pigs. It is difficult to imagine that they could have been in direct contact with any of the peoples whose myths we have so far studied, although Jensen did suggest the possibility of indirect diffusion from Mesopotamia.[5] Jensen was probably influenced by the ideas of Robert Heine-Geldern, who argued for diffusion from a Mesopotamian hearth, not only as far as Indonesia, but clear across the Pacific to the high civilizations of Mesoamerica and Peru.[6] Part of his argument rests upon the fact that pigs, in particular, are not part of the native fauna of this area. They were domesticated in South Asia and were most likely brought to the islands by boat. There is considerable debate as to how long ago this might have taken place, but some recent evidence from New Guinea, just to the east of Ceram, indicates that pigs were being raised there at least as early as 4000 B.C., and possibly as early as 8000 B.C., suggesting that these animals have been part of the local cultural repertoire for a very long time.[7]

Here, for the first time in our series, we are presented with a female protagonist as the subject of transformation. Unlike Actæon and Dumuzi, her male counterparts in Stories Two and Three, who are turned into animals, Hainuwele is transformed both out of, and back into, vegetation. It is possible that this is due to the tendency we have already observed in hunter–gatherer societies for males to be most closely associated with hunting while females gather plants. However, Jensen points out that in the related mythological systems of several nearby groups, the sacrificed plant-being is male.[8] As we have seen, Dumuzi and his later Middle Eastern correlates (Adonis, Tammuz, Christ, etc.) also symbolize the grain. Furthermore, while Wemale men exclude women from their hunting activities (and from dancing in the Maro ritual), the men do take part in the cultivation of vegetal foods, particularly in sylviculture. The women are mostly engaged in raising root crops and tending the domesticated pigs.

In this case, the familiar chase scene is relegated to a relatively insignificant position at the beginning of the story. Most notably in contrast to Bran and Fionn in Story One, neither the dog nor the man presume to enter the water, but allow the wild animal to bring its gift of an unknown thing to the surface—a most appropriate attitude when dealing with contents of the unconscious. Ameta's name means "dark" or "black," suggesting that he already partakes of some of the qualities of the unconscious.

It is also possible to interpret the spiral motions of the Maro dance as a kind of a chase, especially considering that the final result is the same as in Stories One, Two, and Three: death and dismemberment. Other familiar themes are also present: *hybris,* the wrath of the goddess, death, and the association of the slain figure with economically important foods. There is an important difference: the throng which causes the death of the protagonist is not a pack of dogs or demons, but the ancestors of the present Wemale people themselves. This imposes a burden of guilt upon all future generations, both like and unlike that associated with the Biblical Fall, as we shall see. Accepting that guilt and its consequence—human mortality—is an important part of the Wemale's collective adjustment to the ambiguities of life.

Alert readers may be led to ask how it was possible for Ameta to be out hunting boar when these animals had not as yet been created by Satene. The only answer that may be given to this question is that myth is not necessarily internally consistent in its logic. In oral tradition, there is no such thing as copy editing, and the versions recorded by Jensen and Watson may not be the only ones extant at one time or another within the culture. Since myths work upon both the intellectual and emotional level, we should not always expect logic to dominate affect—a point often overlooked by the structuralist school, which tends to see myths as entirely the products of mentation. Furthermore, as we shall see, the myth is groping to explain a state of affairs prior to the present one, which lies at such a conceptual distance from the present that words and logic fail to describe it adequately. As a creation myth, it partakes of the quality of *transcendence,* which Joseph Campbell regarded as one of the chief functions of myth:

> It antecedes and defies definition. It is, on the primitive level, demonic dread; on the highest, mystical rapture; and between there are many grades. Defined, it may be talked about and taught; but talk and teaching cannot produce it. Nor can authority enforce it. Only the accident of experience and the sign symbols of a living myth can elicit and support it; but such signs cannot be invented. They are found. Whereupon they function of themselves.[9]

In Story Four, the transcendent is retrojected back into a mythic past, a stage which is eloquently referred to in the mythology of the nearby Australian aborigines as *Dream-time* or *Dreaming.*[10] These terms are so evocative that anthropologists often use them as general descriptions of the mythic past in all cultures in preference to the "once upon a time" of European folktales.

Gifts of Unknown Things: Trade and Exchange

Another feature of the myth that may seem discordant is its reference to certain objects that are definitely not native to the Wemale culture. Chinese porcelains and gongs are very dramatic motifs, especially when they are derived from the excrement of the main character, but they are unlikely to have reached Ceram prior to the European expansion of the China trade in the seventeenth century A.D. The myth appears in even more modern dress in Lyall Watson's account, where the conflict between Hainuwele and the people is retranslated into a controversy between native religious beliefs and the imposed Indonesian state religion of Islam. The latter is personified by an imam with the fantastical name of *Marduk,* who destroys the feminine power of the Hainuwele-character by offering up his own right eye as a sacrifice, an ultimate gift, with the result that the dancer's legs are paralyzed so that she can no longer dance. Perhaps Watson was applying pseudonyms too liberally here—as he admits he did for the name of the island itself—for the dancer's name is *Tia* (as in Tiamat)! [11] We shall see in Story Five how a sacrifice of the upper part of the body is related to the crippling of the lower part, but we have already viewed this in reverse in the case of the Welsh king Bran.

This particular kind of free substitution illustrates a very important feature of myth. Storytellers are continuously recasting tales into terms that relate to the present, and myth loses nothing of its force by being retold in this manner. One of the tasks of mythological analysis is to attempt to place the myth within a specific cultural context, but as long as the story continues to be told it will keep evolving. So the context may be either that of its current audience, that of the culture in which the myth first arose, or anything in between. German mythologists call this placement its *Sitz im Leben*, or "situation in life." Modern artists are well aware of this process when they borrow classical themes and rework them into modern settings. Think of the close connections between Picasso's paintings and the cave art of the Paleolithic in his home area of Catalonia, or the grafting of Mozartean and Middle Eastern musical styles in Corigliano's opera *The Ghosts of Versailles*. One of the functions of creative artists is to update perennial themes, using free substitution, so that the essential ideas continue to relate to us in whatever cultural setting we may happen to live. We shall return to this idea in Chapter Nine.

Doubtless whatever version of Story Four was told prior to Chinese contact portrayed Hainuwele's gifts as some other articles of value for which the trade goods were later substituted. Doubtless this was also not the original form either; indeed, all search for the "original form" of a myth is bound to be fruitless, because myth is always changing. Unlike canonical texts, the original form is not necessarily the truest. For anthropologists, as social scientists, truth is a relative concept that is contingent upon the culture in which the myth is found, that culture occupying a particular niche in time and space. As Lévi–Strauss puts it, every telling of a myth is equally valid.[12]

The only pieces of ethnographic information that Jensen gives us concerning the specifics of these gifts is that for the Wemale, gongs are lunar symbols, while porcelain dishes are used in ceremonies to overcome female barrenness and are said to be related to Hainuwele's genitals.[13] We may well suspect that, whether or not these kinds of associations apply to the other items in the list, whatever items occupied the positions of gongs and porcelains in previous versions would also have had a lunar or sexual significance. Thus the inherent meaning is likely to look or feel somewhat the same in every version, regardless of the details. This reworking is a transformative process which we have already observed in comparing Stories One, Two, and Three.

In this case, the intent is surely for the gifts of unknown things to be valuable items that increase sequentially in value, just as the intent of

Inanna's disrobing in Story Three is that the positions of her items of apparel are in sequentially descending order. Myths revel in *sequential repetition.* It is used to heighten the tension of the story, but it is also a way of playing with cultural concepts of number, as we saw in Story Three.

Number Symbolism among the Wemale

In Story Four, the important numbers are obviously three and nine. The cocopalm tree and Hainuwele grow in increments of three days, and the entire cycle is completed in twenty-seven days, or 3 × 3 × 3. This number is roughly equivalent in days to a lunar month, suggesting once again an association with the menstrual cycle. There are three important Dema-goddesses (the term "Dema" is actually not native to the Wemale but describes similar divinities among the Marind-Anim of nearby West Irian, where Jensen also collected ethnographic data) among the Wemale: Hainuwele, Satene, and the Moon-maiden Rabia, who, like Persephone, was abducted into the underworld, by the Sun-man.[14] There are other correspondences between the Dema-goddesses and the Persephone myth: the worship of the Greek goddess involved the sacrifice of pigs and serpents. Persephone's association with the latter is also suggested by her Roman name, *Proserpina.*[15] The families of humankind that take part in the Maro dance are nine, as are the nights of the dance, Hainuwele's gifts (the last being herself), and the types of plants that grow from the nine parts of her dismembered body. One of the two societies formed by Satene is called the "Niners," and Satene resides beyond nine mountains. We may also guess that nine, itself a multiple of three, refers to the duration in months of human gestation, and this association will turn out to be central to an understanding of the myth.

The number two is also important to the story. Satene effects a double division among the original people. First, she causes them to be divided into humans and animals, when before all were described as people. Second, each of these two groups is further divided in two: the animals into herbivorous and oviparous groups; the humans into Fivers and Niners. The latter are dance societies among the Wemale; they also represent social groupings whose division is extremely important to the functioning of the whole society.

Anthropologists have long observed these kinds of divisions within social groups in many tribal societies throughout the world. A careful comparative study by Lévi–Strauss has shown that the division of a local group into two parts, called *moieties* (from the French word *moie,* "half"), serves the function of satisfying a need for balanced reciprocity between the groups, thereby ensuring cooperation.[16] Members of one moiety perform certain functions for members of the opposite moiety, who are restricted from performing the same functions for their own members. The most important of these functions are the exchange of gifts and food at feasts, marriages, and burials. These activities are frequently structured so that they *must* involve people from the opposite moiety in prominent roles. Any attempt to engage in any of these activities *within* the moiety would meet with very strong opposition. In the case of marriage, it would be considered incest, which in many tribal societies is one of the very few crimes punishable by death. We shall consider the motif of incest in more detail in Stories Six and Seven.

While marriage exchange is absent from Story Four, the myth certainly features both gift exchange and burial. Both of these are represented in the form they are conceived to have had before the establishment of moieties. We might summarize the latter part of the story thus: *unregulated and excessive gift exchange results in unregulated burial.* After she produces her outrageously valuable gifts, Hainuwele is buried alive, the first murder victim, without a proper ceremony. It remains for Ameta and Satene to create a ritual appropriate to the occasion. This ritual, or one derived from it which the Wemale currently employ, is regulated by the Fivers for the Niners, and vice versa. So the myth relates not only the manner in which the division between people and animals took place, but also the way in which the existing social order came into being. It thereby validates that social order within the framework of a universal design based upon a primal act of violence. Not that the aboriginal populations of this area refrained from ritual murder: the Wemale were head-hunters at the time Jensen studied them. Among the Marind-Anim, the cocopalm is said to have grown from the head of the first man to die, Jawi, clearly indicating a connection between the head-shaped coconut and the practice of ritual head-hunting.[17]

A Comparison with Indian Mythology

The association of gift exchange with decapitation is one which is also found in Indian mythology, in the fantastic story of the *Amrtamanthana,* the churning of the primordial cosmic milk ocean (Figure 18):

Figure 18: The Amrtamanthana. Engraving, Rajput, 18th century A.D. (Corbis)

The lunar cup of amrta, which ensures immortal life to those who drink it, has fallen into the cosmic milk ocean, and the gods and demons agree to cooperate to retrieve it. The god Vishnu incarnates as a giant tortoise, Kurma, and dives to the bottom of the sea. The gods uproot the cosmic mountain Mandara to use as a churning stick, and wrap around it the world-girdling serpent Vasuki as a churning rope. The gods take hold of the tail of the serpent, and the demons of the head, and they churn. Fourteen wonderful gifts arise out of the ocean, including the sun and the moon, and various divine animals. The last of them is the cup of amrta borne by the god Vishnu, now in the form of a beautiful young maiden.

As the gods and demons line up opposite one another, the maiden dances back and forth between the lines with the cup, teasingly offering it to each of the parties but then withdrawing it. Finally, she gives it to the gods only, and the demons are furious. In the ensuing battle, the gods are victorious, but not before the demon Rahu swallows the cup. The warrior god Indra immediately decapitates Rahu, so that the cup passes out through his severed neck and is retrieved by the gods, who now alone enjoy immortality. Though his body falls to earth and decays, the severed head of Rahu is also immortal, since it came in contact with the amrta, and from time to time again swallows the cup, resulting in a lunar eclipse.[18]

Amrta (literally, "deathless," cognate to Greek *ambrosia*) is a substance which ensures the immortality of the gods, but is not apportioned to humans unless they have attained the highest levels of yoga, or union with the divinity. That divinity appears in the myth in many forms: the god Vishnu, the enticing maiden, the tortoise, the mountain, the serpent, even the Cosmic Milk Ocean itself. We may also suspect that using a serpent to churn the ocean has something to do with the Kundalini, especially since it results in twice seven gifts of unknown things. We shall see more associations between the decapitated head and the moon in Stories Five and Six, but, of course, we have already encountered the deathless heads of Bran and Orpheus.

Ætiology: An Attempt to Explain Origins

When we encounter a myth that attempts to explain how things came to be the way they are, we refer to it as an *ætiology*. Some myths appear to be wholly ætiological in purpose, while in others this is only one element of the mythic structure. For example, the Tzeltal Maya folktale in Chapter Two contains ætiologies for pools of water and earthquakes. Ætiologies are useful to society, not so much because they accurately describe the origins of either the people or the world in which they live, but because they describe these matters in functional, easily remembered terms which relate to the current life of the people. They fit the prevailing cultural trends and thus provide satisfying explanations—which serve as *models for* present behavior.

Ætiologies are inherently open-ended in that they allow the truly curious to pose more profound questions. While everyone is more or less interested in their roots, where they came from, not everyone wants or needs to know this in a deep philosophical sense. Some of the Wemale may have been well-content to accept the premise that they came from ripe bananas, and, aside from being entertained by the story, this may be all they got out of it. But for others, William James' tender-minded, the conditions of life and death pose more difficult questions, to which the ætiology gives equally hard answers.

One of the ways to distinguish genuine myth from its Madison Avenue imitations with which we are continually bombarded in our culture is to see whether an image can be pursued from level to level while retaining the same basic form. Genuine myths, like the pool in Story One, should prove to be bottomless. The analytical process through which we have been exploring myth in the past several chapters is a means of approaching this—though, certainly, we cannot assert that we have succeeded in plumbing all the depths any of these myths have to offer. That, indeed, would be *hybris!* All one can state with accuracy is that *every* statement which claims to be definitive about myth, *including this one,* is only relatively true. Readers are encouraged to reach their own conclusions, to plunge into the pool themselves and undergo the transformation, thereby discovering what the forces of the collective unconscious may have in store for them, personally.

The Vegetative Analogy

The particular crux of Story Four revolves around the nature of life and death in the dream-time. It involves what Frazer and others have referred to as the "vegetative analogy": the idea that life is (or was) in some sense cyclical, rather than progressing in a linear manner as Western historians would suggest; that, as with plants, death results in life, and life results in death, in a never-ending spiral much like the patterns of the Maro dance.[19] The goddess Hainuwele began as a food plant, was transformed into a tree, then into a human being, then was killed and dismembered, and finally again became food plants. The dismemberment motif in this case is isomorphous to the method used by Wemale women to plant yams: a seed yam is divided into several pieces and each is planted separately. It is probably no accident that yams head the list of plants springing from the dismembered parts of Hainuwele, since the yam is one of the chief staples of their diet.

Aldous Huxley referred to this kind of cyclical world-view as the "perennial philosophy," both in the sense that it views life as perennially reconstituted out of death and dismemberment, and that it appears to have great staying power, particularly among the agricultural villagers of the Third World.[20] But the same philosophy was also found among the urban civilizations of the ancient Near East, and it resulted in similar cyclical myths. For example, the coffin of the Egyptian grain god Osiris, murdered by his enemy Set, floats down the Nile, across the Mediterranean Sea, and is caught up in the branches of a tamarisk tree which is used by a local ruler as the support column of his palace. There Isis, Osiris' sister-wife, finds it after a search analogous to Demeter's quest for Persephone, and revives the dead god sufficiently to conceive a child from him. On their return to Egypt, Set and his henchmen attack Osiris and dismember him, then bury each of the parts of his body in a different province. Like Ameta and Satene, Isis and her sister Nephthys seek out the parts and reunite them, except for the phallus which has been swallowed by a fish and is replaced by the wooden *djed* pillar. Because of this, Osiris is unable to return to the living and thus becomes the judge of the dead.[21] The goal of the Egyptian afterlife, at first only for the pharaoh but by the Ptolemaic period even for peasants, was to be judged among the righteous and reunited with Osiris—a journey guided by the *Book of the Dead*,[21] and very similar to the one which the Wemale take to reunite with Satene after death. Similarly, Inanna and Geshtin-anna search for the slain Dumuzi to resurrect him, and in the Mesopotamian Sacred Marriage texts Dumuzi is referred to in vegetative terms as *Ama-ushumgal-anna,* "the one great source of the date clusters,"[23] while the cuneiform ideogram for phallus also is used as a determinative for objects made of wood.

The Spiral Dance of Life

The double spiral of the Maro dance is a symbol found in many cultures' artistic representations of the processes of birth and rebirth, as well as in actual dance figures. For example, in the Earth Renewal ceremony of the Cheyenne (parallel to the Sun Dance of other Plains peoples which we shall observe in the next chapter), the Chief Priest instructs the pledgers of the ceremony (a married couple) in the forming of double spirals in the floor of the central lodge; as these spirals increase in size over the first four days of the ceremony they indicate the expanding creative process. This culminates in an act of ritual intercourse between the Chief Priest and the female pledger, symbolic of the descent of spiritual energies from the sacred mountain to humankind, via a woman.[24]

The spiral duplicates the figure of the maze or labyrinth, a powerful and ancient feminine symbol. Perhaps Salome's Dance of the Seven Veils was also based upon this pattern. Geoffrey Ashe has documented many such spiral drawings and rituals, dating as far back as 24,000 B.C. in Central Asia, from whence he feels the entire corpus of shamanic practice was diffused.[25] It is interesting to observe that this "dance of life," replicated on the scale of the very small and the very large, has been rediscovered by modern science in the double helix structure of the DNA molecule and the spiral form of the galaxy. While we cannot credit the ancients with the factual knowledge of such isomorphisms, they do represent the possibility for the reunion of science and myth suggested by Fritjof Capra in his remarks about the dance of Shiva cited in Chapter One.

From the Above to the Below and Back Again

Hainuwele's burial alive in Story Four has strong affiliations with other myths we have examined, particularly Story Three. The virgin Antigone, too, was buried alive for her illegal attempt to bury her brother, and we should not overlook the fact that her name means "against generation." Though in Sophocles' play she has a suitor, Creon's son Hæmon, this is merely a veil for her nubility, since *his* name simply means "blood."[26] This takes us back to Diana's purificatory pool. The hole in the ground into which the Dema is thrown is a grave, but since burial is isomorphous to planting, the fertile ground is also a symbol of the goddess' power to regenerate.

This brings to mind the Old Testament story of the "witch" of En-Dor whom Saul visited in order to contact the ghost of the prophet Samuel, thereby breaking his own law against witchcraft.[27] Actually, the old woman is simply described as *Ba'lat 'Ov,* "The owner of a hole in the ground," and En-Dor means "Well of Generation." The reader may suspect that she is none other than the hag whom Niall encountered at the well at the crossroads! But the original meaning of the word "hag" is "sacred," and refers to the ancient wisdom of the Earth goddess (*hagia sophia*), while the word "witch" derives from the Indo-European root *wic,* meaning "to know." These aspects of feminine power were suppressed by the emergent Iron Age patriarchies of Europe and West Asia. In the Sumerian story of Inanna and the *huluppu* tree, after the goddess had made her throne and bed, she gave what was left of the wood to the hero Gilgamesh, who made of it two musical instruments, a *pukku* and a *mikku,* the first of which is a shaman's drum. He placed these over a hole that led to the entrance to the underworld and began shamanizing, summoning spirits much as Odysseus did at the nadir of his voyage.[28] This activity angered the elders of Uruk, who appealed to the gods. The latter contrived to widen the hole, so that the instruments fell in; and when Gilgamesh's friend Enkidu went down to retrieve them he broke all the inflexible laws of the underworld and was held fast, and died.[29] Thus, Hainuwele's grave brings us back to the start of Story Three, with its complex series of underworld gates.

The transformations in Story Four shuttle back and forth between the above and the below. The boar, starting on the earthly plane, descends to the below, then rises to the surface with its precious gift. The tree grows high and Ameta must climb it to retrieve Hainuwele, just as the Wemale sylviculturalists climb trees to retrieve coconuts and bananas. Hainuwele descends into the below and Ameta must retrieve her from there, and then plant her again so she can grow, as plants, both upwards and downwards. Finally, to find Satene the people must first die and be buried in the earth, and then climb upwards, crossing nine mountains. Thus, the myth is much more complicated in its directionality than Story Three, which only had two descents and ascents, one each for Inanna and Dumuzi.

The coconut is the perfect mediator of this opposition between the above and the below. Coconuts float on the surface of the water; this is the way in which they colonize new islands in the Pacific. Jensen's informant stated that before the events of this myth, cocopalms were unknown on Ceram.[30] Hainuwele's name means "frond of the cocopalm," and she is therefore also a mediator. She furthermore is capable of producing items of value from that which is valueless. This may explain why she is depicted as the product of Ameta's blood and the sap of the cocopalm blossom. As we saw when examining Story Two, many peoples consider menstrual blood itself to be the substance of life, because without a microscope it is impossible to distinguish the unfertilized ovum from the endometrial lining which was prepared to nourish it. Conception in this view is caused by the combination of two essences, female blood and male semen, just as, in the Babylonian creation story cited in the last chapter, the god of the sweet waters and the goddess of the salt waters mingled their essences. But of course these substances are red and white, respectively, whereas Hainuwele is conceived by inversion, from male blood and the white sap of the female blossom.

The study of these bodily substances is most detailed and explicit in the Tantric texts of India. The *Dhyanabindu Upanishad* describes the control (*bindu*) exercised by the yogic adept over them:

> The selfsame *bindu* is of two varieties: the white and the reddish. The white they call *shukra* (semen); the name of the reddish variety is *maharajas* . . . The union of the two is very rarely attained. The semen is Shiva, the *rajas* is the Shakti; the semen is the moon and the *rajas* is the Sun; it is only by the union of the two that this exquisite body is attained.[31]

Rajas is the fiery principle, associated with the Kundalini fire. Shiva and Shakti are the masculine and feminine expressions of divinity, respectively. Curiously, seminal fluid is slightly alkaline whereas the pH of the vagina is slightly acidic! In Medieval alchemy, the union of the Red King (sulphur) and the White Queen (salt) is fundamental to the production of the Philosophers' Stone, an inversion isomorphous to what we find in Story Four.[32]

A Wemale Philosophy of the Universe

This suggests that in the deeper view which the myth takes of the precultural era, reproduction is conceptualized as having been just the opposite of the present condition—a common inversion of the current state of affairs found in many ætiologies. The structural logic of many ætiologies is simple: state an observed condition, question its origin, propose its opposite as an antecedent, and then posit a critical event which caused the inversion. This process of transformation is known in Jungian psychology as *enantiodromion,* the interplay of the opposites, and it is as common to dream processes as it is to myths.[33] There is a further strong hint of the prior absence of gender separation within the myth itself: Hainuwele produces her gifts anally, because she possesses no other orifice through which to birth them! Freud would doubtless have suggested that this corresponds to the developmental stage of *anality,* in which the child confuses excretion and procreation and considers "its own excrement as a thing of value, suitable for presentation as a gift."[34] In the Indian Tantric system of the chakras introduced in Chapter Five, excretion is governed by the Muladhara Chakra at the base of the spine, from which we derive the epithet "filthy moolah" for money! Once again like Antigone, Hainuwele is a marriageable maiden who is "against generation."

Perhaps this notion of presexuality is the reason that the two beings Enki creates of clay in Story Three, who are capable of rescuing Inanna while not being subject to the laws of the underworld, are depicted as sexless (or, in the Assyrian version of the story, as eunuchs). In Talmudic speculations on the Garden of Eden story, the original Adam was also considered to be androgynous, with male and female bodies joined back to back. "Since this posture made locomotion difficult, and conversation awkward, God divided the androgyne and gave each half a new rear."[35] Probably this myth was influenced by Platonic philosophy, particularly the passage in Plato's *Symposium* where Zeus splits the primal "round" doubled human beings in half to form male–female, male–male, and female–female pairs, who have ever afterward gone seeking their missing halves.[36] In the *Symposium*, this story is used as a rationalization for homosexuality: Alcibiades, who is speaking, is trying (without success) to seduce Socrates.

Joseph Campbell cites other Wemale myth fragments which assert that the sexual organs did not appear until Satene had divided humankind into Fivers and Niners.[37] That Hainuwele had just achieved puberty (at three days of age!) at the time of the Maro dance is an incongruity similar to the appearance of the boar at the beginning of the myth, before Satene had created these animals. Jensen informs us that the division into gender roles among the Wemale is most strongly emphasized at the time of women's menstruation, when they are expected to segregate themselves beneath their pile-dwellings. Menstruation is further related to the third of the Dema, Rabia, whose periods coincide with the dark of the moon. Like the New Moon which disappears from the skies for three days, menstruating women are expected to hide themselves in the realm of the below for this amount of time. The violation of this taboo is viewed as tantamount to the forgetting of the original drama of creation, for which the appropriate expiation is a blood-sacrifice.[38]

But if there is no birth in the ordinary sense in the Dream-time, there is also no death. The murder of Hainuwele is cast as the crucial event that separates Dream-time from the present. That murder is presented in the myth as morally ambiguous, since it is based upon a double act of *hybris*. Hainuwele, like the dog Bran, is outstanding; she alone is able to produce wonderful gifts for the Maro dancers. Her increasingly ostentatious excellence marks her for destruction, as it does for her modern counterpart in Lyall Watson's narrative. But her murder is also an act of *hybris* on the part of the people, who are punished for it accordingly by the introduction of death as the normal terminus of life, and as a precondition for regaining the favor of the goddess Satene. Previously, all the people were plants, in accord with the vegetative analogy of perennial renewal. Henceforth, some of them are transformed into animals, subject to birth and death; the others are transformed into mortal humans, equipped with a social structure which is designed to regulate birth and death through marriages and burials. As Jensen puts it:

> With the end of primal time, the Dema cease to exist. In place of immortality enters mortal, earthly life, the ability to propagate, the need for food, and a form of existence when life is extinguished. The murdered Dema-deity transforms himself [*sic*] into the useful crop plants but also embarks on the first journey into death and transmutes himself into the realm of death as represented by the terrestrial image of the cult house. Moreover, we are told, the deity turns into the moon, symbolizing in its waning and reappearing the constant renewal of life.[39]

The End of Primal Unity

That this transformation takes place within the context of a primal act of violence is characteristic, and nearly universal, of ætiological myths of this sort. We find it in the Genesis account also, although there the banishment from the Garden, the curse of mortality, and the first murder appear in inverted order.[40] Like Abel, Isaac, and Jesus, Hainuwele is a sacrificial offering—the *yam* slain from the foundation of the world.[41] Doubtless she is a vegetal offering rather than an animal as in the biblical cases above because the Wemale emphasize planting rather than stock-breeding; though they do raise pigs, it was on a wild boar's tusk that the coconut first appeared.

This kind of transformation from sacrificial offering into food is found in many mythologies. For example, the Ojibway people of Ontario explain the origin of the maize they plant by a myth in which a green-plumed god descends from the sky and asks a youth to wrestle him to the death, then to plant him in the ground. When he emerges again, it is as the corn plant.[42] Sheep, or, even better, lambs assume this role in the Biblical *Sitz im Leben* of pastoral nomadism—and note that Abel, like Dumuzi, is both sacrifice and shepherd—as, in a metaphorical sense, is Christ. The events of the New Testament are set at the close of the period during which the Sun rose at the spring equinox in the sign of Aries, the Ram, and the start of the age in which it would rise in the sign of Pisces, the Fish: the fish is an early symbol for Christ.[43]

Primal unity is a state presupposed by many mythological systems to underlie or precede the current world of opposites. Scientific cosmologies are no exception to this. Getting from that primal state wherein all the opposing forces are at rest to the present situation is a difficult philosophical problem, no less for Western physicists and biologists than for Indonesian planters. For physicists, the idea of a single point of emanation for the universe is implicit in the Big Bang theory. For evolutionary biologists, the origins of both sex and death are linked to an ecocatastrophe some 2 billion years ago, in which the introduction of oxygen-breathing life-forms (eukaryotes) rapidly replaced the aboriginal prokaryotes which reproduced asexually and were, from one perspective, immortal. In both cases, a violent breach from the original state is posited, with concomitant organization into dualistic pairs of opposites.[44] Since the people Jensen and Watson encountered are hardly likely to have been familiar with the writings of Western scientific cosmologists and evolutionists, we are fairly safe in assuming that some mechanism other than diffusion must have produced the striking similarities in outlook between these two cultural systems at the deeper levels that transcend their obvious superficial differences. Either the universe actually *did* proceed from unity to duality, and the myths and modern cosmologies both show an awareness of this (independent invention), or every human psyche is so riven at birth that we are incapable of seeing the universe other than dualistically (psychic unity)—or both. For in an inherently dualistic universe, what other sort of human psyche than a dualistic one would be likely to develop?

This idea is at the center of a controversial theory in physics, known as the *anthropic principle:* the idea that certain constants in the universe are so finely tuned that, were they even slightly different, intelligent, carbon-based life forms capable of exploring them could not possibly exist.[45] The "strong" version of this theory suggests that the universe contains these constants *in order* for intelligent life to exist and discover them. Perhaps the reason this theory has gained any following at all among physicists is its close isomorphism to what the myths tell us: recall the statement in the Maya *Popol Vuh* that, "there shall be neither glory nor grandeur in our creation and formation until the human being is made, man is formed."[46]

The Sacred Mountain

The myth does more, however, than to posit the creation of duality: it also provides a suggestion of a way in which one might escape from this peculiar predicament. The Wemale may be reunited with the goddess after death by crossing a series of nine mountains. It should come as little surprise to the reader to learn that these mountains are not to be found on the island of Ceram, which boasts only the central peak Nunusaku, about 3,000 meters high, and two much lower summits at about 900 and 800 meters. The central mountain does have symbolic importance to the Wemale, since at the birth of a child the father must climb a coconut tree which stands mountainwards with respect to his house and pluck a coconut which he wraps in a special cloth, much as Ameta does with Hainuwele. The coconut cannot be permitted to touch the ground, and the fate of the child is said to be associated with it. But the dead are carried toward the sea, rather than toward the mountain; so the mountains which the Wemale are to scale after death cannot be on the island.[47]

The symbol of the mountain is frequently used in myth to represent the residence of divinity, whether it be Olympus, Ararat, Horeb, Sinai, Everest, Mandara, or, as in the Lakota holy man Black Elk's vision, Harney Peak in South Dakota, which he described as the center of the world, and then added cannily, "but anywhere is the center of the world."[48] It should be added that Black Elk had long since converted to Catholicism when he related his vision to Neihardt, and as catechist for the Lakota reservation, he was very probably aware of Nicholas of Cusa's definition of God as "an intellegible sphere whose center is everywhere and whose circumference is nowhere."[49]

The diffusionist perspective on this, as recently developed by Geoffrey Ashe, is to search for the geographic location of the *original* mountain from which all these legends sprung. Ashe believes he has identified this mountain as Mount Belukha, an impressive 4,600 meter high peak in central Asia. It does seem as if some myths point in this direction, particularly the Indian stories about Mount Meru, which can be approached only after crossing the Himalayas and then a sea of sand.[50] However, from the Jungian perspective this misses the point, for Meru is a coded reference to the human spinal column (the *meru-danda*) and to the practice of Kundalini Yoga alluded to in the preceding chapter.[51] The adept who can raise his consciousness to the crown chakra, the peak of the mountain, experiences the unity which underlies the apparent duality of the manifested world. Jane Austen Pratt, a Jungian analyst, describes the common use of the mountain symbol in the Flood stories of Israel, Mesopotamia, and India:

> That the mountain in these stories represents the self is evident from the role that it plays in the tales themselves. . . . Of what, then, is the bulk of the psychic mountain composed that it should be so relatively indestructible and thus serve to unite the pre- and post-diluvian eras? The answer, I believe, is archetypal stuff. Indeed, if the waters represent unconsciousness, no other explanation seems possible for the mass of psychological material that coheres beneath their surface when consciousness is swept away, and reappears again after the flood is past . . . They fill, between heaven and earth, the same sort of intermediate position that Dr. Jung assigns to the archetypes between spirit and the instinctual. Moreover, many of them do it for the same purpose, namely that light, or consciousness, may appear.[52]

We may conclude that there is a relationship between the mountain and a return to a primal condition of psychological unity, one which is afforded only to the dead in Wemale belief, but which in many other cultures is not necessarily inaccessible to all the living. Perhaps this is because the Wemale lay so much emphasis upon "the urge to adapt to this bisectioning of the world," as Jensen puts it.[53] They do not wish to present to humans, who were after all guilty of something akin to Original Sin in the murder of Hainuwele, the opportunity of escape. But as we shall see in succeeding chapters, the mythological figure who scales the mountain and bridges the gap between unity and duality has a significant role to play in revitalizing society and restoring its connection to its psychic roots.

Chapter Seven

A BRIDE TOO FAR

We now continue eastward along our mythic journey to the New World. As the titles of this chapter and the next suggest, their stories form a complementary pair, variants of which are found throughout the Western Hemisphere in one form or another. Rather than concentrating on a single cultural milieu as we have done in previous chapters, we shall now have to follow both familiar and new themes through a number of permutations as they occur in different cultural settings throughout the hemisphere. This sets up an axis at right angles to the one we have been following, a south to north orientation, and I will play upon the cultures along it much like a chord on a keyboard instrument, rather than concentrating on a single note as we have mostly done until now. The key variants for both Stories Five and Six which I have chosen derive from three very different environments: the western part of the Amazon basin, the Great Plains, and the high Arctic (see Figure 19). To flesh out the analysis, I will draw in additional myths from the cultures we have already visited, as well as from other cultures, particularly, Australian aboriginal societies. All this adds a level of complexity to these chapters, but if readers have followed the thread of connections this far through the labyrinth, they should not become completely lost. All of the stories in this chapter have in common a figure, usually female, who fails to fulfill society's expectations for marriage, but is determined to seek a distant, individual destiny instead.

The first version of Story Five is told by the Cashinawa people, who live in the remote rainforest region of western Brazil and eastern Peru. It exists in several variants which have been collected and republished, along with commentary, by Claude Lévi-Strauss in the third volume of

Figure 19: New World map, showing distribution of cultures mentioned in the text. (Adapted from a map distributed by the National Oceanic and Atmospheric Administration)

his *Mythologiques*. Since the original written versions are in Portuguese, a language with which I am not familiar, I am forced to rely upon the accuracy of the English translation of Lévi–Strauss' translations from Portuguese into French, which in turn rely upon the accuracy of the ethnographer's translations from the native languages. This degree of distance from the sources makes me somewhat uncomfortable, because each translation may have introduced its own misinterpretations. I am far more confident of my interpretations of Stories Two and Three, because I have a working knowledge of both Latin and Sumerian. However, I have been able to confirm many of my impressions of the life of the Cashinawa from Kenneth Kensinger's descriptions of his work among the Peruvian branch of this people. The variant I have chosen to start with was recorded by the Brazilian ethnographer Capistrano de Abreu in 1915.

Story Five: The Ascent of Iaça

Once there was neither moon, stars, nor rainbow, and the night was totally dark. This situation changed because of a young girl who did not want to get married. She was called Iaça. Exasperated by her obstinacy, the mother sent her daughter away. The young girl wandered for a long time in tears, and when she tried to return home the old woman refused to open the door. "You can sleep outside," she cried. "That will teach you not to want to get married!" The young girl ran frantically about in all directions, beat on the door and sobbed. The mother was so infuriated by this behaviour that she took a bush knife, opened the door and cut off her head, which rolled onto the ground. Then she threw the body into the river.

During the night the head rolled and moaned round the hut. After wondering about its future, it decided to change into the Moon. "In this way," it reflected, "I shall be seen only from afar." The head promised the mother not to bear her any ill-will, provided she gave it its balls of thread; by holding one end between its teeth, it got the vulture to take it up into the sky. The eyes of the decapitated woman became the stars and her blood the rainbow. Henceforth women would bleed each month, then the blood would clot and children with black bodies would be born to them. But if the sperm clotted, the children would be born white.[1]

One of the things the reader should notice as we proceed from highly literary, canonical myths such as Stories Two and Three to orally transmitted tales of non-literate peoples like Stories Four, Five, and Six is that certain themes which had only been implicit in the former are often made explicit in the latter. While we have been dealing with beliefs about menstruation and its isomorphism to the lunar cycle all along, this is the first time that we have actually seen it mentioned explicitly in the text of a myth. In part, this is due to assumptions about propriety that imbue the products of civilized societies: it is certainly not usually considered tasteful to mention bodily exudations in polite society! One of the characteristics of the literary versions of myths is that they have tended—at least until the twentieth century—to reinterpret the graphic representations of bodily functions, giving them a more refined significance. To ignore this development would be tantamount to the Conquistadors' error of confounding the mystery of the Mass with Aztec cannibalism. However, neither can we ignore the fact that Christian myth and ritual have their origins, via forms like Story Three, in something like the cannibalistic love-feasts that still persisted in the Indonesian archipelago at the time that Jensen recorded Story Four.

Following Giambattista Vico's philosophy of four ages, it may be suggested that by attempting to eliminate all such references from acceptable art and literature, civilized societies (products of Vico's third age) have stripped language and representational art of their power to transform their citizens. But the more that narrow-minded conformists try to repress these elements, the more powerful the explosion when they erupt from the unconscious where, as Freud has amply shown, they still reside. Vico thought that this would lead to the "Recorso" phase in which society collapses into chaos, only to reemerge at the start of the next cycle.[2] While Vico (who was at least nominally an Italian Catholic) did not presume to apply his model to European society, preferring to separate "people of the revelation" from all other present and previous cultures, we should have little difficulty in observing that the reaction in the arts and literature to Victorian prudery has become increasingly strident over the past seventy years, starting with artists of the stature of James Joyce and D. H. Lawrence but ultimately reaching the banality of 2Live Crew or Snoop Doggy Dog. Can anyone doubt that we are in the maelstrom of a Recorso?

In Story Five, we leave the refinements of civilization behind altogether, or perhaps it would be less ethnocentristic to say that the Cashinawa are not as preoccupied as we are with maintaining them. The frame of the myth, its *Sitz im Leben,* also becomes more intimate, related to the tensions within the family, yet the results are just as cosmic as those in Stories Three and Four.

Social Expectations for Young Ladies

Left behind also (very largely) are the familiar chase and animal transformation motifs we have been pursuing throughout this series, although we shall reencounter the chase in other variants. Except for Iaça's rather aimless wandering through the village, both before and after her decapitation, there is no sense of flight. I reserve further discussion of the rolling head motif until the next chapter. For once, also, there is no collective pursuit. There are only two characters in the entire story: Iaça and her mother. Yet once again we are faced with a confrontation between a young person who flaunts conventionality and a senior female figure. This results in the dismemberment, death, and transformation of the former at the hands of the latter, but in a different order than we have seen before. Unlike the protagonists of Stories One, Three, and Four, who move back and forth between the "Great Above" and the "Great Below," Iaça is depicted as being *permanently* disjoined: like Humpty Dumpty, the parts can never be put back together again. In Story Two, Actæon was subjected to this treatment by the goddess of the Moon, but Iaça *becomes* the goddess of the Moon. Actæon chanced upon a women's post-menstrual bath and was killed because of his illicit desire for a goddess who shunned marital relations. In the present story, Iaça's death is caused by her illicit unwillingness to participate in marital relations, and it results in the onset of the phenomenon of menstruation. Once again, it seems as if the same set of symbolic counters is being read in a different order. Lévi–Strauss comments that Iaça's *hybris* lies in her desire to be distant from human (or at least, male) society.[3] This is certainly contrary to cultural expectations, for Kensinger reports that Cashinawa women

> are married for the first time by the age of thirteen, males by sixteen. Widows and divorcées, even elderly ones, rarely remain unmarried for more than a few days. . . . Unmarried adults, whatever the reasons for their being unmarried, are viewed as potentially more disruptive to the society than is a bad marriage.[4]

However, is not freedom from the requirement to marry precisely what Diana and her maidens desired? Marion Woodman has made the interesting suggestion that virginity is a positive state of mind to be acquired, rather than simply a lack of sexual experience.[5] It may not even necessarily imply physical abstinence from sex, as we saw with Diana's relationships with Pan and the Priest-Kings of Nemi. This is also in accord with the sense of the Hebrew word *betulah,* which is usually translated as "virgin," as in the Old Testament prophecy of the birth of the Messiah,[6] but which more accurately designates a young woman who is not under the domination of a husband. This figure is often portrayed in myth as the mother of the Hero. In Story Five, she has a more active role. Iaça's insistence on retaining her virginity would certainly not be as offensive to a female as it is to a male audience, and in a curious way she attains her goal at the end of the myth. Her dismemberment results in the distribution of her parts to the opposite poles of the vertical axis: her body, the lower part of her (whose physical needs she sought to deny), is deposited in the river, while her head, the seat of her determination to remain inviolate, ascends to the sky.

The Differentiated Sky

Throughout his *Mythologiques,* Lévi–Strauss has illustrated the importance for Native American mythological systems of the dichotomy between river/below and sky/above, with the social world of humans forming the intermediate term.[7] If the purpose of society is to resolve the dichotomy between the above and the below as he claims, then Iaça's rejection of social expectations is portrayed as the original cause of that dichotomy by the disjunction of her body into high and low parts. The result is the origin, not only of the heavenly bodies, but also of the social customs which mediate this dichotomy.

Unlike Hainuwele's death, Iaça's dismemberment does not result in the creation of food plants, even though the Cashinawa, like the Wemale, are swidden horticulturalists. Kensinger indicates that they depend about equally on hunting, fishing, and gardening for their food supply.[8] The only ætiologies in the myth are of the Moon, the stars, the rainbow, and the onset of menstruation, along with the peculiar description of infant skin color as the result of the clotting of the two magical essences we have viewed before: women's menstrual blood and men's semen (surely not "sperm"—the Cashinawa lack microscopes!).

It is possible that this last part of the story is a reaction to the recent intrusion of peoples of African and European descent into Cashinawa territory. Many cultures devise myths to account for the differences in skin color that they observe when contact occurs with distant peoples. For example, the Pima people of southern Arizona tell a story of how the Creator had an oven in which he baked dough into human form:

> *After molding the dough, he noticed that they could not increase, so he added their genitals and then put them in the oven. The first time he greatly underestimated the time required and the result was white-skinned people; the next time he greatly overestimated the time and the result was black-skinned people, but the last time he left the dough in for just the right amount of time, the result being the Pima people.*[9]

Not surprisingly, similar stories are told among European and African cultures, though of course with outcomes favorable to themselves! However, according to Kensinger, the Peruvian Cashinawa have no explicit reference to Peruvians or Brazilians in their mythology or cosmology.[10] It may also be that this part of Story Five refers to the rare incidence of albinism among the Cashinawa, or to the presence of the blue-black Mongolian spot at the base of the spine in infants of Native descent, as Lévi–Strauss rather weakly suggests.[11] However, we shall shortly see that the differentiation of people into well-defined social groups is consistently related to the central theme in other variants of this myth, as it was in Story Four.

The relationship of the Moon to both birth and menstruation in this myth suggests that the Cashinawa think of the conditions preceding the events of the myth as something like the Australian Dream-time, during which procreation in the present sense did not exist. It is true that Iaça has a mother (but no father), and that marriage is portrayed as an expectation of society, but nowhere in the myth are we told that these relationships are linked to reproduction. The Peruvian Cashinawa draw a distinction between *atiwa,* sexual intimacy, and *benewa,* marriage, and allege that only in the latter is sexual activity likely to result in pregnancy.[12] By rejecting marriage, Iaça is by the Cashinawa's own definition rejecting the possibility of further generations beyond herself. A further hint of this Dream-time state is the depiction of the night sky at the beginning of the myth as *undifferentiated.* It is only after the events of the myth that stars, moon, and rainbow (and therefore also time, as measured by their cyclic or sporadic appearance) make their appearance. Like Story Four, Story Five is striving to express something about the inexpressible unity which many cultures believe must underlie the observed duality of the present world.

All the Colors of the Rainbow

In Story Five, the red of menstrual blood, indicating the onset of the periodicity of time, divides the monochromatic universe into colors. This is why Iaça's blood gives rise to the rainbow. Of course, rainbows cannot be seen at night, nor can either the *aurora borealis* or *australis* at the near-equatorial latitude where the Cashinawa live. The absence of rainbows prior to the events in Story Five may simply refer to a lack of cultural differentiation of color, which is perhaps why the myth ends with a statement about the origin of skin colors. We might reflect upon the fact that the principal operations of calculus are *differentiation* and *integration.* It is differentiation which breaks up circles into short line segments; integration restores the unity by reversing the process. As we saw in Chapter One, the calculus was developed in the cultural context of European imperialist expansion, contemporaneous with the emergence of social theories of racial inferiority and superiority. So it is interesting to observe that the name Jesse Jackson has given to his major effort to integrate the races in this country is the *Rainbow Coalition,* linking the symbol back to the social sphere.

Rainbows are such remarkable symbols that we shall have to spend some time considering them in cross-cultural context. While we tend to take seven-colored rainbows for granted, the number of colors people see in the rainbow turns out to be partly a matter of cultural conditioning. Physics tells us that the visible light spectrum is actually a continuous band, without coherent divisions between wavelengths. When light bouncing off an object activates the optic nerve, it sends impulses to the brain which then must interpret them, not in a linear way but based upon trains of associations which are neither entirely inherent in the object nor inherited biologically by the subject, but are mediated by shared experience and discourse.[13] Each culture determines how to divide the band of visible light into discrete colors, and these may not necessarily be the divisions which seem obvious to us. For example, the ancient Egyptians referred to the Mediterranean Sea as "The Great Green." In Sumer, the word for the dark blue stone lapis lazuli meant "dark stone." For the Sumerians, there were only five principal colors—white, black, red, yellow, and green—each of which corresponded to one of the World's Four Quarters plus the center, Nippur.[14] Homer repeatedly refers to the Aegean Sea as "the wine-dark sea." The dye known as Tyrian purple, derived from the *murex* snail and used to color the garments of members of the imperial family in Rome, looks crimson to our eyes. It is surely no accident that the number of colors Westerners perceive in the rainbow is the same as that of the days of the week and also the same as the number of "moving" heavenly bodies, the planets, which are visible to the naked eye: the Sun, Moon, Mercury, Venus, Mars, Jupiter, and Saturn. These also correspond to the chakras in the Tantric system of India, as we shall see below.

To tie this motif of color symbolism back to Story One, an old Irish poem describes Fionn's wolf-hound in the following terms:

Yellow legs had Bran,
Both sides black and her belly white,
Above her loins a speckled back,
And two crimson ears very red.[15]

The division of the colors into black, white, yellow, and red is very common among Native American peoples, but it is also emblematic of the four stages of the alchemical process in Medieval Europe: *nigredo, albedo, citrinitas,* and *rubedo.*[16] Jung notes that eventually the citrinitas phase dropped out of common usage, leaving only black, white, and red. It would be interesting to know how many colors the Cashinawa see in the rainbow, but unfortunately it does not seem to have occurred to either Abreu or Kensinger to ask this question. Lévi–Strauss cites associations of the rainbow among these people with, on the one hand, the Milky Way; and on the other, the "path of enemies"—a correspondence we shall explore in the next chapter.[17] The stars are indeed not uniformly white, but display a range of spectral colors especially visible in the unpolluted skies above Amazonia.

The color red is often used by cultures as a mediating term in the fundamental opposition between light and darkness, white and black, and it often stands for color generally. Even as objective a researcher as Sir James Frazer made use of these three colors as a metaphor to describe the historical progression of human thought from magic (black) through religion (red) to science (white).[18] Victor Turner has explored the widespread cultural classification of colors into white, black, and red. Among the Ndembu of Angola and Zambia whom he studied:

> [t]hese are the only colours for which [they] possess primary terms. Terms for other colours are either derivatives from these . . . or consist of descriptive and metaphorical phrases, as in the case of "green," *meji amatamba,* which means "water of sweet potato leaves." Very frequently, colours which we would distinguish from white, red, and black are by Ndembu linguistically identified by them. Blue cloth, for example, is described as "black cloth," and yellow or orange objects are lumped together as "red."[19]

The significations of these three "primary" colors for the Ndembu is much the same as noted above: red is feminine and is associated with menstrual blood, while white is associated with masculine political and ritual power, and black with death and sorcery.[20] Turner has followed this common set through the mythologies of many cultures, ethnographic as well as archaeological.

The Rainbow Serpent: A Bridge to Australia

Among many Australian aboriginal groups, the rainbow is considered to be a great serpent. For some northern groups, this Dream-time serpent is depicted as a cosmic female figure, who, like the Mesopotamian mother of all sea-serpents, Tiamat, contained all life within her. As a result of her dreaming, life was born. This figure is depicted in some myths as both male and female: i.e., antecedent to the division into sexes.[21] Among the Kurnai of extreme southeastern Australia, the male rainbow serpent Mungan-ngaua, specifically identified as the *aurora australis,* emerged in anger because women had illicitly obtained access to sacred-secret lore:

> Men then went mad with fear and speared one another, fathers killing their children, brothers their brothers, husbands their wives. The sea rushed over the land and most of the people drowned. Those surviving became the Ancestors of the legends, many as birds, animals, and fish. . . . And it was then that Mungan-ngaua left the earth, ascending to the sky, where he remains.[22]

Here we have the association of the rainbow with women's power, with social and environmental chaos, and with a disjunction of the serpent-being into the sky—as Iaça's ascension follows her death and disjunction at the hands of her mother. Notice how similar the violence in this story is to that at the start of the Tzeltal myth, where it was also associated with the Flood. Similarly, the Genesis narrative of the Deluge is preceded by a story about illicit sexuality (the sons of God cohabiting with the daughters of men) and ends with the establishment of the rainbow as a covenant against future floods. In the biblical account, the Flood is also associated with a prohibition on the consumption of meat with blood in it, and also with the commandment to "be fruitful and multiply."[23] A Talmudic legend states that "when a single truly pious man is alive on Earth, the Rainbow no longer needs to remind God of his promise, made in Noah's day, that he would never again flood the whole world as a punishment of its wickedness."[24] We shall see the association of the Moon with bloodshed again in the next chapter.

The best known Australian story about the rainbow serpent is that told by the Murngin of North Australia, whose primary myth concerns the Wawilak sisters, the younger one pregnant and the older one carrying her young child:

> *As the women traveled through the desert, they hunted animals and named them as they killed them. After the younger sister gave birth, they traveled until they came to a waterhole. As the younger sister prepared to cook the animals and plants they had hunted and named, the food items came back to life and jumped into the waterhole. The older woman pursued them into the hole, but she was menstruating and her blood contaminated the waterhole, awakening the giant rainbow serpent Yurlunggur. As he arose out of the well, the water rose also and began to flood the earth. As the rain began to fall, the sisters began to sing the secret songs of each of the Murngin clans to stop it; as this had no effect they decided they must sing something even more powerful, more taboo. They sang Yurlunggur and menstrual blood. This resulted in the snake actually entering their camp and swallowing both them and their children. He then uncoiled himself and stretched up high into the sky. All the other totemic serpents also raised themselves into the sky, and were addressed by Yurlunggur by their clan names. He inquired of each what it had eaten (each of the foods relating to clan taboos). Finally, one of the other serpents asked Yurlunggur what he had eaten. At first he was reluctant to admit it, because his victims were members of his own moiety, but he finally confessed to having eaten the two women and their children. With this, he fell to the ground and the flood ceased. He spewed forth the women, who in spirit form instructed the men of their moiety in the performance of clan rituals that regulate Yurlunggur and the rain.*[25]

The association of clans with food taboos is particularly notable, as we shall see in the next chapter. Like many other hunter–gatherers, the Murngin do not permit women to hunt large game, because of menstrual taboos, so this story is an inversion of present conditions.

In each of these Australian examples, the rainbow symbolizes differentiation and the transition out of the Dream-time state of asexuality into present conditions of duality. I certainly do not wish to suggest that these similarities are due to diffusion between Australia and South America. As far as we know, the Australian aborigines were absolutely isolated once they arrived on the island continent about 50,000 years ago until the arrival of Europeans in the seventeenth century. But it is possible that their distant ancestors and those of the people who crossed over the Bering Straits to the Western Hemisphere may have shared a common cultural heritage which included ideas about the origins of culture. For example, the differentiation into animals and humans of the survivors in the southeastern Australian myth, or of the objects of the women's hunt in the Murngin myth, is reminiscent of the end of Story Four, in which the categories of both the natural and cultural world were established. The ascent of the primordial serpent into the sky is similar to Iaça's ascent after her violent differentiation into upper and lower parts at the hands of her closest relative.

The Cashinawa also have a rainbow serpent motif, which they associate with spirituality and healing. Their diagnostic practice is related to the use of the hallucinogenic brew *ayahuasca* to achieve shamanic trances, which often include visions of multicolored snakes. The vine whose extract is the chief ingredient of this brew (*Banisteriopsis caapi*) itself has a serpentine appearance, and both figuratively and literally links the Above and the Below in Amazonian beliefs.[26]

With the Murngin waterhole we have returned, in a curious fashion, to the transformative pool of Stories One and Two. Like the Irish, the Greeks, and many other peoples, the Murngin associate deep waters with dangerous, chthonic powers. Jung asserts that deep water is archetypal, i.e., universal, in its signification of the unconscious:

> Water is the commonest symbol for the unconscious. The lake in the valley is the unconscious, which lies, as it were, underneath consciousness, so that it is often referred to as the 'subconscious', usually with the pejorative connotation of an inferior consciousness. Water is the 'valley spirit', the water dragon of Tao, whose nature resembles water—a *yang* embraced in the *yin*. Psychologically, therefore, water means spirit that has become unconscious.[27]

The Murngin specifically state that Yurlunggur is the chief of the serpent spirits because he resides at the greatest depth in the pool, and ascends to the greatest height in the sky.

Rainbows in Other Mythological Contexts

Elsewhere in myth, rainbows have a similar significance. In the Mesopotamian Gilgamesh legend, the protagonist must pass the rainbow-girded scorpion-man guardians of the mountains to reach the paradisal isle of Dilmun where the Flood hero resides.[28] In Norse myth, the rainbow bridge Bifrost leads from the lower realms to Asgard, where the Aesir (gods) rule and where the dead heroes shed each other's blood each day and are revived by sacred mead served by demi-goddesses each night.[29] Among the Jicarilla Apache, the Sun and the Moon are said to have disappeared through a hole in the sky due to the exaggerated practices of their shamans, and the gods directed the people and animals, whom they differentiated from one another, to construct ladders of rainbow light to reach into the upper, current world. They then differentiated the people into clans, as Satene did in Story Four.[30] The Tlingit people of southern Alaska, who, like the Apache, speak an Athabascan language, tell a related story:

> *Two young boys, close friends, were walking in a meadow one night under the full moon. One of them insulted the moon, though the other warned him not to. Suddenly, a strange rainbow descended out of the sky around the first boy, and when his friend looked for him, he had vanished. The moon had taken him. Not knowing what else to do, the second boy took out his bow and arrow and shot at a star. The arrow did not return, so he shot more and more arrows until the dawn, when his arrows formed a ladder leading to the upper world which he climbed. There he obtained the help of a grandmother spirit, who gave him four magical objects. She then sent him on his way to the lodge of the moon. When he reached the moon's lodge he heard his friend screaming out in pain. He saw his head emerging from the smoke hole. He rescued him, and the angry moon, a gigantic rolling head, pursued them. One by one the boy cast his magical objects in its path to slow it down. Finally, he cast the last object, a small whetstone, and it turned into a cliff so steep that the moon could not climb it, but kept rolling helplessly up and down, again and again. The pair were blessed by the grandmother spirit and returned in safety down the arrow ladder to their village. There, they had been taken for dead, and people were both surprised and overjoyed at their return.*[31]

Here, the arrow ladder replaces Iaça's hair-string balls as a means of ascent. Once again we have *hybris* on the part of a young person leading to the emergence of a rainbow, and then his punishment and pursuit by the lunar deity (in reverse order of Story Two). Joseph Campbell calls the motif of escape by throwing obstacles in an ogre's way *Obstacle Flight*.[32] However, the moral sense of this tale is quite different from Story Two, for the Tlingit say that because the Moon was blocked by the whetstone they can now insult it with impunity.

The rainbow in each of these myths seems to reflect the idea of a bridge which connects the differentiated world back to its undifferentiated root—the proverbial "pot of gold" at its other end, the "somewhere"-land which is attained only by the few, under unusual circumstances (Figure 20). As Jung points out:

> Only the gods can walk rainbow bridges in safety; mere mortals fall and meet their death, for the rainbow is only a lovely semblance that spans the sky, and not a highway for human beings with bodies. These must pass under it. But water flows under bridges, too, following its own gradient and seeking the lowest place.[33]

But in Tibetan yogic discipline, the Rainbow Bridge or *Antahkarana* connects the consciousness of the initiate with divinity, and specific practices for constructing it are provided for Westerners in the writings of Alice Bailey:

> In the beautiful Eastern symbology, "The Bridge of Sighs" which links the animal world with the human world and leads all men into the vale of tears, of woe, of discipline and of loneliness, is rapidly being replaced by the radiant Rainbow Bridge, constructed by the sons of men who seek pure light. "They pass across the bridge into the Light serene which there awaits them, and bring the radiant light down to the world of men, revealing the new kingdom of the soul; souls disappear, and only the soul is seen."[34]

The same author comments upon the two polarities at either end of this bridge, matter and spirit:

> It is as if a magnetic field were then established and these two vibrating and magnetic units, or grouped energies, begin to swing into each other's field of influence. In the early stages, this hap-

Figure 20: Christ enthroned upon the rainbow. Monastery of St. Catherine's, Sinai Peninsula, 2nd century A.D. (Corbis)

pens only occasionally and rarely. Later it occurs more constantly, and thus a path of contact is established which eventually becomes the line of least resistance, "the way of familiar approach," as it is sometimes esoterically called. Thus the first half of the "bridge," the antahkarana, is constructed. By the time the third initiation is undergone, this way is completed, and the initiate can pass to higher worlds at will, leaving the lower worlds far behind; or he can come again and pass upon the way that leads from dark to light, from light to dark, and from the under, lower worlds into the realms of light."[35]

The Way of the Shaman

The spirit journey of the two Tlingit boys resembles a shamanic initiation, especially since their relatives are convinced that they have died. Like the adepts who construct the *antahkarana,* the shaman is a communicator between the worlds, and the manner in which these remarkable individuals achieve their powers is described, throughout the world, as the result of a psychological crisis which feels like death and resurrection to the person undergoing it. In myths and folktales about shamans, the death and rebirth are presented as literally having taken place. As we have already seen among the Arunta, during the liminal state between death and rebirth various operations are alleged to take place which involve the replacement or rearrangement of the shaman's internal organs.[36] Knud Rasmussen's Inuit (Eskimo) informants told him much about the initiatic ordeals they endured, and one concluded that:

> The only true wisdom lives far from mankind, out in the great loneliness, and it can be reached only through suffering. Privation and suffering alone can open the mind of a man to all that is hidden to others.[37]

Siberian shamans plant a tree in the ground at their seances in memory of the cosmic tree which unites all the worlds, and they metaphorically climb up and down this tree when they shamanize. They are also conversant with a division of both the upper and lower worlds into seven levels. This has suggested to Geoffrey Ashe that there is a shamanic substrate to Story Three—though he interprets this in terms of diffusion rather than independent invention or psychic unity.[38]

While apparently in some societies only males are permitted to become shamans, the Inuit definitely have female *angakoqs* who are entitled to the same powers as their male counterparts. Indeed, this is the only prestige position permitted to women in this society, since men alone are permitted to hunt and to make decisions for the larger group. This is partly due to familiar hunter-gatherer beliefs about the incompatibility of menstruating women with hunted prey, but mostly because women's traditional role as food providers through gathering is almost completely inconsequential in the tundra environment, where there are simply no plants to gather for ten months of the year.[39] We must be cautious about the association of male gender with shamanic abilities, since almost all of the early ethnographers were also male and were only shown that half of the sacred life. Geoffrey Ashe suggests that in Siberia, at least, female shamans may actually have preceded males in the craft.[40] Diane Bell has documented the importance of female secret-sacred practitioners among the Walbiri of central Australia, a group previously thought to reserve secret-sacred teachings only to males. But she was not permitted to view any of the men's secret-sacred rituals.[41] Among the Cashinawa, shamanism may be undertaken by any person, male or female, who has a propensity for dreaming, although the more powerful form of the craft is closely related to the use of *Banisteriopsis* and is exclusive to males.[42]

The Serpent and the Eagle

Like all of the myths we have considered, the action in Story Five turns upon a violent pivot, the murder of Iaça, as the event which precipitates the onset of present conditions. The singular event of the shedding of Iaça's blood by her mother, using a *cultural* item, a knife, leads to the regular monthly shedding of blood by all women, *naturally*. As in Story Four, the moral responsibility for this act of murder is entirely ambiguous. Iaça does not punish her mother for decapitating her, as we (and very certainly the Cashinawa!) would have expected. Instead, she merely asks for her balls of hair-thread (woven from human hair, from the highest part of her body) which she uses as her means of transport to the sky. Ironically, she calls upon the vulture, the highest-flying bird of the Amazonian region but also an eater of carrion, to serve as her means of ascent. We have already had a hint of this symbolism in Story Three, where Dumuzi dreams of being carried off by an eagle. Raptorial birds (eagles, hawks, falcons, vultures, etc.) almost always seem to signify contact with, or transition to, the realm of the above. Hence the word "rapture" is associated with flights of mystical imagination. The universal experience of mystics is that they have been seized and carried off into another world. The appearance of the eagle in Dumuzi's dream might at first appear to be an inversion, since he is in fact taken downward into the Great Below, not upward. However, in other Sumerian myths Dumuzi is depicted as one of the two gatekeepers of the heavenly world. He shares this honor with the winged serpent-god Ningishzida, whose name means either "Lord Right Tree" or "Lord Erect

Phallus"—most probably, both—and who is also a fertility figure.[43] They may even be the same god, for we know that Dumuzi sometimes has serpent limbs. We also find nearly everywhere in myths an association between serpents and winged beings. Both of these are alternative symbols in European and Near Eastern mythology for the astrological sign of Scorpio, which stands for both sex and death, the pair of opposites which characterizes this world of dualities. Presumably, their association in myth antedates and underlies the symbolism of the astrological system popular in the West, since it is much more widespread.

In Middle Eastern myths, the eagle/serpent pair is often associated with the symbol of the tree. For example, before the hero Gilgamesh chopped down the *huluppu* tree so that Inanna could make her couch and throne, and his musical instruments, its root had been infested by a snake which knows no charm; its trunk by the pure maid Lilith; and its crown by the lion-headed eagle Anzu.[44] In Jewish Talmudic literature, Lilith was Adam's first wife, whom he divorced because she would not assume a subordinate position to him in intercourse. She later copulated with the serpent from the Garden of Eden and became thereby the mother of hosts of demons, and dances in the ruins of cities. Like Diana, she lives in the unsettled lands, with a company of animals.[45] In Sumerian, her name, "Virgin of the Air" (*ki.sikil.líl.lu*), is associated with the air element (*líl*), the mediator between the Above and the Below, and thus her place on the tree is medial. In Norse myth, the world ash tree, Yggdrasil, is infested by the same serpent and eagle combination, but in Midgard, the middle world, it is plagued by deer who eat the buds. Once again, the deer is the mediator between the above and the below. In Mesopotamia, deer were sacred to Ninlil, "Lady Air," the consort of the mediating god Enlil, "Lord Air." We have already seen the role of the deer as a transformative symbol in Stories One and Two.

There is also a curious Akkadian tale about a serpent and an eagle who shared the habitation of a *sarbattu*-tree, and formed what we would today term a reciprocal daycare arrangement:

> *While the serpent was out hunting, the eagle took care of its young, and while the eagle was out hunting the serpent took care of its young. But one day the eagle's young demanded food, and the eagle fed them the young of the serpent. When the serpent returned, it was enraged and swore vengeance. It killed a bull, dug a pit and covered it with branches, placed the bull's carcass on top of the branches, and lay*

in wait for the eagle in the pit. When the eagle descended to the carrion, the serpent grasped hold of its talons with its coils and imprisoned it there. Etana, the king of Kish, was wandering through the wilderness in search of divine guidance because he had no son, and he heard the eagle's cries. He freed the eagle, which as a reward flew him up to the heaven of Anu.[46]

There, presumably, he was granted his wish. Unfortunately, the end of the tablet is broken and we do not know how the story concludes. In Sumerian, the word for bird is *mushen.* While we are unsure of the etymology of this word, it is likely that the Sumerians would have noticed that this can be a play on the words *mush.en,* "noble serpent"—even if this is not its actual derivation. Again we see the herbivore (the bull in this case) as the middle term between the serpent and the eagle. These myths also have a persistent relationship to sexuality: the serpent, maiden, and eagle must be dispersed to their respective directions before Inanna can have her couch for the Sacred Marriage; and the eagle must be released from the serpent's pit before Etana can figure out how to have a son. Indeed, his ascent is a perfect inversion of Iaça's, for she ascended so as *not* to procreate.

These stories relate the serpent and eagle symbols to the sacred tree in a way which suggests a relationship to the caduceus symbol of Hermes, formed by a pair of serpents intertwined five times about a staff, surmounted by eagle's wings and a sphere. In Greek myth, this symbol stood for healing, for it was given by Hermes to Asklepios, the healing god, who in turn gave it to Hippocrates. This is how it came to be the emblem of the medical profession. This is perfectly isomorphous to the Indian Kundalini system, with the lower five *chakras* associated with the spinal column, about which the serpents *ida* and *pingala* are wound, the sixth *chakra,* at the brow, having two "petals" like the wings, and the crown *chakra* being represented by a sphere of light, or the all-seeing eye (Figure 21). The heart chakra, at the center of the system, is symbolized by a deer. In the view of Kundalini yoga, the imbalance of the centers is the cause of all disease, and healing involves their proper realignment.[47]

There is a fascinating Greek myth that relates sexuality to the origin of the caduceus:

Tieresias of Thebes, as a young man, was wandering about in the mountains when he saw a pair of serpents copulating. He thrust his staff

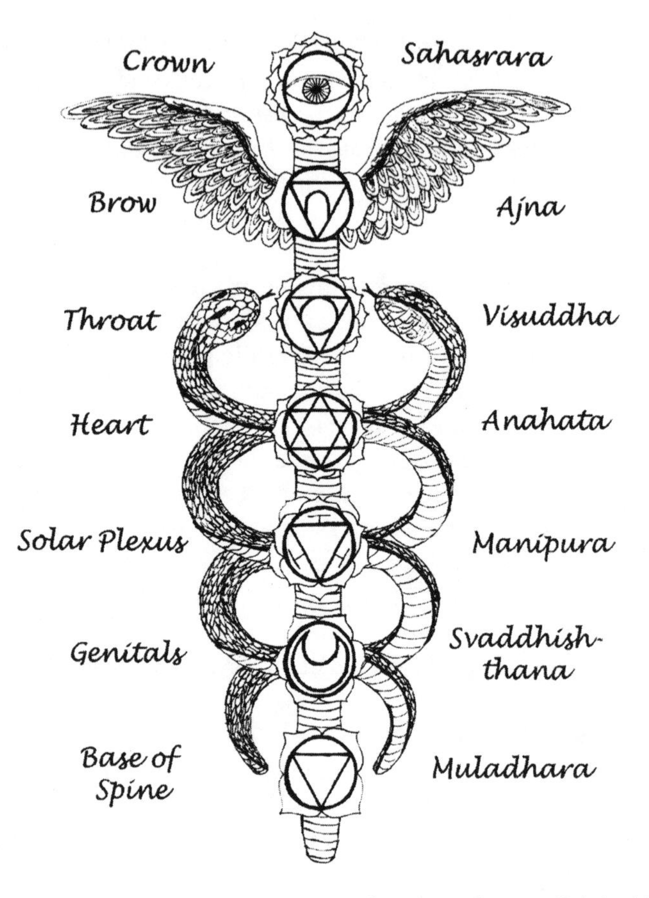

Figure 21: The Kundalini system compared to the caduceus. Original line drawing. (Darrel Hoffman)

between them, and was transformed into a woman. After seven years in this state, she was again wandering through the countryside and again saw a pair of serpents copulating, thrust her staff between them, and was transformed back into a man.

Now Zeus and Hera were having a marital spat over the issue of whether it is the male or the female who derives greater pleasure from sexual intercourse; each claimed it was the other gender. Having no independent means of confirmation at their disposal, they consulted Tieresias, who replied that of twelve parts of pleasure, the man has three and the woman nine. Hera was so angry at having lost the argument that she blinded Tieresias; but Zeus was so pleased that he granted him long life and inner sight.[48]

As Jesus said in the Sermon on the Mount, "If thine eye be single, thy whole body shall be full of light"[49]—a condition which, in Kundalini Yoga, is achieved when one has opened the Third Eye at the summit of the *chakra* system. But there is also another story about how Tieresias became the blind seer (an oxymoron!) of Thebes, which ties in neatly with Story Two as well as with the serpent/eagle symbol complex:

As a young man, Tieresias chanced to see the virgin goddess Athene bathing. In anger, she blinded him. However, his mother was a friend of Athene and interceded on his behalf with the goddess. She was moved by his mother's plea, so she took the serpent Erechthonius from her aegis, ordering it to cleanse Tieresias' ears with its tongue so that he might understand the speech of birds.[50]

Unlike Actæon in a similar situation, Tieresias is spared, and even gifted, because the feminine intercedes for him. He uses his gift to prophesy to all of the rulers of Thebes, from Pentheus to Creon, and his life is as long as the life of the city. As for Erechthonius, he was created when Haephestus vainly tried to rape Athene. His seed fell on her thigh, whence she wiped it off with a piece of wool and cast it to the ground where it fertilized Gæa, the Earth Mother. When born, the child was half human, half serpent, and frightened the Athenian royal women so much when they saw him that they leaped from the Acropolis to their deaths. Athene agreed to place Erecthonius on her aegis, and he later became king of Athens and introduced chariotry, silversmithing, and the worship of the goddess. He then ascended to the sky to become the constellation Auriga, the Charioteer.[51] Graves interprets his name as "wool on the earth"—recall that Iaça's means of ascent to the sky was via her hair-string balls—but another interpretation is possible. The Greeks referred to the ancient city of Uruk as Erech, so we may suspect that there is a Mesopotamian connection once again, like that of the Theban dynasty of Kadmos. Uruk, the city of snake-footed Dumuzi, was sacred to Inanna, who, as we saw in Story Three, is a warlike goddess like Athene. In Sumer, too, we find the earliest chariots, and the first silver currency standard.

The serpent's method of hunting eagles in the Etana story is very peculiar, since the identical method (with buffalo instead of bulls) was described in the eighteenth and nineteenth century by ethnographers and other travelers visiting Native peoples on the American Great Plains as the means by which men obtained eagle feathers for their regalia. This exceedingly dangerous pursuit happened only during the fall, a liminal time between the large summer group encampments which engaged in collective buffalo hunting and warfare and the small group camps of the wintertime which concentrated on individual hunting and raiding.[52] In this case, the object of the enterprise was not to be taken up to heaven, but to obtain a hard-won favor from the most sacred of the Winged Beings.

A Plains Variant of Story Five: Sun and Moon Go Courting

The emphasis by the Plains peoples upon the powers of the Above is also related in a widespread story about the search for wives by the Sun and the Moon, here depicted as brothers. I give an Arapaho version:

> *The Sun and the Moon decided to leave their father's lodge to search for wives. The Sun disliked human women, since whenever they looked at him they squinted. So he traveled eastwards down the Eagle River until he reached a swamp, where he found a frog wife, who could look at him without squinting. The Moon, by contrast, found human women beautiful; they certainly didn't squint when they looked at* him! *So he traveled westwards up the Eagle River for four days until he came to a big camp circle. Seeing some young women coming his way, he, transformed himself into an albino porcupine, near a tall cottonwood tree. A young Arapaho woman was out gathering with her friend and spied the porcupine, which was a rare and valuable source of quills for ornamenting garments. The porcupine ran up the tree, and she began to climb after it, but by his magic the Moon caused the tree to grow upwards as she climbed, until it reached the sky. When she reached this far, he transformed himself into the handsome Moon and proposed marriage, which she accepted. He brought her to his father's lodge, taking care to cover the opening where she entered the sky world so that she might forget its position. The Sun had already returned with his frog bride, whom they named Water Woman.*
>
> *The Arapaho woman quickly proved her industriousness, but the frog wife was lazy, could not chew her food with appreciative smacking*

noises, and was incontinent. Moon was displeased with her, and Sun was fascinated with Moon's human wife. The Arapaho woman suddenly bore a son to Moon, and the father of the brothers then decreed that women would henceforth give birth only after ten moons had passed: "In the beginning the child preceded the flow of blood; henceforth it will follow it after a ten-monthly interval. And each bleeding will last from the first to the last quarter of the moon, that is, the same period of time which elapsed between Moon's departure to look for a wife until his return." In jealousy, Water Woman leaped on Moon's breast, which was the origin of Moon spots. The appearance of the frog on the belly indicates pregnancy of the woman; the face of Moon bears the mark of the first menstruation of the woman.

After a time, the human woman developed a longing for her own people, but the Moon did not want her to leave. So she began making sinew strings into a long rope. She discovered the hole which led to this world and stole out with her young son and tried to climb down to the earth plane via a rope. However, the rope was not long enough and she remained dangling from the end. Moon looked down and saw her there, and cast down a sacred stone which struck her on the head which caused her to fall and die. Her son, falling, was borne up by a meadowlark and safely reached the ground, and nursed from the dead body of his mother until it decomposed. Then he was found by Old Woman Night, who claimed to be his grandmother. She adopted him and raised him as her own, and made him a special lance decorated with eagle fathers. After a while, he discovered a great horned serpent eating the old woman's food cache and killed it. He later discovered that this water monster was her husband.

After a time he decided to leave her to seek his father. Traveling east along the river, he came upon many sleeping snakes and killed many of them with his lance. Some of them gave the alarm and soon the serpents covered the entire earth so that he could not find a passage. He eventually became sleepy and lay down. A large serpent came up, crawled slowly into his rectum, up his spinal column, into his skull, and then completely coiled up within the skull and remained there, immobilizing the boy until he turned into a skeleton. But the ligaments kept his bones together, and he called upon the rain and the sun to descend upon him. This made the serpent so restless that it emerged from his mouth, whereupon the boy grasped its head and pulled it out and was about to kill it with his lance when it appealed to him to spare it if it gave him its skin to wrap about the lance. The boy agreed, and let the serpent go. From this time forth, snakes shed their skins annually.

Eventually he reached the lodge of his uncle, the Sun, who would not admit him because his lance was "lawless." So he placed his lance above the door and transformed himself into the morning star, which follows the Sun and the Moon.[53]

In this story, we have another woman whose marital aspirations are outside of the human sphere—too high for her own safety. As in the Cashinawa version, the unregulated flow of menstrual blood is transformed into an orderly calendar by the birth of the child. The Sun's wife comes from the river, the place where Iaça's body is deposited, and is of a distinctly lower order of life forms than the Moon's wife—she belongs to the oviparous class which we have observed before. The cottonwood, which grows tall and straight and favors river environments, is the tree used by the Arapaho and other Plains tribes as the central pole of the Sun Dance lodge, hanging from which individuals sacrifice portions of their flesh to the Sun.[54] As we shall see in Story Six, there is a widespread belief in the Americas that the Sun (like Yurlunggur) is a cannibal. Among the Mandan, with whom the Arapaho lodged for several generations during the seventeenth century, the tale was told that the only survivors of a great flood brought by the "Foolish One" in the Sun were those who escaped in a boat which lodged in the branches of a cottonwood tree. In the Okipa ceremony which celebrated this escape, they, too, offered up their flesh as they danced around the central cottonwood lodge pole.[55]

The serpent transformation in the second half of the story is also reminiscent of Yurlunggur's swallowing of the Wawilak women, except that here the serpent follows precisely the course of the Kundalini to lodge in the boy's head, causing his shamanic death and resurrection. This is symbolized thereafter by the wrapping of the snake skin about the sacred lance, which is a part of the Arapaho Sun dance ritual. It is also reminiscent of the composite symbol of snake and staff in the Tieresias story. In Lakota versions of the story of the wives of Sun and Moon, the child is called "Stone Boy," and brings the people the sacred pipe before he likewise ascends into heaven. Pipestone, which is the red clay mineral catlinite, is used to carve smoking pipes used in sacred ceremonies to conduct the tobacco smoke from the earth plane to the sky plane, carrying with it the prayers of the people. It is referred to by the Lakota as "blood turned to stone."[56] Lévi–Strauss comments extensively on the role of tobacco in Native American societies as a symbol of the above, the hypercultural (overcooked), whereas ordinary food is merely cultural (cooked).[57] The meadowlark, as he has noted, is a bird which flies neither high nor low, and thus mediates between the Above and the Below.[58]

An Inuit Variant of Story Five: Sedna

The Arapaho story allows us to bridge to the last series of New World variations on our distant bridegroom theme, a widely dispersed set of Inuit myths about the mistress of the sea beasts, known most popularly as Sedna. Sedna stories are told from Thule, Greenland to Nome, Alaska, and in this case their wide distribution is definitely due to the diffusion and rapid migration of the ancestral Inuit across the Arctic from west to east, for they are a biologically distinct population, and their innovative technology, indeed their whole way of life is a fine-tuned adaptation to one of Earth's most inhospitable regions.[59]

> *Sedna was a young woman whose father wished to marry her to a man in the village called Dog (or an actual dog). She refused, because she wanted to marry a seabird, and the pair eloped. The bird took her up to his sky realm, and she was happy there for a while. But eventually she discovered that the pleasures of the sky kingdom were not as attractive as she had been told, and she desired to visit her family, so he permitted her to return to earth. It happened that she arrived just as the villagers were getting into their kayaks to begin their migration to their summer hunting grounds (i.e., at the spring equinox). She saw her father's kayak in the water, and plunged in and swam to it, grasping the gunwales with her fingers. Her father was so enraged to see her that he took his ice axe and cut off her fingers, and she sank to the bottom of the sea and drowned. Her fingers became the sea beasts: the whales, porpoises, and walruses upon whose flesh the Inuit depend for survival.*[60]

This story fits into a ritual context. The Inuit attribute misfortunes within their community to the breaking of taboos by individuals—most often, by women's attempts to control reproduction. Concealed abortions are considered to be especially heinous sins. These offenses cause the hair of Sedna, who now lives under the ocean, to become tangled. Because she no longer has fingers, she cannot comb out the tangles, and she therefore becomes distressed and withholds the bounty of the sea, her beasts. To alleviate this problem, the *angakoq* or shaman must enter into a trance state in which he travels psychically down to her house under the sea, being sure to take with him the means to placate her father and the dog, who stand as guardians at the door. He then combs out her hair, and she informs him of the particular breaches of taboo which have distressed her. On his return, he communicates these to the people and prescribes penances—mostly in the form of food taboos upon the women.[61] Jensen, commenting on this myth, associates Sedna's inability to comb her hair with the frequent prohibition on menstruating Native American women against scratching their hair with their fingers.[62]

Sedna is known by many names across the Arctic, one of which means "she who would not have a husband"; her father is known by a name which means "the man with a knife"—further parallels to the Cashinawa version.[63] In some variants of the story, Sedna actually was originally married to the Dog, and her canine children were sent over the seas to become the ancestors of Europeans, while her human children spawned the Inuit, a detail that once again connects us to the end of the story of Iaça with its ætiology of different skin colors.[64] The differentiation among humans followed by that of the sea beasts inverts the order found in the story of the Wawilak sisters, as well as that in Story Four. The result of Sedna's disobedience is the imposition of taboos upon women, particularly related to their reproductive function: if they disobey society's expectations by secretly aborting their unborn children, the productivity of the sea is withdrawn. Just as Iaça forgave her mother for killing her under the condition that she give her her hairstring balls to unravel so she could ascend, Sedna forgives her father and permits him to serve as the guard to her undersea abode. She also forgives the Inuit women for killing their children if they observe the penances the *angakoq* who descended to unravel her hair prescribes.

Once again, we are dealing with the polarity of the Above and the Below. This is made clear by Sedna's original ascent into the sky kingdom and her subsequent catastrophic descent, not only to the earth plane like the Arapaho woman but to a subaqueous underworld. Like Iaça, she disobeys her parent's wishes for her marriage and is therefore murdered; only in this case her ascent into the sky is not permanent and precedes her dismemberment. Like Hainuwele, her parts become food—for the coastal Inuit, whose environment does not permit the cultivation or even the gathering of plant foods for most of the year, the sea mammals into which her fingers are differentiated are the mainstay of the diet.

As we have seen, the wounded or dismembered deity is often a source of foods necessary to the people to avoid starvation; she suffers or dies that they might live. For example, among the Pano, close linguistic relatives of the Cashinawa in Peru, a daughter abandoned by her parents is visited by a bird who takes the form of a boy. When she cannot satisfy his demands for food, he makes her strike his knees with a stick, and ripe bananas fall from them. On later visits, other crop plants are produced in the same way.[65] This may remind us of Hainuwele's sacrifice, but the bird motif links us to Iaça and Sedna; like them, the Pano girl has a distant, avian suitor (and we may recollect that the Virgin Mary also conceives immaculately upon a visitation from the dove of the Holy Spirit; the Latin word *macula*, "spot," is also used to describe moon spots). The sexual symbolism of the Pano story is almost too obvious for comment. We will explore the relationship of sexuality to the motifs of hunger and cannibalism in the next chapter.

The Cheyenne, like their Arapaho, Lakota, and Mandan neighbors, celebrate the Sun-dance with sacrifices of their own flesh as they hang suspended from the central cottonwood tree of the ceremonial lodge. They attribute the origin of this ritual to a period of famine, associated with the breakdown of the family. The foundation myth tells how the culture hero Erect Horns eloped with the chief's wife to Harney Peak to find the cave of the Powers of the World, who gifted the pair with a ceremony which calls out the buffalo for the annual hunt by means of an act of extramarital sexual intercourse.[66] In the Mesopotamian *Atra-hasis* epic, too, conditions of a seven-year famine lead to a breakdown of the family similar to that described in Story Five:

In the fourth year of the famine
The mother watched the scales at the sale of the daughter;
The daughter watched the scales at the sale of the mother.
In the fifth year they served the daughter for dinner . . .
Each house consumed their neighbors.[67]

There is a striking parallel to the Sedna story in a fifteenth century European alchemical text, the *Vision of Arisleus:*

The philosopher Arisleus journeys to the land of the King of the Sea, in which only like mates with like; consequently nothing is begotten and nothing prospers. Arisleus advises the king to mate together his mentally conceived son and daughter, Gabricus and Beya. During intercourse, Gabricus is swallowed into the womb of Beya, and dissolved into atoms. As a punishment, Arisleus and Beya are banished to a hothouse under the sea. There they remain imprisoned for eighty days until they are rescued by the androgyne Harforetus, a disciple of Pythagoras, who feeds them the fruit of the immortal tree which gives salvation. Beya gives birth to her own brother, resolving the king's problem.[68]

This fantastic tale is closely isomorphous to Story Three as well as to the Sedna stories, though once again the order of the motifs is transformed. Jung comments that the name of Beya derives from the Arabic *al-Baida,* "The White One," which in addition to its obvious relationship to the White Goddess is a specific reference to *salt,* one of the three alchemical essences, representing the absorbing, inert, receptive, feminine physicality. Gabricus is *sulphur* (< Arabic Kibrit), the red, penetrating, active, invigorating masculine essence of mind.[69] The third essence, *mercury,* is the androgynous, healing, and equilibrating spirit, and is represented in the alchemical story by Harforetus. Jung equates this myth with the process of individuation, whereby the union of mind and body in the darkest part of the unconscious results in a temporary extinction of consciousness, followed by its redemption through the divine intercession of the Self.[70] Pythagoras, regarded by the alchemists as the greatest of philosophers, plays the role of Enki in Story Three, dispatching his androgynous acolyte to save the day with the sacrament of the Tree of Life. But Harforetus also replicates the role of the *angakoq,* braving the descent into the sea to bring about a solution related to birth in a land which has been blighted by infertility, like the conditions in Sumer following Inanna's descent. We shall return to the motif of sibling incest in detail in the next chapter.

The Ritual Context of the Sedna Story

Franz Boas relates a ritual to control Sedna among the Baffin Island Inuit which is set around the time of the winter solstice, when the sun disappears below the horizon completely for several weeks:

The spirits of the dead, the *tupilaq,* knock wildly at the huts, which they cannot enter, and woe to the unhappy person whom they can lay hold of. He immediately sickens and a speedy death is regarded as sure to come. The wicked *qiqirn* (author's note: a huge hairless dog) pursues the dogs, which die with convulsions and cramps as soon as they see him. All the countless spirits of evil are aroused, striving to bring sickness and death, bad weather, and failure in hunting. The worst visitors are Sedna, mistress of the under world, and her father, to whose share the dead Inuit fall. . . . The hardest task, that of driving away Sedna, is reserved for the most powerful angakoq. A rope is coiled on the floor of a large hut in such a manner as to leave a small opening at the top, which represents the breathing hole of a seal. Two angakut stand by the side of it, one of them holding the seal spear in his left hand, as if he were watching at the seal hole in winter, the other holding the harpoon line. Another angakoq, whose office it is to lure Sedna up with a magic song, sits at the back of the hut. At last she comes up through the hard rocks and the wizard hears her heavy breathing; now she emerges from the ground and meets the angakoq waiting at the hole. She is harpooned and sinks away in angry haste, dragging after her the harpoon, to which the two men hold with all their strength. Only by a desperate effort does she tear herself away from it and return to her dwelling in Adlivun. Nothing is left with the two men but the blood sprinkled harpoon, which they proudly show to the Inuit.[71]

In this ritual, we find all the symbols of the myth, played in reverse: the dog, the father, the seal, the emerging demoness; but here Sedna struggles to escape from the attack of the *angakoqs* back to her world of the Below, rather than chasing her father who then proceeds to attack her and send her there. Of course, the point of the ritual is that the trio of *angakoqs* have caught her quite deliberately in order to force her to cease tormenting the living. The ghosts who precede Sedna repeat the motif of Iaça's aimless wandering around the village. Also, Sedna's descent into the sea is keyed to the spring equinox, while her emergence in this ritual is at the darkest time of year, when it is feared the Sun will not return. The Yu'piq, who live at the extreme western end of the Inuit range near Nome, Alaska, have a similar ritual "to please the animal spirits" at the winter solstice. For this ritual, their shaman wears a complex mask (which very likely represents Sedna herself) which has a seal face, flippers, and human hands.[72] Interestingly, Boas cites an earlier ethnographic account of what he assumes to be the same ritual among the mainland Nugumiut in which

Sedna is replaced by "the evil spirit of the deer," (presumably the caribou?) which is pursued through the village and speared to death.[73] This should remind us of the many chase scenes we have already seen. Sedna, like the deer in Stories One and Two, is a mediator between the worlds of the above and the below. For the coastal Inuit, she provides from her body the sea beasts which are their food; for the caribou hunters of the mainland, she provides these animals also. A hunter who has participated in this ritual is considered extremely lucky, for his arrows will always find their mark.

A Danish Version of Story Five: The Little Mermaid

Since Sedna descends from the sky world to earth, and then to the bottom of the sea, the reader should by now be unsurprised to find yet another permutation of this story in Hans Christian Andersen's fable of the Little Mermaid:

> *An adolescent mermaid rises from her comfortable home in the sea kingdom and gazes upon the likeness of a prince, her exact counterpart in age. She aspires to his love, rescues him from a violent tempest, but cannot join him on the shore because of her fishy tail. Her sisters advise her to consult a sea witch, who gives her a potion which will cause her tail to split into legs. But the price for this is that she will lose her tongue and will bleed from her feet. She accepts this suffering, knowing that she risks her life if her prince should marry another. When he innocently does so, considering her only as a companion, one of her sisters gives her a knife from the sea and tells her to sacrifice him and his new bride so that their blood will run over her feet and rejoin them into a tail. When she finds herself unable to do this, she casts herself into the sea and her spirit is borne up into the air by the sylphs, as her corporeal body turns to sea foam.*[74]

The figure of the mermaid or *melusina* is well known from art and literature. Jung considers it to represent a man's *anima*, tempting him into the unconscious realm but not, ultimately, able to deliver on her offer.[75] However, this is an exclusively masculine perspective, one which might be typical of Fionn and Actæon, who pursue her into the unconscious at their peril. The male *angakoqs*, too, undertake a perilous journey, and succeed in placating the archetypal feminine. However, in Andersen's tale we get a feel for what it might be like to *be* a Melusina. From the feminine perspective, the figure takes on an entirely different charge, tinged with a sense of willing sacrifice for the distant beloved which is absent from the masculine versions, but which is very reminiscent of Geshtin-anna's sacrifice. This is the feminine equivalent, for Jung, of *anima*-possession: a woman's preoccupation with her inner masculine side, or *animus*. While the elusive and seductive *anima* appears from the Below (like Sedna), the *animus* is intellectual and judgmental, and appears from the Above, like the seabird. A woman who becomes preoccupied with finding the perfect sky-mate may indeed undergo a fall once the blinders are removed—as they always are in real relationships. Unless she is able to ground herself in her own being, and especially in her body, she may have the metaphorical (or even literal) experience of dissolving into mist—through conditions like *anorexia nervosa*.[76]

Not all mer-people in myth are female: the earliest literary and artistic representations of such mixed creatures we have derive from Sumer. According to the Babylonian priest Berossus, the first of the antediluvian sages, Oannes, was a fish-man who came from Enki's paradise, Dilmun, to teach the people the arts of civilization. As we have already seen, Dilmun is the place where time's impact is not felt.[77] While Oannes himself is not described as such in the cuneiform literature, his successors, the culture heroes called *apkallus*, are described and depicted on seals as fish-men (*ku.lilu*).[78] This word is also used to describe drowned humankind in the lament of Inanna in the Flood story. According to Berossus, the *apkallus* instituted unions with mortal women, resulting in *Mischwesen* of various sorts.[79] This was followed by the Flood—as in Genesis, where the mating of the sons of god with the daughters of men is the immediate precursor to the Flood.

The undivided tail of the mermaid/merman is symbolic of a presexual, and therefore pre-cultural state. Like the realm of the Sea King in the *Vision of Arisleus*, the mermaid's kingdom is one in which there is no procreation (though she has sisters), because the lower part of her body has not been separated and the bleeding of her "feet" has not yet begun. In this she resembles Hainuwele, who can only produce her gifts anally. Interestingly, one of the symptoms of *anorexia* is the cessation of menstruation: the body's internal clock shuts down when fat levels are insufficient to sustain a pregnancy. Immanuel Velikovsky, in his discussion of the myth of Oedipus, whose feet were pierced at birth, suggests that:

> In folklore feet may stand for legs. Many languages do not have different words for legs and feet. In Greek, the word *pous* stands for both; in Egyptian, too, the word *r-d* (foot) stands also for leg. In Hebrew, as well, *regel* is the lower limb and likewise the foot . . . In the riddle that Oedipus solved concerning the creature that walks on four legs, on two, and on three (the staff being the third), the Greek word used is *pous,* and thus the name Oedipus could, and even preferably so, mean "swollen legs."[80]

The substitution of feet for genitals is also present in the Pano story above. As we shall see in Chapter Ten, the wounding of the Hero in this part of the body is very common in mythology, and usually refers to a sexual and/or moral dysfunction.

The emergence of the *melusina* beckons the consciousness into a timelessness free of human responsibility, much as Oisin follows his bride into the timeless world of Tir-na-n'og across the sea. The tragedy of Andersen's story is that the mermaid herself yearns to leave this paradisal state and enter the painful world of time and sex and (necessarily also) death—a world where she does not belong. She longs for a bridegroom too far removed from her own society even to notice her affection. Like Iaça, she aspires to the heights; also like Iaça, she cannot attain them without sacrificing the lower portion of her body—first literally, using the potion, then figuratively, as an air spirit. Her transformation is in an exactly opposite direction from Sedna's—from undersea to earth to air.

The mermaid's wounding in Andersen's tale only affects her own psyche, but that is typical of the limited scope of Andersen's literary renderings of folk-tales. No doubt it also reflects his own troubled psyche, his despair of achieving happiness—as another famously neurotic Dane exclaimed, "O, that this too too solid flesh would melt, thaw, and resolve itself into a dew."[81]

It is also no accident that hers is the only one of the stories I have chosen for this chapter which derives from the industrial age. As Joseph Campbell has noted in the final volume of his tetralogy on myth, in modern Western civilization the scope of myth is similarly limited to the individual, who becomes increasingly split off from the whole and must achieve what Jung refers to as individuation without much support from the larger society, or else be ground under the wheel of conformity.[82] The dreams and visions of schizophrenics are rarely perceived to have a relationship to life in normative society. Orthodox Freudians would certainly include the initiatory experiences of *angakoqs* in this category.[83] They would argue that because these neurotic individuals fail to fit society's expectations, they must be put out of our sight until they can regain a sense of the "reality principle," by force if necessary.

We shall see in the final chapter that this perception may be a fundamental error, a pernicious misjudgment of the tender-minded by the tough-minded who dominate the "normal" world. Each of the female protagonists in Story Five has thwarted the norms imposed by that world, and each has paid a price for her disobedience. But at the same time, with the exception of the Little Mermaid, each of them has gained a power over the periodicity of time and the division of society as a result of her actions. They partake of the strength reflected in their sisters from Stories One, Two, Three, and Four: the hag, Diana, Inanna, and Hainuwele. They are not victims. By contrast, we shall see the female protagonists of Story Six take on a more passive role, one which will lead us to some very equivocal conclusions about the nature of society.

Chapter Eight

A BREED TOO NEAR

The key myths we will consider in this chapter, as I stated before, derive from the same culture areas as the variants of Story Five, some of them from the same peoples. If the myths from Amazonia, the Great Plains, and the Arctic considered in the last chapter formed a kind of major chord, those in this chapter are distinctly darker, as if set in a minor key. The composition here is less structured than before, more like a set of seven free variations on the general theme of *incest*. As we ranged northwards to find Inuit parallels for the Amazonian version of Story Five, we shall have to range back southwards to Amazonia to find parallels for the Inuit version of Story Six. And, once again, we shall pause among the Cheyenne, while casting frequent glances back westward along our route to the cultures we have studied before, as well as to the Australian continent.

The first key myth of this series was told by the Thule Inuit of Greenland to Peter Freuchen and recorded by him in The Book of the Eskimos.

Story Six, Inuit Variation: The Origins of the Sun and the Moon

For entertainment during the long arctic nights, the young people would assemble in a special semi-subterranean lodge. The whale-oil lamps would be extinguished, and everyone would engage in indiscriminate intercourse. Contrary to the expected randomness of the couplings, one woman noticed that she was continually visited by the same man. She therefore took care to put some soot from her lamp on her fingers, and on the next occasion she rubbed it on his forehead. In this way, she dis-

> *covered when the lamps were relit that her lover was her own brother. Blushing red with shame, she fled from the lodge. To pursue her, he transformed himself into the Moon, but she in turn became the Sun. He continues to pursue her across the sky forever; but as his moss-whisk lamp was lighted hastily, it glows with a dimmer light than hers.*[1]

This myth has a very specific temporal association: the sun is invisible above the Arctic Circle for much of the day from the autumnal to the vernal equinox. The emergence of the flaming red sun above the horizon corresponds precisely with the timing of the celebration of the death of Dumuzi at the New Year's Festival in Sumer. As we saw in the last chapter, in the Arctic this marks the time of the disappearance of Sedna from the world of men; here it also marks the removal of the Sun Goddess from the social sphere, this time to the Above rather than the Below. Boas, in recounting the winter solstice ritual for banishing Sedna, indicates that on the day following her harpooning by the *angakoqs*, a ritual tug-of-war takes place between those born in the summer and those born in the winter (the Inuit do not have moieties, so this is the only dual division of society available to them). This is followed by the appearance of two strange transgendered figures who assign men and women to one another for a period of sexual license, after which the Inuit pretend to ritually kill and dismember the figures. All the fires in the village are extinguished and then relit in the course of this ritual. An informant, when asked the meaning of this, replied, "New sun—new light,"[2] indicating that the Sun is rekindled by the ritual, in association with sexual license, which also characterizes the opening of Story Six.

Though there is no obvious association here with menstruation, the sister is reddened with shame by her realization (as was Diana when she noticed Actæon spying on her), and this results in her flaming forth as the sun. The same moral ambiguity that characterized the Cashinawa and Inuit variants of Story Five is apparent: the brother is not punished for his crime any more than Iaça's mother or Sedna's father were, and he continues to pursue his sister across the skies.

Story Six, Kuniba Variation: The Origin of the Moon

We may compare the Inuit myth with the following variant on the rolling head story of the last chapter, recorded by the Brazilian Jesuit ethnographer Nimuendaju from the now extinct Kuniba tribe and first published in an anthology by Baldus in 1946. It was subsequently republished by Lévi–Strauss in the third volume of his *Mythologiques*, along with the story of Iaça. This is probably an example of local borrowing or sharing of mythic imagery, since the Kuniba and the Cashinawa territories were within only a few days' river journey of one another:

> *A young Indian woman was visited every night by a stranger whose face she rubbed on one occasion with the bluish-black juice of the genipa tree. In this way, she discovered that her lover was her brother. The culprit was driven out; and, as he fled, enemies killed him and cut off his head. Another brother, who was trying to rejoin him, offered the head shelter. But it never stopped asking for food and drink; the man resorted to craft, abandoned it and fled. It managed to roll as far as the village and attempted to get inside his hut. As it was not allowed to enter, it considered in turn several possible metamorphoses: into water, stone, etc. Finally, it chose to become the moon, and rose into the sky unrolling a ball of thread as it went. In order to be revenged on his sister who had denounced him, the man, now changed into the moon, inflicted the curse of menstruation on her.*[3]

In another version, the brother tries to wipe the stain from his face with leaves, resulting in the creation of the dark Brazilian cuckoo, *Crotophaga ani*[4]—restoring the relationship between the severed head and the bird which is absent from the first version.

It is hardly likely that direct diffusion can be called into play to explain the similarities among the Inuit and Kuniba variants of Story Six, or between them and the other myths in our unfolding series. The Amazonians are biologically one of the most isolated groups in the world, having nearly 98 percent incidence of Type O Positive blood.[5] They are thought to have arrived in South America by migration from the north no later than 10,000 years ago, and recent discoveries on both sides of the Andes suggest a much earlier date.[6] Several researchers have suggested the possibility that Japanese or Polynesian fishermen reached the western coast of South America,[7] and the association of the rolling head with sibling incest is found in Polynesia. In a myth from the Tonga Islands, Eel attempts to mate with his sisters, who reject him and flee, and are turned into two rocks. He swims off to Samoa, where he impregnates a virgin bathing in a pool. When the people decide to kill him for this, he tells the girl to plant his head, which grows into the first coconut tree.[8] The wide-ranging Polynesians are thought to have begun their voyaging in Melanesia, where they could have become familiar with variants of Story Four, with its emphasis on coconuts and ritual dismemberment.

More remotely, Phoenicians may have reached the eastern coast of Brazil bringing with them the myths of the Near East,[9] but most archæologists dismiss the evidence for transoceanic contact as insufficient, and even the most ardent diffusionists do not argue that such peoples would have had any interest in penetrating very far into the interior jungles. My own feeling about this is that there is more Shadow projection than tangible evidence on both sides of the argument.[10] But it is likely that there has been at least a generalized sharing of mythological ideas within the Amazonian basin, and between it and other regions of South America, including both coasts.

The Inuit are thought to have entered the Western Hemisphere by boat from Siberia as recently as 4,000 years ago, and to have spread quickly across the Arctic, but they had very minimal (and usually unfriendly) contact with the earlier entrants to their south.[11] They are biologically and culturally quite distinct from other Native populations in the Western Hemisphere. Lévi-Strauss nevertheless felt that all of the Native peoples of the Americas participate in a single mythological community, with shared myths reaching from one end of the hemisphere to the other.[12] A process which may account for this is called *stimulus diffusion*. It does not require actual contact between any particular pair of peoples for the transmission of traits and ideas between them, but instead the information flows through intermediaries. The question left unanswered by such an explanation, as is usually the case with diffusionist hypotheses, is just why such transmission should have taken place at all. That can only be approached on a case-by-case basis, unless we are prepared to invoke psychic unity as the underlying ground for the acceptance of mythological ideas.

On the local level, the relationship of the Kuniba variant to the Cashinawa version of Story Five should be obvious, either directly or through inversion, and details which are inexplicable in one variant are clarified by the other. For example, the hair-string ball in the Kuniba variant makes no sense as a means of ascent unless one notes its association with the vulture in the Cashinawa version of Story Five. On the other hand, the rolling head is much more a part of the action in this version than in the story of Iaça. Story Five is about a young woman who wishes to distance herself from human sexual relations, but this is unacceptable to society. Both of the versions of Story Six I have presented so far are about a young man who wishes to engage in sexual relations with a person not sufficiently distant from him for this to be acceptable to society: his own sister.

The Crime of Incest: Brothers and Sisters

The question of incest is one about which a great deal of myth revolves, as readers familiar with the work of Sigmund Freud doubtless know. We have not yet encountered it explicitly before in our series, outside of the *Vision of Arisleus,* but, as was the case with menstruation in Story Five, it is a motif which lurks behind the scenes of the canonical texts and appears here undisguised for the first time. All human societies without exception define categories of sexual relations or marriage which are forbidden, based upon the kinship proximity, real or alleged, of the participants. These rules dictate both the maximum and the minimum acceptable distance, but the greatest emphasis falls upon defining the latter of these two, the violation of which is defined as incest. This is one of the very few universals in human culture.

If asked, most people in our society will say that the reason for the incest taboo is the need to avoid the appearance of recessive genetic mutations in the next generation. However, given the relatively low birth rate for humans, it is unlikely that any small population of hunter–gatherers, or even swidden horticulturalists, would have had the opportunity to draw cause-and-effect conclusions of this kind. This is especially unlikely for Amazonians, because they are not involved in breeding domestic animals (except for dogs), which have shorter gestation periods and larger litters. The chances of a recessive gene appearing in the succeeding generation from a brother-sister cross is only about 25 percent for each conception anyway; for live births it is actually much less, since most deleterious mutations result in spontaneous abortions *in utero.*

De Abreu recorded that the preferred minimal distance for marriage partners among the Cashinawa is between first *cross cousins* (cousins whose kin links are through parents who are brother and sister, but are married to other people).[13] Kensinger indicates that a man's sexual relations with any closer kinswomen are "strongly prohibited and generally are prevented or terminated by beating or death."[14] The Inuit also prefer cross-cousin marriages, or secondarily between first *parallel cousins,* whose kin links are through parents who are same-sex siblings, but they do not permit brothers and sisters to marry. Brothers and sisters are supposed to relate to one another with "considerable respect, reserve, and distance."[15] In our society, the marriage of first cousins would itself be considered incest, and we do not distinguish between cross cousins and parallel cousins. We legally permit only second cousin marriage, and some religious sects are more restrictive than that. In terms of genetics, first cousin marriage allows for only a one in eight probability of recessive traits emerging, and the difference between cross cousin and parallel cousin marriage is infinitesimally small: for the trait to appear it would have to be on the sex chromosome, for which the chances are only 1 in 23. So it is very unlikely that any biologically adaptive advantage is the basis for these rules.

Nor is it likely that we can call upon the explanation given by Freud for the universality of the incest taboo. He posited a primordial social structure for protohumans similar to that of the Hamadryas baboon, in which a single alpha male controls all sexual access to females and drives off his male offspring when they mature. Freud thought that eventually the younger males ganged up on their sire, killed him and ate him, and then participated in an orgy with his wives and daughters—their mothers and sisters—after which they felt so guilty that they created taboos on incest and on foods which tasted like human flesh, and invented a religion centered on a vengeful father-god.[16] Freud's views of primate society are now considered suspect because they were based upon studies done in zoo environments, not in the wild. The model for protohumans was most likely closer to chimpanzee society, where there are no permanent alpha males and where relatively unrestricted patterns of mating occur which are determined by mutual consent of both partners rather than being controlled by males only.[17]

Lévi–Strauss has argued for an alternative explanation of the incest taboo based upon the importance of *exogamy*, or "out-marriage," to human society, not only in terms of expanding the gene pool, but because the value to all human societies of marriages is that they unite not just couples, but families. The families in question need to know that they can depend upon one another for future cooperation before they are prepared to exchange personnel. Marriage exchange thus allows for the expansion of kin networks, which results in a kind of safety net for every member of society. In a *unilineal* kinship system which reckons descent through one parent (in the Cashinawa case, the mother), cross cousins are necessarily members of opposite moieties, and, therefore, are legitimate marriage partners. We do not have data on this for the Kuniba, who are now extinct. However, most Native American tribal societies are organized into matrilineal descent groups like the Cashinawa. Incest—a marriage within rather than between moieties—simply does not allow these extended kin networks to form, and thus violates one of the most important prerogatives of culture. This argument is made stronger by the existence of marriage prohibitions that also limit the maximal distance for exogamy. Marriage too far beyond the society is also less likely to result in reciprocity, since the in-laws are too distant from one another for reliable future exchanges.[18] Though it has nothing to do with recessive mutations or a primal father complex, it is also forbidden or at least severely restricted in most traditional societies as we saw in the previous chapter.

Certainly, brother–sister marriage would not have been permissible among either the Inuit or the Kuniba, as the myths illustrate. In each case, it is clearly the violation of a taboo, since the brother tries to get away with it by concealing his identity under the cover of darkness. The only known societies in which such close matings were permitted—indeed, obligatory—were the royal lines of ancient Egypt, Hawaii, and Peru, where the ruler had to marry his sister in order to assume the throne. In Egypt, the throne itself was the goddess Isis, and it descended through the female line. The pharaoh while alive was likened to her son, the solar hawk-headed god Horus, and after his death to her brother–husband, the lunar god Osiris.[19] In Peru, the first Inca and his sister–wife were considered Children of the Sun, and were thought to be of a different race than their subjects.[20] In each of these three cases, the ruling couple were considered divinities, directly associated with the Sun and/or the Moon, and not mortals. Their extraordinary marriage form was therefore a symbol of their extraordinary status, for in myth, gods and goddesses often are joined in brother–sister marriages; e.g., Zeus and Hera. Like the Mesopotamian kings participating in the Sacred Marriage, these figures were regarded as having stepped out of the realm of ordinary society into a nonhuman, superior world. They were considered to be living in a kind of Dream-time which was considered outside the domain of dualistic human existence with its requirements for reciprocity. In highly centralized societies like those of the Egyptians, Incas, and Hawaiians, *endogamy* (in-marriage) also keeps property and status within the family, which is why European royalty have favored cousin-marriages for so long. For ordinary people to break this essential taboo would also render them nonhuman in the eyes of society, but in an inferior sense, since it is commonly believed that the incest rules are peculiar to humans and do not affect the behavior of animals. However, Robin Fox presents data for large, slow-breeding mammals that suggests that the opportunity for incestuous encounters is very limited,[21] and Jane Goodall has found that adolescent male chimpanzees will not mate with their mothers.[22]

Incest also violates another prerogative: the need for each person to establish individual identity. Lévi–Strauss and other structuralists have mostly studied the incest taboo from the perspective of the group, portraying marriage exchange as if it were a kind of game played only by the males of the society, with the females moved around like counters. But it is just as important to consider its psychological effect upon the individuals involved. Many accounts of childhood sexual abuse are now emerging as women, in particular, find the courage to recall the traumas of victimization to which they were subjected at an early age. These illustrate the important principle that incest violates the victim's sense of selfhood, preventing or retarding emotional maturity and, all too frequently, resulting in the repetition of the victimization upon the next generation.[23] Unfortunately, Freud thought that all the accounts he was receiving from his female patients about child abuse were merely wish fulfillment, associated with the Electra-complex in which the female child competes with the mother for her father's attention; he thus set back the treatment of familial child abuse by fifty years![24]

Totemism and Food Taboos

It appears to be essential for all human cultures to have a clear-cut system of categorization of all things, both within and outside of the culture. In this way, the individual can know his or her place in the social and natural world, within a complex network of interacting principles.[25] We have seen that systems of zoological classification, such as the one we examined in conjunction with Story Three, and also the one hinted at by the division of the animals at the end of Story Four or the differentiation of Sedna's digits in Story Five, accomplish this for the natural world. Systems of kinship, including the incest taboo, accomplish the same for the social world. What is most interesting about these two systems is that they are often made to be isomorphous to one another. For example, a moiety or clan is often named after a species in the natural world and enjoys a special relationship with the members of that species, which requires its members to be the providers of that species for the other moiety or clans while they themselves may not partake of its flesh. This relationship is expressed as an alleged kinship relationship between the clan and its species. This is referred to by anthropologists as *totemism*, from the Ojibway *ototeman*, "my ancestor," which originally signified a blood covenant—often considered to be at the level of brothers and sisters—between a human group and an animal species.[26]

In this sense only, Freud was correct to associate exogamy rules with food taboos, though he was incorrect in attributing a historical causality to this relationship. It is more a matter of metaphor: sexual passion is likened to a consuming hunger. Lévi-Strauss has shown that in many myths there is a fundamental isomorphism between the alimentary and reproductive functions.[27] Even in our own popular speech, we use words like "dish," "tomato," and "beefcake" to describe attractive persons of the opposite gender, and we have also seen that the Wemale consider their porcelain food dishes to have sexual references. It is doubtless because of this association between eating and sexuality that the brother in the Kuniba version of Story Six is depicted as having a voracious appetite—like the Foolish One, the cannibal Sun of Mandan myth. Lévi-Strauss has further suggested that cannibalism is to hunting as incest is to exogamy and cites some cases in which this analogy is consciously expressed among hunter-gatherers.[28]

In one variant of the Inuit version of Story Six, set "in the old days, when everything began," the sister cuts off her breasts with a knife and throws them at her brother, saying, "As you seem to enjoy me, as you seem to have a taste for my body, eat these!"[29] Perhaps Arctic myth is not so far from the land of the Amazons as we might have thought! In Greek myth, the Amazons (Greek, "without a breast") were warrior women descended from Lysippe, whose son had committed suicide rather than yield to an incestuous desire for her. They bore half-moon-shaped shields and cut off their left breasts, which otherwise would have impeded their skill in archery; they also broke the legs of their male children to incapacitate them for battle. And they were devotees of Artemis—they erected the famous temple of Diana of Ephesus, one of the Seven Wonders of the ancient world, with its many-breasted statue of the goddess.[30]

Gender Inequality Among Hunter-Gatherers: Ignoble Savages

In the case of Story Six, we are not dealing with kings or gods but ostensibly ordinary mortals. The desire of the Inuit and Kuniba brothers to breed too close is an antisocial behavior similar, through inversion, to Actæon's desire to couple with the goddess: it is an act of *hybris*. The brothers' behavior is also an inversion of that of the giant Bran in the *Mabinogion*, who becomes an oracular head as a result of his altruistic desire to protect a sister who has married too far afield to guarantee reciprocity. But, unlike Actæon, who was bloodied and slain at the height of the solar day by the menstruating goddess of the Moon, the Kuniba and Inuit men visit their innocent sisters at night, become the Moon, and then the Kuniba man inflicts menstruation upon all women, transforming them into beings caught within the trammels of temporality as revenge for his sister's having denounced him. Even more startling, they get away with it. It is almost as if the Kuniba myth is suggesting that the brother's act of incest is somehow justified, because he continues to receive help from his brother until he makes a total nuisance of himself, and since after his decapitation no punishment other than a temporary (and unenforced) exile is imposed upon him. It is the innocent sister (and, by extension, all women) who must pay the price. This is what we would call "blaming the victim," and is a very frequent behavior in cases of actual incest. In another Cashinawa version of this story, the male protagonist has again been decapitated by unspecified "enemies." His severed head, after rejecting various transformations which would have been useful to society, addresses the village:

> *"With my blood I will make the rainbow, the path of the enemies; with my eyes I will make the stars, and with my head the moon. And then your wives and daughters will bleed." "But why?" asked the frightened Indian women. And the head replied, "For no reason."*[31]

With this implacable answer, we find ourselves faced with the startling conclusion that the oppression of women, which we associated in Chapter One with the advent of the Iron Age canonical religions of the Near East, is in fact much older in origin, occurring in societies which have had little or no exposure to Western values. This conclusion was anticipated by the stories of the Mehinaku and Wogeo flutes cited in Chapter Two. At least among the Mehinaku the whole issue of gender conflict is accompanied by a great deal of good-natured banter and farce perpetrated by both sides.[32] Among the Cashinawa, the carefully maintained illusion of male dominance is often punctuated by female assertiveness, and intergender hostility is defused through the public use of sexual stereotypes which depersonalize real emotions to group behavior.[33] But we have to wonder whether stories with ambiguous morals like these are simply reflections of these tensions, or whether they actually reinforce them. This is a familiar issue for our society with its rampant graphic depictions of sex and violence in the media!

In general, the degree of gender inequality that exists in hunter–gatherer societies is minimized by the absence of much inequality of status at all, unlike state societies with their steep wealth gradients and permanent inherited positions of political and religious authority. But gender inequality there is, and in many hunter–gatherer societies it is rather extreme. For example, among the Arunta of Central Australia, the culminating initiation, *athnata puriltha,* consists of a subincision of the penis for boys—whereby they discover that they transcend gender, having both male and female parts—and a clitorodectomy followed by a gang rape for girls—whereby they discover their permanently subsidiary status to the adult males. Both operations are physically painful, but their social consequences are exact opposites: in the view of the Arunta they provide the male with a female part and remove from the female a male part.[34]

To further illustrate this idea, another version of the origin of the Moon is told among the Yanamamö, who live in an environment similar to that of the Cashinawa and Kuniba along the upper reaches of the Orinoco River along the Brazil–Venezuela border:

> *The spirit of the moon liked to descend to earth to eat the souls of children in cassava-bread sandwiches. Two brothers decided to shoot him to stop this, and one of them wounded him in the abdomen, which caused him to bleed profusely. When this blood fell to earth, it changed into male humans, who became the ancestors of the modern Yanamamö. Because they have their origin in blood, they are fierce and are continuously making war on each other. Women were not introduced until one of these primordial male's legs became pregnant, producing women and cowardly men.*[35]

Here, as in the Kuniba story, we have a cannibalistic male Moon, who bleeds profusely from the lower part of the body (suggesting menstruation), resulting in the creation of men. Like many of the other Amazonian (and Tlingit) rolling heads, he is inimical to humans—just as Artemis, in her guise as Hecate, the waning Moon, was accused of stealing the souls of children for sacrifice.[36] This nasty habit was also attributed in the Talmud to Lilith, Adam's first wife, whom we have already met as one of the beings who infested the Sumerian *huluppu* tree.[37] The motif of the fighting adolescents is reminiscent of the Tzeltal Maya story in Chapter Two, where Santo Cristo destroys the people because they shed each other's blood when they reach puberty. The curious motif of birth from the leg of the god is also found in Greek myth, where, after his dismemberment by the Titans, Dionysius is placed in a pocket in Zeus' upper left thigh (his "male womb") to gestate.[38] The unisexual nature of this first creation suggests a Dream-time state before the differentiation of the opposites, as we saw in Story Four.

That the Moon here, as in other versions of Stories Five and Six, is depicted as masculine should not be seriously questioned. The genders attributed to the Sun and Moon in myth are very variable. In Mesopotamia, for example, both Utu and Nannar are male, while in Norse myth the Sun is female and the Moon is male. The Hebrew word for Sun, *shemesh,* is the only noun in the language which can be of either gender; the most common words for Moon, *yareach* and *levanah,* are masculine and feminine, respectively. Certain African tribal societies have myths parallel to Story Three, in which a male Dumuzi-like figure (whom they ritually sacrifice) is identified as the Moon—as, indeed, is the slain Egyptian god Osiris.[39]

The Motif of Displacement

There is another peculiar feature of the Kuniba variant of Story Six. In every other myth we have studied, the death of the protagonist is a very personal event, in which the perpetrator is usually the goddess in her Crone aspect, either directly or indirectly through her minions. Story Four includes this motif through the medium of Satene's judgement and departure from the world, resulting in death for humans. But in the Kuniba myth, while the brother is indeed pursued and flees as in Stories Two and Three, his death and dismemberment are attributed to impersonal "enemies." This is an example of another aspect of mythological construction, *displacement.* This is the removal of the cause of a morally questionable event from the sphere of responsibility of the culture.

As stated above, in many tribal societies, including the Cashinawa, the punishment for discovered incest is death. Unfortunately, the Kuniba are extinct so we cannot know for sure whether this was the case for them also. It is likely that at the very least they would have exiled such a person for his antisocial acts, as Oedipus was exiled from Thebes for his unwitting incest with Jocasta. It is possible that the displacement of responsibility for the man's death here is due to the blame being laid at the feet (metaphorically, as with the Little Mermaid!) of the sister. Unlike Story Five, where the mother is pardoned for her infanticide, the sister in Story Six, a victim of covert incest, is further victimized by the "curse" of menstruation. One has to wonder whether Nimuendaju, who was a Jesuit priest, was interjecting Catholic values into the account he was recording. In most Native societies in the New World, menstruation is not considered to be a curse, but simply a formidable power exclusive to women.[40] The Cashinawa, like many tribal societies, certainly consider menstrual blood to be dangerous to hunters.[41]

Story Six, Cheyenne Variation: The Pursuit of the Rolling Head

This leads us back to the Great Plains, where the Cheyenne have a variant of Story Six that combines many of the elements we have been observing:

> *Once in a lonely lodge near a lake there lived a man, his wife, and two children: a girl and a boy. Every day the man went hunting, but before starting he would paint the woman red all over, ostensibly to protect her from harm. Not being a good hunter, he never brought any meat, and when he returned each night he found that the paint that he had put on his wife in the morning had disappeared. One day he asked his daughter where her mother went when he was gone. She replied that the woman went down to the lake for water. The next day, the man painted his wife as usual and then took his bow and arrows and left the lodge. But instead of going off hunting, he went down to the lake shore, dug a hole in the sand, and buried himself, leaving a little place where he could look out. The man had not been hidden long when he saw his wife coming with a bucket. When she was near the water's edge, she slipped off her dress and called to a lake spirit, which crawled out on the land, crept up to the woman, wrapped itself about her, and licked off all the red paint that was on her body. Enraged, the man emerged from his hiding place and rushed down to the pair. With his knife he cut the monster to pieces and cut off his wife's head. The pieces of the monster crept and rolled back into the water and were never seen again. The man cut off the woman's arms at the elbow and her legs at the knees. Saying, "Take your wife!" he threw these pieces and her head into the water. He cooked the rest and, return-*

ing to the lodge, offered the meat as antelope to the children, who both ate, though the boy, just weaned, complained that the meat tasted like his mother. Then the father left the lodge, never intending to return. After he had gone, the children heard a voice outside say, "I love my children, but they don't love me; they have eaten me!" The children looked outside and saw their mother's head rolling toward the lodge. The girl quickly picked up her possessions, while the head had rolled against the door and called to her to open it. The head would strike the door, roll partway up the lodge, and then fall back again. The girl and her brother ran to the door, pushed it open, and stood to the side. The head rolled into the lodge and clear across it to the back. The girl and boy jumped out, the girl closed the door, and both children ran away as fast as they could. The head pursued them, and the girl repeatedly saved her brother, who ran slower than she, by casting her possessions behind her as obstacles for the rolling head. Eventually she tricked it into rolling into a ravine, which closed over it. On reaching their peoples' camp, the siblings were wrongfully accused by their father of having killed their mother and were left staked on the prairie to die. They managed to befriend the Dog and the Bear who rescued them, avenged their wrongs on their father, and cleared their names with the tribe.[42]

In another variant of the story, the girl tells the people to form a council of 44 Peace Chiefs, which is empowered to banish murderers from the tribe to prevent this kind of family violence from recurring. She tells them to honor the Dog, which saved her life, and then ascends into the sky and becomes a star.[43]

Here we have the clear association of the rolling head with the distant bridegroom, in this case a serpent from the Below, which emerges from the pool and cleanses the wife of her red paint. The paint is obviously analogous to menstrual blood, because by keeping his wife in a continual "red" state the husband is incapable of hunting. Recall that the Cheyenne do not permit women to hunt because they fear their menstrual blood would frighten away the game. The only game he can catch is his adulterous wife, and he can only do this by setting a trap, a hunting method permitted to women. The scene of this action, on the shore of the lake, may recall Actæon's hiding place, though in Story Two it was he who was transformed into a hoofed animal and dismembered while here it is the woman. While the rolling head is not the moon in this story, its persistent pursuit of the children recalls the Tlingit tale of the previous chapter. The motif of cannibalism also recalls the Inuit sister's offer of her breasts to her brother, especially since the brother realizes the nature of the meat because it tastes like his mother's breasts.

The Cheyenne paint people red for ritual purposes, most especially corpses prior to scaffold burial. The motif of throwing the mother's limbs into the water saying "This is your wife" recalls a ritual form of divorce practiced by Cheyenne males in their warrior society lodges: a man who is displeased with his wife can participate in the Omaha dance in which he throws a drumstick in the air, representing her, saying "I throw her away; whoever catches her can have her." The other men are expected to scatter away from the falling drumstick lest they be teased by their fellows.[44] The situation prior to the formation of the Council of 44 Peace Chiefs is like the undifferentiated state in Stories Four and Five in which murders can go unavenged or unpunished.

There is yet another inversion of the Cashinawa version of Story Five in this variant, for there the mother tried to keep her roving daughter who wanted no marriage out of the lodge, and then decapitated her, while here the daughter tries to keep her decapitated mother's roving head out of the lodge; the mother had tried to have too many marriages! As in the Inuit version, the sister outruns her brother, and she has to keep throwing objects behind her to keep the rolling head from catching him. We may compare this with a Netsilik Inuit version of the story of the Sun and the Moon, in which the brother and sister *voluntarily* engage in incest after killing their evil mother, who wanted to murder them.[45] Finally, we have the transformation of the wayward mother into three parts: her limbs, which descend into the below with the serpent; her head, which emerges out of the water but ends up rolling into a dry ravine; and her middle part, which is turned into antelope meat, just as Dumuzi was transformed into a gazelle, and as deer nibble the Midgard buds of Yggdrasil in Norse myth. In this case, incest with the mother is metaphorically displaced to unwittingly eating her, but we have already seen the isomorphism of incest and cannibalism.

One cannot help but recall the familiar European folktale of Little Red Riding Hood, who is consumed by a wolf who had already eaten and disguised himself as her grandmother! Like the woman in the Cheyenne story, the girl wears red. In a French folk version which antedates Perrault's tale, she is invited by the wolf to partake of her grandmother's flesh and blood as if they were meat and wine, take off her clothes garment by garment (like Inanna!), and get into bed with him. In this version, the girl escapes by pretending to need to defecate outside. The wolf attaches a rope to her leg, but she reattaches it to a tree and runs away. When he discovers the ruse, he pursues her, but she reaches home safely.[46] In symbolic terms, Red absorbs her grandmother's wisdom, and thereby escapes the dangers of sexuality by descending to a level of anality (in Latin, *anus* also means "grandmother"!) antecedent to it. She therefore disconnects the rope—like the hair-string balls in the Amazonian versions of Stories Five and Six—which tied her to the adult stage. Anality, according to Freud, precedes the sexual stage of child development, and the Muladhara chakra is below the Svaddhishthana chakra in the Kundalini system—just as Hainuwele's fertility is on a presexual level.

Story Six, Iroquois Version: Falling Woman

Many of these themes are rehearsed in the multi-generational Iroquois creation myth. I give here a condensation of the Mohawk version (Figure 22):

> *In the sky kingdom, a brother and sister spirit couple lived together in the same lodge. Each morning, the sister would braid her brother's hair. Eventually, she realized that she was pregnant, but she would not reveal the name of the father. When the child was born, her brother died. This was the first death, and the sky people placed the body on a scaffold in the back of the lodge. The child, a daughter, seemed very attached to the corpse, which did not decay, and eventually she was heard talking to it and addressing it as her father. When it came time for her to marry, her father instructed her to seek a groom far to the east, and instructed her on how to behave herself. Her prospective husband, an old chief, tested her by having her make a mush of corn and told her to remove her clothes. As she stirred the mush, her body was splattered with it. He then called in his two large dogs and ordered them to lick the mush from her, and their tongues were so sharp that when they were done she was bathed in blood. He informed her that had she flinched during this procedure it would have been a sign that she was not ready to marry. After they had been married for a time, the chief fell ill and ordered his people to uproot a tree to provide a place for him to lie down so he might recover. He asked his wife to sit with her legs dangling over the edge of the hollow, and then asked her to look into the hole to see what was there. While*

Figure 22: The descent of Sky Woman. Original acrylic painting based on the Iroquois myth. (Jean–Jacques Rivard; photo by Darrel Hoffman)

she was doing this, he pushed her into the hole and she fell from the sky toward the earth. At that time there was no land, only water, and the birds saw the woman falling and resolved to bear her down on their wings. They summoned the turtle, asked him to float, and placed the woman on his back. They then asked the diving mammals to bring up mud from the bottom of the ocean to place around the turtle's carapace. In this way the earth was formed. The woman later gave birth to a daughter, who grew rapidly into a young woman. Her mother instructed her on whom she should accept as a husband, but when the right man arrived he did not lie with her; he only placed one of his arrows beside her body and departed. Nonetheless, the girl became pregnant with twins. One of these, Flint, was evil, while the other, Maple Sapling, was good. The good twin emerged from his mother in the usual way, but the evil twin burst forth from her armpit, causing her death, which he then blamed on his brother. Their grandmother then cut off her daughter's head and hung it and the body on separate trees. The head became the moon, and the body the sun. When the boys were grown, they were enemies, but the grandmother always believed Flint and exiled Maple Sapling. The latter engaged in numerous heroic exploits, including an adventure in which he released the sun and the moon from their trees and set them into the sky. He eventually overcame his evil brother and turned him into the Adirondack Mountains.[47]

The incest motif is once again associated with the onset of birth and death, the departure from the Dream-time conditions which we have been following since Story Four. As in the Cheyenne story, the body of the mother is reddened, this time through the agency of the dogs (who helped the Cheyenne heroine). This reddening is symbolic of her sexual maturity, for it indicates her readiness for marriage, as does her ability to cook food. As in the Arapaho tale, the woman falls from the sky and birds contrive a safe landing. At the end, she decapitates her daughter and transforms the head into the moon. The battling brothers, as stone and tree, recall the opposition of the Sun and the Moon in the Arapaho myth as well as the antagonists in Joyce's *Finnegans Wake,* Shaun and Shem, who are also stone and tree.[48]

Some of these themes recur in the Japanese tale of Izanagi and Izanami, to which I briefly alluded in connection with Actæon's flight in Story Two:

Izanagi and Izanami, a brother–sister pair, had engendered between them the various levels of the universe, but eventually Izanami gave birth to a fire-spirit which exhausted her, and she died. After dismembering the child with his sword, her brother went to the underworld in search of her;

but he angered her by viewing her rotting corpse, and she pursued him. He escaped by throwing obstacles in her path which she devoured, and finally emerged in the outer world and rolled a large rock in front of the entrance to the underworld. The pair addressed each other from opposite sides of this rock: Izanami declared that she would strangle to death 1,000 of his people; Izanagi replied that in return he would cause 1,500 women to give birth.[49]

An inversion of this ratio is used as the solution to overpopulation in the Mesopotamian *Atra-hasis* story, where after the population has rebounded from Enlil's plagues of disease, famine, and flood, Enki creates one-third of women barren.[50]

The Shadow on the Moon

The motif of the sister's discovery of her lover through the use of a stain or dye (charcoal or *genipa*) is significant, and allows us to link up with several other stories. The color produced by these stains is always very dark, so it reveals the perpetrator, whose attempted concealment using the color of darkness is carried into the daylight side. The application of the stain makes the brother a piebald, a combination of light and dark. It should be remembered that at the start of the Cashinawa version of Story Five the night sky was undifferentiated and uniformly dark. Perhaps this staining is a parallel to the motif in that story of the varying skin colors of infants. As we have seen, cultures may use any number of devices, including ethnic slurs, to account for and thereby reinforce the differences between themselves and members of other cultures. For example, among the Nuer of southern Sudan, the white skins of Europeans are said to be due to an act of incest committed by their ancestor with his mother.[51] One can find similar, but inverted rhetoric in the writings of White Supremacists in this country. While we certainly should not approve of racist ideas like this, at least they do help people to know who they are by recognizing who they are not, which can be a useful tool in establishing identity.

In the terms of Jungian psychology, what has happened in Story Six is that the sister has revealed her brother's Shadow—the undesirable elements of his character that he would prefer to conceal in the darkness.[52] Most people deeply resent having their Shadow revealed, because they are unconscious that they have one. Normally, they project their Shadow onto "enemies," an act of displacement. The most common reaction to this kind of disrobing is precisely the Kuniba brother's: to blame the person who was responsible for the revelation rather than accepting one's dark side and integrating it. As the *I Ching*, a famous Chinese oracular treatise, says:

> When evil is branded, it thinks of weapons, and if we do it the favor of fighting against it blow for blow, we lose in the end because thus we ourselves get entangled in hatred and passion.[53]

However, as Lévi–Strauss notes, this darkening is also a Kuniba ætiology of the Moon's spots.[54] Along the dimension of time, the Moon alternates between light and dark, but this alternation is also characteristic of its appearance in space, particularly at the Full Moon. The origin of moon spots is variously described in New World mythologies, but it is often associated with a dye or stain of some sort. For example, in the Arapaho myth about the wives of the Sun and the Moon, the Sun's lazy frog wife becomes jealous of the Moon's wife, who is an industrious Arapaho woman, so she places a piece of charcoal in her mouth in order to simulate teeth to be able to chew. This ruse is discovered, so she jumps onto the face of the Moon, disfiguring him with spots.[55]

Lévi–Strauss noted that the association of moon-spots with inappropriate marriages spans the Western Hemisphere,[56] while Joseph Campbell has suggested that the association of the Moon with sibling incest has a specifically northern distribution across both hemispheres.[57] However, the distribution is actually much wider than either of these claims. The Kaytej Arunta of central Australia have a variant of the Rainbow Dream-time stories cited in the last chapter:

> *A pair of Rainbow brothers search for wives despite the advice of their father, Rain, that they remain at home. The two women they pursue are in fact members of their moiety and thus their own classificatory sisters. The men stain themselves with red ant-hill paste so as not to frighten them. The older brother woos his sister decorously while she is digging for yams, but such is his brightness that she closes her eyes. The younger brother approaches his prospective bride while she is swimming in a waterhole. She is afraid of him and attempts to flee, but he captures her by spearing her in the leg. To counter their exploits, their mother feigns illness to lure them home. On their return, they die.*[58]

We should recall that the Murngin Rainbow Serpent also lived in a pool and was attracted to the surface by the menstruating Wawilak sister (much as the water spirit in the Cheyenne version of Story Six was attracted by the "reddened" wife), and that his eating of the women and their children was taboo because they were of his moiety—another substitution of improper eating for incestuous sex. The Arunta specifically attribute the origin of red ochre to two menstruating kangaroo-women during the Dream-time.[59] In their quest for wives, the men resemble the brothers, Sun and Moon, who seek distant brides in the Arapaho myth—an inversion of the Arunta brothers' desire for their classificatory sisters. The men deliberately stain themselves with red paste, while the Cheyenne husband stains his wife when he goes hunting. The elder sister shields her eyes, like the Arapaho women when they view the Sun.

The story of the Arunta sisters' differing reaction is also similar to a scene in the great Indian epic *Mahabharata,* in which the sage Vyasa, blackened with soot, visits a pair of sisters because his half-brother, their husband, had died before he could consummate his marriage. The first closes her eyes and conceives Dhrtarashtra, who is blind. The second turns pale at the sight of him, and conceives Pandu, "pale." The sons of Dhrtarashtra and Pandu, the Kurus and the Pandavas, are the warring brothers at the center of the epic.[60]

If we ask what the Sumerians thought about the origin of moon spots, we encounter a curiously isomorphous myth about Enlil, the king of the gods, who approaches the young goddess Ninlil as she bathes in the river. When she rejects him, claiming her vagina is too small, he rapes her. For this deed he is temporarily banished by the council of gods to the underworld. Ninlil follows him there, and gives birth to her child Sîn/Nannar, the Moon God, who, because he was born in darkness of Ereshkigal's realm, lacks the luminosity of his son Utu, the Sun God. To allow Nannar to ascend to the sky, Ninlil consents also to bear children to the gatekeeper of the underworld who remain below as Nannar's substitutes, as Geshtinanna does for Dumuzi.[61]

Enlil's younger brother, Enki, was also known for his propensity to impose himself sexually upon his own kin. He, too, rapes a series of women who are bathing in the river in Dilmun—only they are his daughter, granddaughter, and great-granddaughter, successively. Finally Enki's wife, Ninhursag, is roused to action and removes Enki's seed from the body of her great-granddaughter and causes it to sprout into eight plants, which Enki, ever ravenous, eats—with the result that *he* becomes pregnant, and consequently deathly ill, a fitting retribution for his misdeeds. The mother goddess, perhaps reflecting an older substrate of the religion, agrees to place him in her own vagina so she can give birth to the eight children, each of which is named for a part of Enki's body. Thus we have again the association of differentiation and dismemberment with the incestuously rapacious, ravenous god. The myth ends with a hymn of praise for Enki's generative potency, though he is so thoroughly humbled by the goddess that his subsequent behavior is more circumspect.[62]

Story Six, Naga Variation: Arboreal Amour

Yet another curious variant of the mysterious lover story is found in a folktale from the Naga culture of northern India:

> *A young girl was visited each night by a handsome but mysterious suitor who left before dawn. She failed to recognize him among the village bachelors, so at the advice of her parents, she tied a belt around her lover's waist at night. To her surprise, the next day she found the belt tied around a tree at the bank of the stream below her house. Her suspicions aroused, she placed an indigo shawl around his shoulders on the next night. In the morning she found the shawl hanging from a forked branch of the same tree. Then she recalled that she used to bathe in the stream by the tree, and that the branches used to move up and down, as if blown by the wind, whenever she came there. Her father then resolved to cut the tree down, and gathered all the villagers to help with this task, telling his daughter to remain in the house. The tree proved impossible to fell, but finally a small chip of wood flew off and passed through a hole in the wall of the house and struck the girl in the eye. She died instantly, and the tree fell with a crash.*[63]

While this is a case of wrong marriage in the direction of a bride too far, note the curiously consistent association of the dark indigo color with the identifying mark on the mysterious lover. Like Actæon, he observes her in her bath surreptitiously, but he is able to transform himself from human to tree form, and only falls to the crowd of *galla*-like axemen when the daughter has also been wounded in the upper part of the body, like Iaça.

From these myths we may bridge back to the realm of Greek mythology. The transformation of a mortal into a tree by the riverside may remind us of the tale of the nymph Daphne, daughter of the river god Peneus, who appeals to the Earth Mother to turn her into a laurel tree in order to escape the amorous pursuit of Apollo. The god had previously arranged for the death of his rival Leukippos, who had disguised himself as a woman in order to approach Daphne, by ordering all the women to bathe naked. When they discovered his ruse they tore the unfortunate Leukippos to pieces, as Pentheus and Orpheus were dismembered by the *maenads*. Having been foiled by Daphne's transformation, Apollo subsequently awards the laurel-leaf crown to the winners of footraces.[64] Laurel (Greek *daphne*) was chewed as a mild soporific by Apollo's oracular Pythian priestesses at Delphi, and there it is associated with another Daphne, the first of these priestesses, whose rite was originally associated with the great serpent Python whom Apollo slew. She is said to be the daughter of none other than the gender-changing seer, Tieresias.[65] Max Müller was convinced that this story derived from the Sanskrit myth of Savitri, a sun god who pursued the goddess of the dawn, Dahana, until she expired in his arms, because Sanskrit *dahana* is cognate to both Greek Daphne and English "dawn."[66] This should remind us of the Moon's pursuit of the Sun in the Inuit story or the chase scenes in Stories One, Two, and Three.

Story Six, Greek Variation in the Major Key: Psyche and Eros

The Inuit sister's oil lamp which reveals the identity of her mysterious lover is reminiscent of the Graeco–Roman romantic tale of Psyche and Eros (Figure 23):

> *Psyche was a beautiful princess who was chained to a rock by her father as a sacrifice to alleviate an act of hybris she had committed—she had permitted herself to be compared to Aphrodite in beauty. She had been led to believe that the mysterious lover who visited her by night was a beast. Despite his warnings not to look upon him, her curiosity eventually got the better of her. Gazing at the divine form of Eros in the light of her oil lamp, she accidentally dropped some hot oil on his face, at which point he awoke, cursed her, and departed. She had to undergo severe trials at the hands of his mother Aphrodite before she could be reunited with her lover.*[67]

Most of Psyche's tests relate to problems of discrimination (e.g., separating wheat from chaff) for which she was able to enlist the aid of animal helpers (i.e., instinctual components of the Self), like the Cheyenne children. Eros, of course, is as notorious an archer as Artemis, though his arrows inflame passion rather than cause disease. In this case, he had made the mistake of wounding himself when his mother sent him to punish Psyche. Then again, in Buddhist mythology, the archer-god Kama-Mara, "desire-death" has five arrows (Inflamer, Parcher, Infatuator, Inciter of the Paroxysm of Desire, and Death) which provide a bridge between the two Greek archer-divinities. These arrows can only be resisted by the Buddha, whose subsequent illumination is associated with the Full Moon of Taurus, the celestial Bull.[68]

Psyche, of course, is hardly Eros' sister; like Sedna and the Arapaho, Cheyenne, Iroquois, and Naga women, her husband is as distant from the mortal as possible, irrespective of whether he is in the form of a beast or a god. Her mistake is in a sense isomorphous to Actæon's: she thought her lover to be an animal, inferior to herself, when he was her superior. She is spared Actæon's transformation, humiliation, and death, or even the deferred revenge of a descent into temporality inflicted upon the sister in the Kuniba version of Story Six, for several reasons. First, her conjunction with the god was not casual; they had been married long enough before she discovered his identity for her to realize that she had conceived a child. Second, her *hybris* in seeking to unveil the god is displaced in the myth onto her wicked sisters, who tempt her to inquire into her lover's true nature. They carry her Shadow much as do the step-sisters in the Cinderella story, while Psyche herself is depicted as the incarnation of innocence and innate goodness. But most important, her misappraisal of Eros as the Beast nevertheless was occasion for as much genuine awe on her part as her correct vision of him as Beauty incarnate. Her acceptance of him into her bed was as the Beast, and—just as in Beaumont's well-known fairy-tale[69] or in the stories of Niall and Oisin—this worked to her advantage. One begins to suspect that had Actæon's gaze been devotional rather than leering, his fate would have been far different, more like that of the city rulers who were spared by Inanna for their humility.

The story of Eros and Psyche also works on the level of allegory, as is clearly intended by their names: Psyche, the Soul, is confronted with the dark power of eroticism, which can indeed be either elevating or degrading. Her determination to discover the source of the mystery leads her to the use of the mind (the lamp), which forces the relationship from its dreamy, mystical, romanticized beginnings onto another plane, where any achievement of unity must be worked for. Yet it is by using her mind, as

Figure 23: Psyche discovering Eros. French, 18th century A.D. (Corbis)

well as by obtaining help from the animals, that she passes Aphrodite's tests. Seen in this light (literally and metaphorically), Actæon's problem is that he had never before experienced anything that would inspire the sense of mystery, trusting rather in his own mortal strength—the very essence of machismo. Thus, he never gets to experience growth, only absorption into the beastly, dark side of his own Eros.

Story Six, Greek Variation in the Minor Key: Myrrha and Cinyras

Behind the edifying story of Eros and Psyche, a darker variant lurks in Greek myth, and it is another double inversion of Story Six:

> *Myrrha, a princess of Arabia, conceived an illicit passion for her own father, Cinyras. Abetted by her nurse, she inveigled herself under cover of darkness into her father's bed, not once but several times, until at length Cinyras, curious to know who was his mistress after many meetings, brought in a light and recognized his daughter. Speechless with woe, he seized his sword from the sheath which hung nearby and prepared to kill her. Myrrha fled, escaped death by grace of the shades of the night, and fled into Sabaea (Yemen), where she pled with the gods for a just punishment. They transformed her into a myrrh tree, whose aromatic sap is likened to her weeping.*[70]

This myth, with an incest theme which would warm the cockles of the most patriarchal Freudian's heart, contains another example of displacement, this time of its entire plot onto an alien culture. Before giving all the lurid details, Ovid advises the reader to be thankful that this took place in a country far removed from Rome! This is perhaps one of the reasons that myths are often set in Dream-time: by displacing the misdeeds of mythic figures to a distant place or time, the story-teller avoids the problem of evoking the Shadow archetype in the listeners, thereby resulting in a rejection of the myth's message. But displacement does nothing to solve the problem of Shadow, which can return with a vengeance if it is denied. Within a generation after Ovid's day, three successive Roman emperors engaged in scandalously incestuous relations with their sister, niece, and mother (the same woman in all three cases; Agrippina certainly got around!).[71]

In the urban, industrialized late twentieth century, the myths of all cultures are sometimes regarded as belonging to Dream-time, for which reason a cross-cultural approach seems innocuous enough because it employs the same type of displacement to the cultural "other." But if we begin to take myth seriously, we shall have to recognize that in a real sense there *is* no "other" to which these stories can be displaced. All of them are *our* stories, and the potential for misbehavior which they depict also resides within us. That is perhaps one reason why so many people discredit myth today—they fear to discover its utter relevance to their lives. Myths have always been vehicles for social transformation, at both the personal and the collective level. Denying their power is tantamount to denying the opportunity to be transformed, which will make the inevitable transformation we each will face at death all the more difficult when it comes.

It is also possible that Ovid's displacement of this story into the Arabian desert is a reflection of the Genesis story of Lot's daughters, who, after the destruction of Sodom and Gomorrah, believed themselves to be the last women alive. Lest the human race die out, they got their father drunk and lay with him; each conceived a son who was the ancestor of a desert nation: Moab and Ammon.[72] In the Genesis story of Lot we have many of the same ingredients as in the *Vision of Arisleus:* the homosexuality of the Sodomites, who would have raped the angels who visited Lot to warn him of the city's destruction, the elements of sulphur (brimstone) and salt (Lot's wife), and the incest motif.

Lest the reader think I am expressing a homophobic attitude here, let me emphasize that Jung's concept of *anima* and *animus* posits the existence of a contrasexual component in each of us, and endocrinology confirms this on the physical level. The psyche is *potentially* bisexual, no matter what the actual manifestation of sexual behavior in one's life may be. There is some evidence that there is a genetic factor in sexual preference, as indeed Alcibiades speculated in the *Symposium.* In some cultures people whose *gender* (defined by anthropologists as a culturally constructed pattern of manifested behavior, irrespective of physical equipment) differs from the norm are respected or even regarded as sacred persons, while in others they are ostracized. The rejection of homosexuality in the Old Testament context may reflect a belief that anything which worked against population increase was undesirable. With close to 6 billion people living on Earth, that is certainly no longer an issue!

Myrrha's child, born from the trunk of his mother tree, was none other than Adonis, whom we have seen is a cognate of Dumuzi. In another variant of the story, Cinyras pursues and apprehends his daughter at the point of her transformation into the tree, and splits the trunk in two with his sword, causing the infant Adonis to tumble out.[73] This may remind us of the dismemberment of Iaca by her mother, but also of the splitting of the primordial mother–serpent Tiamat by Marduk. Or, as Jesus tells his disciples in the Gnostic Gospel of St. Thomas, "Cleave the wood, and I am there."[74] After his death, Aphrodite wept for Adonis, and transformed his blood and the nectar of her tears into a sweet-scented flower, the anemone or "wind-flower," whose head is easily blown off in the wind.[75] Once again we have the decapitation motif! May we not also view this as a permutation of Hainuwele's story—from tree to young mortal to flower through the medium of a boar and a goddess, blood and nectar? Myrrh is an incense derived from the gum of southern Arabian trees which is used throughout the Middle East to mask the stench of decay at funerals; thus it is associated with death and the dying god, particularly with Christ, as foretold by the gifts of the Magi.[76] But it is also an aphrodisiac!

The tree-association is also apparent in the myth of Pentheus, which we viewed in our discussions of Story Two. Since we have seen that the kind of voraciousness associated with the *mænads* is often a symbol for rapacious sexuality, might we not view Agave's decapitation of her son, who had climbed a tree to get a better view of the women's forbidden Dionysian rituals, as a kind of mother–son incest? The hunter hiding on the shore of the lake to watch his wife's invocation of the serpent in the Cheyenne story is similar, though his hiding place is like that used by the Cheyenne to catch eagles, not serpents. The woman who becomes the Moon's wife in Plains myth also climbs the sacred tree and later falls to her death.

Of course, the most famous case of incest in Greek mythology is once again from the line of Kadmos: Oedipus and Jocasta. Oedipus, as we have seen, was wounded in the feet at birth and wounded himself in the eyes upon his self-discovery. Lévi–Strauss has commented on the bizarre names and behaviors of the Theban kings (Labdacus = "crooked"; Laius = "left-handed"; Oedipus = "swollen foot") and speculates that the entire line represents an attempt by the Greeks to resolve the paradox of biological inheritance versus a desire to claim autochthonous creation for their royalty.[77] This has already been suggested by Antigone's name, "against generation," and it brings us back to the problem of duality we have been dealing with since Story Four. All of these Theban monarchs have a peculiar relationship to sexuality: the cursed fate of Oedipus was said to be in retribution for Laius' introduction of pedophilia to Greece. We should also note that the introduction of the alphabet to Greece is attributed to Kadmos,[78] which associates him with the druidic tradition described in Chapter Three. At the destruction of Thebes by the Epigoni, Kadmos and his wife were transformed into blue-spotted black serpents and were sent by Zeus to the Isles of the Blessed—to Dilmun.[79] Perhaps they were the coupling serpents seen by the Theban sage, Tieresias? He travels with them into exile until he suddenly dies when he pauses to drink at a spring. It is then that the victorious Epigoni dispatch his daughter Daphne to Delphi as a prize of war.[80] In any event, Kadmos' and Harmonia's spots are the same color as the *genipa* juice used by the Kuniba sister, the soot used by Psyche, by the Inuit sister, by Vyasa, and the shawl used by the Naga girl.

Story Six, Northern European Variation: Allerleirauh

To complete our set of variations on the incest theme, we return to northern Europe, where the strange folktale of Allerleirauh ("All Kinds of Hides") has recently received a thorough analysis by the Jungian psychoanalyst Marion Woodman:

> *A king has promised his wife on her deathbed only to remarry someone as beautiful as she is. But he discovers that the only person who meets this qualification is his own daughter. She is repelled by the idea and sets him seemingly impossible tasks: to retrieve in succession three dresses displaying the Sun, the Moon, and the Stars, and finally a cloak made of the hides of all animals. When he succeeds in all of these, she conceals herself in the latter garment, taking the others with her, and flees the kingdom. For a while she hides herself in the trunk of a tree, but eventually is discovered by another king, who mistakes her for a wild beast and puts her to work in his kitchen. She falls in love with him and, wearing the three dresses at successive royal balls, lures him into dancing with her. He discovers her identity after the third dance because the hem of the dress of stars shows beneath her cloak of hides. He strips this from her to reveal her true identity, leading to a happily-ever-after relationship.*[81]

This story once again links the incest motif to the heavenly bodies, a period of incubation inside a tree, and the motif of transformation into the beast to escape pursuit. The tasks Allerleirauh asks her father to perform are like those Aphrodite posed for Psyche or like the obstacles the Cheyenne girl, the Tlingit boy, and Izanagi throw behind them to deter their pursuers. In an early episode of the Leinster cycle, the young Fionn and Bran also hide from their enemies in a tree-trunk. Woodman has elsewhere argued for the necessity of a "chrysalis" phase of psychological development in which the victim of sexual abuse finds a place, like Allerleirauh's tree, in which to reconstitute her shattered personality.[82] We might think of the escape into the sky of the violated sister in the Inuit variation of Story Six, or the escape of Myrrha into the desert, as a refuge of this kind, and we might recall that the journey to the Above is the route taken by several of the heroines of Story Five to escape from unwanted masculine attention. If the opportunity for this kind of sanctuary is not available, it often results in the victim becoming in turn a victimizer, repeating the cycle of abuse. Alternatively, it saps the victim's will to live. Woodman shows the clear causal relationship between bodily disorders such as *anorexia* and either physical or "psychic" incest.[83] The "sap" of Myrrha's tree becomes the sacrificed Adonis as well as the incense which bears her name.

Allerleirauh's dance in disguise with the prince—so reminiscent of Cinderella's—is an inversion of the usual concealed lover theme, for here it is the woman who takes the initiative and who is revealed by the dark, starry dress beneath her hide cloak. That cloak is reminiscent of the coronation cloak of Enid in Arthurian legend:

> The fur lining that was sewn into it was from strange beasts that have completely blond heads and necks as black as mulberries and backs that are bright red on top, with black bellies and indigo tails.[84]

This rainbow cloak is quite similar to the description of the dog Bran we saw in the last chapter. To tie this more firmly to Story One, the adventure begins with Arthur's reenactment, fairly late in his reign, of the Quest of the White Hart with which it began. Perhaps, like Shalmaneser III, he was seeking renewal from the goddess? The result is that Enid, a poor woman who at the outset of the story is dressed in rags, is awarded the head of the stag and a kiss from the high king, and then is happily married to Geraint as his queen.[85] Matthews and Matthews comment that its many colors are those of Sovreignty (Royal Rule) and "indicate the strong presence of the Goddess of the Land, whose sacred colours these are."[86] They also suggest that composite cloaks of this sort are used by shamans (like Merlin) when they undergo metamorphosis into their animal forms.[87]

However, no such escape is offered the sister (or womankind in general) in the Kuniba version of Story Six, and this is conceived of as necessary for the current dualistic state of the universe, divided by gender, constrained into mortality by time, and cut off from the sky world. In the Old Testament this condition of separation from Primal Unity is the equivalent of the Fall, which is indeed blamed on Eve,[88] resulting in (or from?) a misogynistic attitude pervasive throughout the Eurasian world. We see now that this attitude of blaming the victim is also found among tribal cultures in the Americas, though the arguments are less strident and are indeed absent from some cultures. This forms a bridge to our final story, in which both brother and sister are trapped into a cycle of abusive behavior from which there is no escape in this life.

CHAPTER NINE

MASTER OF FATE

Resuming our easterly course, we cross the Atlantic and come full circle back to northwestern Europe for our final story. It belongs to a génre nearly unique to our century: a myth created by a mythologist. John Ronald Reuel Tolkien was a scholar of Anglo-Saxon, Germanic, and Finnish myth. His commentaries on *Beowulf* are his chief claim to scholarly distinction. Yet he is far better known to the public as the creator of hobbits and of Middle Earth (Figure 24). The latter, of course, is hardly his own invention; it is simply a translation of Norse Midgard, which refers, as so often in myths, to the mediating world of men, between the upper world of the Aesir (the gods) and light-elves and the lower worlds of the dwarves and giants. However, the history, geography, and languages of Tolkien's Middle Earth are in large part his own creation.

Underlying the novelistic forms of *The Lord of the Rings* and *The Hobbit* is a darker work, never published in the author's lifetime, but subsequently published in numerous variants by his son Christopher under the general title of *The Silmarillion.* It was Tolkien's intention for many years to bring these legends of the "Elder Days" into print under this title, but his publisher felt the work was "too biblical" and would not have a sufficient market—quite wrongly, as it happens; Christopher Tolkien has now successfully published fourteen volumes of his father's unfinished works. It is certainly true that *The Silmarillion* is much more mythological and less "modern" in both style and content. Like the myths of northern Europe from which it draws its inspiration, it consists of layer upon layer of accretion, since Tolkien worked on it discontinuously for the better part of sixty years. In addition, its stories are told to other characters in Middle Earth as something that happened thousands of years before their time—a myth

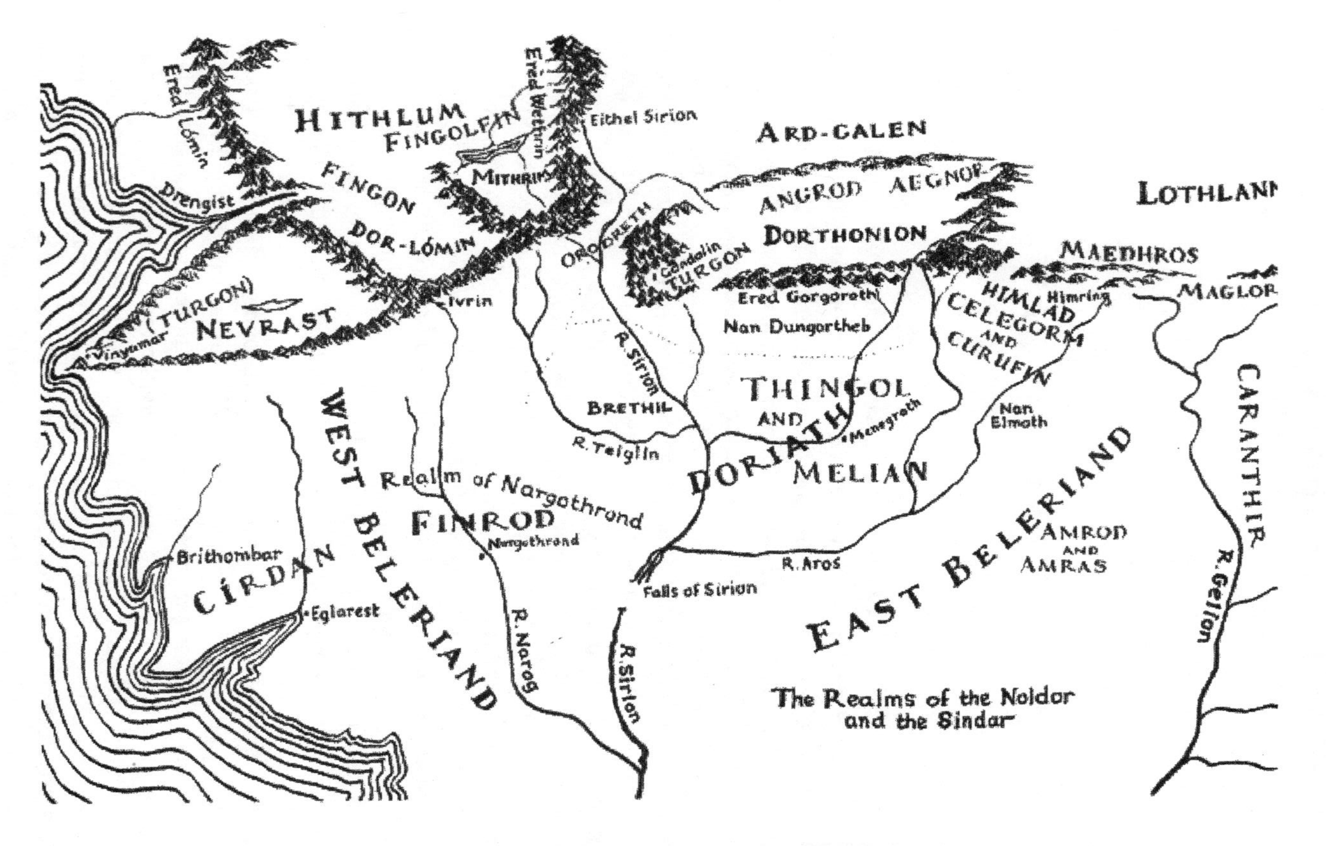

Figure 24: Map of Middle Earth during the First Age. (Christopher Tolkien)

within a myth. It is only now that Tolkien's drafts for these unpublished texts have at last been put forward that it is possible to "pursue the roebuck into the heart of the thicket," as Robert Graves put it,[1] and to observe the philosophy which lay behind the creation of *The Silmarillion.*

Story Seven: Túrin and Nienor

The particular segment I have chosen for our story is drawn from the from the longest of its tales, the *Narn i Hîn Húrin* (The Tale of Húrin's Children), which now exists in at least eight published variants including a long alliterative poem in free verse. Even the shortest of these versions runs for twenty-eight pages and is far too long to quote in full here. Therefore, I have included in my synopsis below only those incidents that most closely concern the theme of this book, largely drawing from the version published in *Unfinished Tales.*

Túrin, son of the great human warrior Húrin, was dispatched from his homeland of Hithlum at the age of seven, after the defeat of the alliance of Elves and Men against the evil lord Morgoth, a battle from which his father had failed to return. He left behind his mother Morwen and his yet to be born sister Nienor ("Mourning"), and was fostered in the Hidden Kingdom of Doriath, ruled by the Elven King Elu Thingol. Thingol accepted him gladly, since his father had done him service, and when he came of age gave him weapons and allowed him to earn his manhood on the marches of Doriath. Not all Thingol's people were so gracious, however. One evening, Túrin returned to Thingol's hall with his hair unkempt and wearing a weather-stained cloak. He was upbraided by Saeros, son of Ithilbor, whose place he had mistakenly taken at the table. Since he did not at first respond to Saeros' taunting, the latter said scornfully for all to hear, "If the men of Hithlum are so wild and fell, of what sort are the women of that land? Do they run like deer clad only in their hair?" At this, Túrin took up a drinking vessel and cast it in Saeros' face, and drew his sword to attack him, but was restrained by Thingol's Company.

The next day, Saeros attempted to ambush Túrin from behind, but Túrin got the better of him, stripped him of his clothing, and said, "There is a long race before you, and clothes will be a hindrance; hair must suffice . . . Run! And unless you go as swift as the deer I shall prick you on from behind." Saeros fled into the wood, crying wildly for help, but Túrin came after him like a hound, and however he ran, or swerved, still the sword was behind him to egg him on, until he came suddenly to a brink where a stream flowed in a deer-leap. There Saeros in his great fear attempted the leap; but he failed of his footing on the far side and fell back with a cry, and was broken on a great stone in the water.

Having unintentionally caused the death of one of King Thingol's chief councilors, Túrin went into self-imposed exile, being unwilling to accept the king's justice. He had many adventures, but all of them led to misfortune, due to his excessive pride and willfulness. Captured by Orcs, he mistakenly slew his best friend Beleg with the latter's own iron sword Gúrthang during a rescue attempt. Beleg's companion, Gwindor, led him to the hidden elvish city of Nargothrond, where he found favor with its king, Orodreth. Gwindor's betrothed, Finduilas, the daughter of the king, fell in love with Túrin; but he spurned her out of friendship to Gwindor. His bad counsel led to the sack of the city by Morgoth's great dragon Glaurung and the capture, torture, and death of Finduilas at the hands of Orcs in the forest of Brethil. Of these events, word came back to Doriath, whither in the meantime Morwen had fled with Nienor. They set out in search of Túrin with a company of Elves, but Nienor became separated from the others in a fog, and chanced to climb a hill where she found herself staring into the eye of the dragon. Glaurung mastered her will and projected onto her a state of total amnesia; she knew nothing, she heard nothing, and she remembered nothing. When she was found by her companions they attempted to return her to Doriath, but they were attacked by Orcs, and suddenly Nienor leaped up and sped away into the forest. The Orcs gave chase, and the Elves after them. But a strange change came upon Nienor and she outran them all, flying like a deer among the trees with her hair streaming in the wind of her speed, and she tore off her clothing, casting away her garments as she fled, until she went naked; and all that day she ran as a beast.

Still in a state of amnesia, she swooned upon Finduilas' burial mound in the forest of Brethil, where Túrin had meanwhile taken up residence under the assumed name of Túrambar (Master of Fate), as the leader of a band of woodmen. There Túrin found her, naked in the woods, and took care of her, and there she found healing, though not memory; and the women of Brethil taught her their culture as if she were a child. Túrin named her Niniel, "Tear-Maiden," and gradually the two fell in love and were married. Within the year she conceived, but at the same time came word that Glaurung had turned his attention toward Brethil, and would soon destroy the houses of the woodmen if not stopped. Thereupon Túrin resolved to slay him, and planned to strike him from below as he crossed the gorge of the river Teiglin, the border of their land. He set out with only two companions, but against his wishes, and without his knowledge, Niniel resolved to follow him. Túrin's plan was successful, and he gave the dragon a mortal wound with his sword, but fell unconscious after looking into the eye of the dragon.

Niniel found him there, by a great chasm in the river known as Cabed-en-Aras, and thinking him dead, wept over him. At this, the dragon stirred for the last time, and spoke to her: "Hail Nienor, daughter of Húrin. We meet again at the end. I give thee joy that thou hast found thy brother at last. And now thou shalt know him: a stabber in the dark, treacherous to his foes, faithless to his friends, and a curse unto his kin, Túrin son of Húrin. But the worst of all his deeds thou shalt feel in thyself." Then Nienor sat as one stunned, but Glaurung died, and with his death the veil of his malice fell from her, and all her memory grew clear before her, nor did she forget any of those things that had befallen her since she entered Brethil. Swiftly she came to the brink of Cabed-en-Aras, and there stood and looked on the loud water, crying "Water, water! Take now Niniel Nienor daughter of Húrin, Mourning, Mourning daughter of Morwen! Take me and bear me down to the Sea!" With that, she cast herself over the brink. Túrin, on awakening and being told of all that had transpired, called upon his sword to slay him, and Gúrthang replied that it would take his life gladly. Thus died Túrin, and the sword broke asunder beneath him.[2]

With Story Seven, we leave behind the ætiologies of Stories Three, Four, and Five and reenter the sphere of the folktale with which we began our journey. Mythological purists might object to the inclusion in this book of a modern story, so clearly the result of literary elaboration, especially since some of its details are drawn from other "real" myths, as we shall see. However, this point of view is unnecessarily biased against myth. In effect, it displaces the activity of myth-making to a prescientific Dream-time and denies the ability of myth to affect us today. What we know about the storytellers of the past suggests that, though their range of knowledge of other cultures' myths may have been much more limited than Tolkien's, they would not hesitate to seize upon a good story if they heard it, and to rework it into the repertoire of their own cultural heritage.

Those who object to Tolkien's creations on the grounds that they contain extracultural elements must also object to Hainuwele's Chinese porcelains and gongs!

The Art of Mythopoeia

Modern fantasy and science fiction are fully as capable of expressing mythological ideas as any génre of the past, and the ability of the modern mythmaker or *sub-creator* to induce belief in a *Secondary World* (Tolkien coined these terms to describe the storyteller's craft and the effect that it should have upon the listener[3]), welding together elements taken from the myths of many cultures, should be seen as an advantage, not a drawback. As the young Richard Wagner wrote in 1845 in a letter to Eduard Hanslick (who would later become his most strident critic):

> The unconsciously produced artwork belongs to epochs remote from ours: the artwork of the epoch of the highest culture can be produced only in consciousness. . . . only the richest human nature can achieve the marvelous union of this strength of the reflective intellect with the fullness of immediate creative power. [4]

And, echoing this sentiment, Tolkien himself wrote in a letter to Milton Waldman in 1951:

> These tales are "new," they are not directly derived from other myths and legends, but they must inevitably contain a large measure of ancient wide-spread motives or elements. After all, I believe that legends and myths are largely made of "truth," and indeed present aspects of it that can only be received in this mode; and long ago certain truths and modes of this kind were discovered and must always reappear. [5]

In a very real sense, the worldwide diffusion of myth through the ethnographic process has made all of the world's myths our common heritage, to be reworked in each generation to meet society's changing demands. George Lucas' *Star Wars* series is a clear example of this process in our own day, and Lucas has publicly acknowledged his debt to such mythologists as Joseph Campbell. One of the advantages of working with

Tolkien's material, now that so many of the underpinnings of the "final" version have been published, is that we can begin to glimpse the creative thought processes that doubtless have characterized the work of storytellers for ages.

Tolkien was quite familiar with classical and Celtic myth, so he was most likely well aware of Stories One and Two, and probably also of at least the Assyrian redaction of Story Three. It is possible that he could have delved into Jensen's ethnographies of the Wemale in his later years; his close friend C.S. Lewis incorporated a scene very similar to Satene's judgement into the last of his *Narnia* books.[6] However, Jensen's work was not published until well after the early versions of the story of Túrin were drafted. Most of the variants of Stories Five and Six would almost certainly have been inaccessible to him. So we can suggest diffusion as only a partial mechanism for explaining some of the similarities between Story Seven and others we have encountered so far. As we shall see, Tolkien very consciously incorporated elements of northern European myth into his work, using something akin to the "intellectual reflection" suggested by Wagner. Certainly, one can also analyze elements of Tolkien's writings as emerging from his personal history. For example, it has sometimes been suggested that his consistent depiction of spiders as monsters (Shelob, Ungoliant, etc.) may have derived from a trauma over a bite from a tarantula during his early childhood.[7] It must be noted that Tolkien himself was not particularly sympathetic to those who held this view.[8]

However, there are moments in his writing when an entirely different, less scholarly sort of methodology breaks through. For example, in a draft letter of 1971 to Carole Batten-Phelps, he relates the following concerning *The Lord of the Rings:*

> Of course the book was written to please myself (at different levels), and as an experiment in the arts of long narrative, and of inducing 'Secondary Belief'. It was written slowly and with great care for detail, & finally emerged as a Frameless Picture: a searchlight, as it were, on a brief episode in History, and on a small part of our Middle-Earth, surrounded by the glimmer of limitless extensions in time and space. Very well: that may explain to some extent why it "feels" like history . . . But it does not fully explain what has actually happened. Looking back on the wholly unexpected things that have followed its publication . . . I feel as if an ever darkening sky over our present world had been suddenly

> pierced, the clouds rolled back, and an almost forgotten sunlight had poured down again. . . .
>
> A few years ago I was visited in Oxford by a man whose name I have forgotten. . . . He had been much struck by the curious way in which many old pictures seemed to him to have been designed to illustrate *The Lord of the Rings* long before its time. He brought one or two reproductions. I think he wanted at first simply to discover whether my imagination had fed on pictures, as it clearly had been by certain kinds of literature and languages. When it became obvious that, unless I was a liar, I had never seen the pictures before and was not well acquainted with pictorial Art, he fell silent. I became aware that he was looking fixedly at me. Suddenly he said, "Of course you don't suppose, do you, that you wrote all that book yourself?." . . I think I said, "No, I don't suppose so any longer." I have never since been able to suppose so. [9]

Even more revealing are the hints given in the pages of Tolkien's recently published "Notion Club Papers," written in 1936–1937 during a hiatus in the composition of *The Lord of the Rings.* Set fifty years in the future, it features a group of academics, thinly disguised members of Tolkien's own literary circle, the Inklings, who debate on the matters of "true" dreaming and time travel. Several of them have had experiences either in dreams or waking trances of a lost world, which is gradually revealed to be the downfallen Númenor of the Second Age of Middle-Earth. Two of his characters begin speaking to one another in unknown languages, which turn out to be Sindarin and Adûnaic, Tolkien's created languages for Elves and Men.[10] The whole scenario resembles what Robert Graves described as "analeptic trance": a method of casting the mind consciously into past cultures to obtain intimate glimpses of them.[11] While I personally do not at all disapprove of this means of mythological prospecting, I would emphasize that after making an intuitive leap of this sort it is necessary to follow it up with sound research. Not all the possible connections are "made of truth" in the sense Tolkien meant—nor can all of them survive scholarly scrutiny!

Whether or not one wishes to acknowledge that this method can be used with accuracy for scholarly research, there is no doubt that it resembles closely the means used by *angakoqs* and other spiritual practitioners to obtain their visions. Robert Moss, an Australian of European descent who has received shamanic training from both Native Australian and Native

North American practitioners, describes how the creative imagination is used by traditional shamanic specialists to enlarge on dream experiences and to retrieve important information for use in healing and other purposes, and gives step-by-step instructions for Westerners to try this practice.[12] And it is clear that Tolkien was aware of this from his own experience. In a candid letter written to W. H. Auden in 1955, Tolkien admitted to having an "Atlantis Complex," and he revealed that a persistent dream of his about the drowning of Númenor/Atlantis had been "bequeathed" by him to a character in *The Lord of the Rings*. Interestingly, he also revealed that, once he had written this dream into his text, his own dreaming about the subject ceased.[13] Perhaps the process of myth creation acts analeptically as a means of exorcising dream images by concretization. We must acknowledge that, whether or not he was fully conscious of it, Tolkien partook of an ancient storymaking tradition, with its roots in what Jung would certainly call the collective unconscious.

Connections to the "Northern Material": The Volsung Twins

If we wish to examine the intellectual roots of Story Seven, with its emphasis on the theme of sibling incest, we shall have to look closer to home than Story Six, to the mythological corpus with which Tolkien was most familiar, and to which he often referred as the "northern material." In the Norse *Volsunga Saga,* Signy conceals herself as a witch to seduce her twin brother Sigmund, in order to conceive a child from him who will avenge her against her brutal husband. Sigmund is unaware of her identity at the time, but later agrees to bring up their son, Sinfjotli. When the child is grown, Signy has him set fire to her house and burns to death in it, along with her children by her husband.[14] Signy's self-immolation is a parallel to the blazing redness of the Sun in the Inuit version of Story Six, or the reddening through menstruation of the sister in the Kuniba version, or the painting of the Cheyenne mother, or the bloodying by dog tongues of the Mohawk woman, or the blushing of Diana from embarrassment in Story Two. Unlike the innocent sisters of Story Six, here it is the female who perpetrates the incest on her unknowing brother, rather than the reverse, and her punishment is self-inflicted.

There is more than a hint of this willfulness remaining in the characterization of her Germanic counterpart, Sieglinde, in Wagner's *Die Walküre:*

his Siegmund (who, like Túrin, has disguised himself under an alias) sings the praises of the *metaphorical* sibling incest of Spring and Love, but it is Sieglinde who recognizes him and maneuvers him into the real thing, symbolized by his release of a magic sword from the tree in which it had been lodged (Figure 25). The pair flee into the forest and are pursued by Sieglinde's husband, there named Hunding (the Dog). Siegmund is slain, his magical sword is broken, and Sieglinde flees into the forest to birth her child, the hero Siegfried.[15]

In Story Seven, the incest is unsuspected by both parties, and their discovery of it leads at once to their self-destruction, as it did for Jocasta in the Oedipus cycle. Nienor/Niniel's downfall takes a form characteristic of the myths we have been following: having been dehumanized by the dragon, she is transformed metaphorically into a deer, and is pursued by *galla*-like Orcs. On achieving self-knowledge, she jumps into the bottomless abyss of Cabed-en-Aras, "The Deer's Leap." These events are prefigured by the fate of Saeros, who, after his all-too-symbolic taunt, is made by Túrin to run like a deer until he, too, falls to his death in a watery abyss. In this part of the tale, as in Story One, the main character takes the role of the dog pursuing the stag; yet, as in Story Four, the stag/boar perishes in the water, while the dog remains on the bank.

Figure 25: Siegmund and Sieglinde. Engraving from the 1876 Bayreuth Production (Corbis)

Unlike Signy/Sieglinde, Nienor carries her unborn child to its death with her; Húrin's line is to have no issue. Like Iaça and Antigone, she denies birth—but by descending into the Great Below like Antigone, rather than ascending to become the Moon, like Iaça. Children of incestuous unions in mythology are frequently heroes and dragon-slayers themselves (e.g., Siegfried Fafnirsbane), or sometimes slayers of the hero (e.g., Mordred in Arthurian romance), underscoring the equivocal nature of such pairings. Tolkien was well aware of this, but evidently he did not wish to involve such moral ambiguity in his story, for reasons we shall explore below.

The Dragon

The role of dragons is distinctly equivocal throughout world mythology. They are depicted at the moral extremes: European and Middle Eastern dragons, like Abzu and Tiamat, or the biblical Leviathan, are depicted as evil, while in the Far East the dragon is the symbol of heaven and the ultimate good. In the New World, we have already met the figure of Quetzalcoatl, the Feathered Serpent, who created man and who brings rain and corn but who also had incestuous relations with his sister, which led to his self-exile. An Aztec creation myth describes how he and Tezcatlipoca, his dark adversary, dismembered the primordial serpent-woman Cihuacoatl as she swam in the primordial waters, placing half her body above as the sky and half below as the earth.[16] This splitting is very similar to Marduk's division of Tiamat, but—as with the Quiche Maya creation story with which we began our exploration of myth—with two protagonists instead of one. Gúcumatz and Quetzalcoatl are probably the same god, for the name of the former also means "plumed serpent" in Quiche Maya.[17] No one seems to be sure whether Tepeu is the equivalent of Tezcatlipoca, however; the name simply means "Lord." We have already seen the equivocal nature of the Rainbow Serpent in Australian myth.

Thus, the dragon is iconographically a profoundly enigmatic figure. As E.D. Van Buren said of its Mesopotamian representations (Figure 26):

> the choice of such antagonistic features and the urge to weld them into a more or less convincing whole must have been occasioned by a need to express pictorially a creature believed to be endowed with diametrically opposed qualities.[18]

Figure 26: Storm god riding on a dragon. Mesopotamian cylinder seal, Akkadian Period. (Yale Babylonian Collection).

Jung describes the alchemical dragon in very similar terms:

> The dragon in itself is a *monstrum*—a symbol combining the chthonic principle of the serpent and the aerial principle of the bird. It is, as Ruland says, a variant of Mercurius. But Mercurius is the divine winged Hermes manifest in matter, the god of revelation, lord of thought and sovreign psychopomp. The liquid metal, *argentum vivum*—"living silver," quicksilver—was the wonderful substance that perfectly expressed the nature of the *stibnon:* that which glistens and animates within. When the alchemist speaks of Mercurius, on the face of it he means quicksilver, but inwardly he means the world-creating spirit concealed or imprisoned in matter. The dragon is probably the oldest pictorial symbol in alchemy of which we have documentary evidence. It appears as the orobouros, the tail-eater, in the Codex Marcianus, which dates from the tenth or eleventh century, together with the legend: *en to pan* (the One, the All). Time and again the alchemists reiterate that the *opus* proceeds from the one and leads back to the one, that it is a sort of circle like a dragon biting its own tail. For this reason the opus was often called *circulare* (circular) or else *rota* (the wheel). Mercurius stands at the beginning and end of the work: he is the *prima materia*, the *caput corvi*, the *nigredo;* as dragon he devours himself and as dragon he dies, to rise again as the *lapis*. He is the play of colors in the *cauda pavonis* and the division into four elements. He is the hermaphrodite that was in the beginning, that splits into the classical brother–sister duality and is reunited in the

> *coniunctio*, to appear once again in the radiant form of the *lumen novum*, the stone.[19]

This description could well be said to characterize myth itself! Note the association with the motif of sibling incest at the end of this passage, reminiscent of the *Vision of Arisleus*. For Jung, such unions within the psyche (but certainly not in his patients' outer lives!) symbolized an important stage in the completion of the individuation process. He also notes that in Medieval alchemy the "work" was normally performed by a male alchemist and his *soror mystica*.[20]

Túrin and Nienor's encounters with the dragon are profoundly equivocal events, unlike most European dragon-slaying quests. This is signaled by the fact that when Túrin goes to battle to save Nargothrond, he wears the helmet of Dor-Lómin, upon whose crest was set in defiance a gilded image of the head of Glaurung.[21] Characters in Medieval myth who bear symbolic tokens into battle are often intimately associated with those symbols; for example, Gottfried von Strassburg's Tristan goes into single combat with the Irish champion Morholt bearing a shield with the heraldic boar of Cornwall, decapitates Morholt, but is wounded in turn in the thigh, like Adonis' wounding by the boar.[22]

Tolkien's dragons are crafty beyond measure, capable of overwhelming the fragile personalities of all whom they encounter. One must speak to dragons carefully, in riddles, concealing one's identity, lest they cast their potent spells on the hearer.[23] Tolkien depicts Glaurung as the first dragon anyone in Middle-Earth had seen, so it is not surprising that neither Túrin nor his sister were aware of these precautions. Though Glaurung is not a winged dragon (those were introduced by Morgoth later), he still manifests some of the traditional ambiguity inherent in this figure. To slay the dragon and partake of its blood, in myth, is to achieve a measure of self-knowledge. Wagner's Siegfried, having done so, immediately understands the speech of the Forest Bird, who gives him excellent advice.[24] Once again, we find the conjunction of the serpentine dragon with the bird, the lower and higher correspondences of the Scorpio symbol. Likewise, Túrin and Nienor's encounters with the dying Glaurung bring them self-knowledge—but it is knowledge which leads to their destruction. Nienor's plunge into Cabed-en-Aras in reaction to the dragon's taunt may remind us of the Athenian royal women who plunged to their deaths from the Acropolis upon seeing the serpent-footed Erecthonius.

The Origins of the Sun and Moon in Middle Earth

The "etymology" (of course all of these languages are Tolkien's secondary creations) of Saeros' name is unclear, but that of his father Ithilbor means "steadfast moon," establishing a lunar connection.[25] However, within this system it is a contradiction in terms, since the Moon is anything but steadfast. The Moon in Middle-Earth is masculine, the Sun feminine, as in Inuit and Norse/Germanic mythology. Much earlier in *The Silmarillion,* there is a peculiarly familiar story about the origins of these heavenly bodies out of the final blossoms of the Silpion and Laurelin, the Two Trees of Valinor, in which the motif of the pursuit of the Sun by the Moon is introduced, though the characters are not in this case siblings:

> *The fruit and flower Yavanna gave to Aulë, and Manwë hallowed them, and Aulë and his folk made vessels to hold them and preserve their radiance . . . These vessels the gods gave to Varda, that they might become lamps of heaven, outshining the ancient stars, and set them to sail appointed courses above the earth. . . . The maiden chosen from among their own folk by the Valar to guide the ship of the Sun was named Ariën; and the youth who steered the floating island of the Moon was Tilion. In the days of the Trees Ariën had tended the golden flowers in the gardens of Vana and watered them with the radiant dew of Laurelin. Tilion was a young hunter of the company of Oromë, and he had a silver bow. He loved Ariën, but she was a holier spirit and of greater power, and wished to be ever virgin and alone; and Tilion pursued her in vain. . . . Now Varda purposed that the two vessels should sail the sky and ever be aloft, but not together: each should journey from Valinor into the East and back, the one issuing from the West as the other turned from the East. . . . But Tilion was wayward and uncertain in speed, and held not to his appointed course; and at times he sought to tarry Ariën, whom he loved, though the flame of Anár withered the sheen of Silpion's bloom, if he drew too nigh, and his vessel was scorched and darkened.*[26]

In later versions, Morgoth himself attacks Tilion's vessel instead, causing moon-spots. To tie this tale even more tightly to the Inuit variation of Story Six, we find that in a late version of the text Morgoth, or Melkor as he was called in the early years of Middle-Earth, himself ravishes Ariën:

> *desiring both to abase her and to take into himself her powers. Then the spirit of Arië went up like a flame of anguish and wrath, and departed ever from Arda. . . . But even as Arië foretold, Melkor was burned and his brightness darkened, and he gave no more light, but light pained him exceedingly and he hated it.*[27]

As we saw in Story Two, there is no eroticism in this attempted rape; only the lust for power and the desire to debase another being.

In the earliest version of the tale of the Sun and the Moon, the solar spirit, there called Urwendi, is not a solitary but, like Diana in her pool, is surrounded by her maidens. The solar vessel Faskalan is so radiant that Manwë, the ruler of the gods, fears that "even the holy bodies of the Valar, meseems, may not for long endure to bathe in this great light." But Urwendi volunteers, along with her maidens:

> *and casting aside their raiment they went down into that pool Faskalan as bathers into the sea, and its golden foams went over their bodies, and the Gods saw them not and were afraid. But after a while they came again to the brazen shores and were not as before, for their bodies were grown lucent and shone as with an ardour within, and light flashed from their limbs as they moved, nor might any raiment endure to cover their glorious bodies any more. Like air were they, and they trod as lightly as does sunlight on the earth.*[28]

Urweni and her maidens then board the solar ship and it is launched into the heavens.

This brings to mind the Aztec story of the origin of the current (fifth) Sun, after the destruction of the previous world by flood (as in the Maya cosmology).

> *The gods created a great fire, but the splendid deity they had offered the opportunity to become the new Sun was afraid to enter lest he be burnt, and an ugly, scabby, unrecognized god, Tonatiuh, volunteered, on the condition that he be given ultimate power. To this, the gods assented, and he plunged into the flames and emerged as the Sun. His cowardly predecessor became the Moon. At first, the two were of equal brilliance, but the gods struck Moon in the face, and his brilliance was dimmed. All the gods then sacrificed themselves in the fire, feeding the Sun with their flesh and blood so it could move through the sky.*

Thus Tonatiuh has acquired a taste for human flesh, and demands massive sacrifices at his temples[29]—the sort of sacrifices which Tolkien depicts as most pleasing to Morgoth.[30] Once again, we see the voracious appetite of the male solar deity.

In the early version of *The Silmarillion,* Morgoth's attack on the Sun-spirit had not yet acquired its later sexual connotations, but its result is that:

> *Urwendi fell into the Sea, and the Ship fell near the ground, scorching regions of the Earth. The clarity of the Sun's radiance has not been so great since, and something of the magic has gone from it. Hence it is, and long has been, that the fairies dance and sing more sweetly and can the better be seen by the light of the Moon—because of the death of Urwendi.*[31]

Thus, her fate is similar to that of Sedna, who, as we have already seen, bears a relationship to the time when the Arctic Sun sinks below the horizon during the winter half of the year.

A Hero with Attitude

In character, Túrin seems to be similar in many ways to Actæon and Fionn (and wayward Tilion). A perennial misfit, a punk hero, he continually blunders into misfortune, both for himself and all those around him. The dragon's description of him is all too accurate. His sojourn in Doriath is described in these terms: "Also it seemed that fortune was unfriendly to him, so that often what he designed went awry, and what he desired he did not gain; neither did he win friendship easily."[32] We might compare this with Siegmund's self-description in *Die Walküre:*

> *Misfortune follows me wherever I flee;*
> *misfortune approaches me wherever I rest. . . .*
> *Whatever I did, wherever I fared,*
> *if I sought friends or wooed women,*
> *I was always despised:*
> *ill fate lay upon me.*
> *Whatever seemed right to me,*
> *others reckoned it ill;*
> *whatever seemed evil to me,*
> *others considered favorably.*

I fell into feuds wherever I was;
wrath met me wherever I went;
though I sought joy,
I only awakened grief.[33]

This condition of *alienation* is a characteristic of the early stage of the Hero archetype's appearance. The young hero is often a nonconformist, for the very good reason that he is one of the tender-minded living in a tough-minded society.[34]

The problem of the Hero, as Campbell has eloquently shown, is to go beyond his alienation to a state of union with that whole from which the tough-minded themselves are alienated; to recognize that it is not he but they who are out of balance; to die the death and to return imbued with eternal life. It is by this means that society is rejuvenated.[35] This process is entirely isomorphous to shamanic initiation, which suggests that the ceremonies which accompany that process are glosses upon a fundamental dissociative and reintegrative psychological catharsis common to all cultures. While Wagner's Siegmund is indeed able to reach for these goals, Túrin never outgrows his "attitude" (any more than Fionn, Actæon, or Iaça do). He is therefore an irresistible target for the disaster which overtakes him; the tragedy is that he draws everyone around him, including his perfectly innocent sister, into the abyss.

The Faithful Sister—of Morgoth!

One element which is clearly missing from Story Seven is the role of the goddess. *The Silmarillion,* like all of Tolkien's works, is an attempt to grapple with the perennial problem of evil, which Jungians refer to as the Shadow. As such, the evolution of its moral framework increasingly required that evil be projected onto the Dark Lord Melkor, "he who arises in might" (the master of Sauron of *The Lord of the Rings*), called by his foes Morgoth, "The Dark Enemy," who in the last analysis is a fallen angel very much like the New Testament's Satan. While Siegmund's bad luck in *Die Walküre* is attributed to the Norns, the fate-weaving Triune Goddesses,[36] Túrin's misfortune is manipulated solely by the malice of Morgoth, who holds his father Húrin captive and wishes to break him to his will.

Morgoth is always depicted as a male deity without a female consort (except in that he feigns to propose such a partnership to Ariën). He does have a temporary feminine partner in crime: the menacing figure of Ungoliant, an archetypal spider who weaves darkness (described as if she were a Black Hole) lurks behind the scenes and appears at a critical moment to suck the life out of the Two Trees of Valinor at his behest. At one point she nearly overcomes him in her lust for the Silmarils, which he has stolen with her aid.[37] However, like Túrin, Morgoth has a sister, and curiously enough her name is *Nienna,* formed from the same root as Nienor and Niniel. Like her sisterly counterparts Geshtin-anna and Antigone:

> *she dwells alone. She is acquainted with grief, and mourns for every wound that Arda has suffered in the marring of Melkor. . . . But she does not weep for herself; and those who hearken to her learn pity, and endurance in hope. Her halls are west of West, upon the borders of the world.*[38]

She waters the soil beneath the Two Trees with her tears, with the foreknowledge of the doom that awaits them. And when Morgoth is first constrained by the Valar at the time when the Elves awaken, it is Nienna who intercedes for pardon on his behalf "because of her kinship."[39]

However, this does not solve the problem of evil, any more than did the gods' struggles by arms against him. Morgoth plants strife among the Elves, and when this becomes known he escapes to the south where he plots to destroy the Trees and steal the Silmarils, the jewels made with their light. He then flees to Middle-Earth where he erects an impregnable fortress from which he rarely again emerges. In the *Silmarillion,* he prefers to work his will through agents like the dragon. "Chance" encounters with him (like Actæon's with Diana) are clearly out of the question, and since he is absolutely evil, there is no possibility of growth from the experiences he inflicts upon others. Túrin can thus commit *hybris* again and again, without learning anything from his mistakes except that there is a superior power who wishes him ill.

Ethical Dualism: Rome's Faith without the Text

What lies behind this transformation of the myth is another form of displacement, one derived from the historical process through which European civilization has passed. The equivocal nature of the goddess' power has been largely eliminated and replaced by *ethical dualism.* The characters in *The Silmarillion* are what they are, morally, from the beginning, and they do not pass as a result of their contact with the divinity to a higher state. Neither do the divinities themselves undergo development; all of them are unchanging, essential expressions of ethical (or, in Melkor's case, unethical) qualities. In this sense, Tolkien's work was clearly cast within the mainstream of the Judæo-Christian tradition, even if the symbols he chose to use derived from an earlier mythological substrate. Tolkien was a devout Catholic all his life. As Nietzsche comments acerbically in his famous critique of Wagner's *Parsifal,* his writing is really an example of "Rome's faith without the text."[40]

Thus, in spite of Tolkien's stated distaste for allegory,[41] Túrin is in reality an allegory for Fallen Man, struggling in vain to achieve Grace and continually tempted away from it by his own pride and Morgoth's malice. His desire to become "Master of Fate" (as reflected in his alias in Brethil) is by its very nature doomed to failure. His parallel cousin Tuor is Redeemed Man, whose continual self-sacrifice and devotion to the powers of good earn him entrance into the most concealed of Elvish realms, the Hidden City of Gondolin, passing successfully through its seven gates.[42] There he weds the king's daughter, Idril Celebrindal, and it is their son, Eärendil, who will provide the salvation of Middle-Earth from the torments of Morgoth.

And yet, in the earliest versions of Túrin's story, Tolkien gave to him and Nienor the distinction of being exempted from imprisonment in the halls where Men go after death (represented throughout his writings as a mystery):

> those twain Túrin and Nienori entered into Fos'Almir, the bath of flame, even as Urwendi and her maidens had done in ages past before the first rising of the Sun, and so were all their sorrows and stains washed away, and they dwelt as shining Valar among the blessed ones; and now the love of that brother and sister is very fair. [43]

In other words, their incest is pardoned, and perhaps even subsequently condoned, after they (like the Inuit sister in Story Six and Signy) have passed through the fire. In a late work on the customs of the Elves, Tolkien provides a possible reason for this: the act of physical union binds together the spirits (*fëar*) as well as the bodies (*hróar*) of a couple for eternity,[44] surely a reflection of the Catholic view of marriage. While the characters under discussion are Elves, not Men, Tolkien suggests that the *fëar* and *hróar* of Men are in many ways similar to those of Elves, being made of the same earthly substance.[45] Certainly, they can intermarry and produce children, though this only occurs in three recorded cases. Thus, having innocently consummated their marriage in Brethil, there was no licit way for Túrin and Nienor to be separated once they were permitted to live in Valinor, in spite of the illicit nature of their union.

Eschatology: the Final Days of Middle Earth

Even more remarkably, Tolkien has an elvish narrator relate a prophecy that in the Final Battle of the World, Morgoth will return from beyond the Walls of Night to the west of Valinor where (like Santo Cristo) the Valar have confined him after hewing off the lower part of his body. After destroying both the Sun and the Moon, he will face the gods in battle on the plain of Valinor, and it is Túrin who will slay Morgoth with his sword.[46] The meteoric iron from which Gúrthang was forged is the only object in the *Silmarillion* tradition which derives from *outside* the world. It thus may reflect the interference of Ilúvatar, the creator, in the processes of history, for Tolkien stated unequivocally in the *Annals of Aman* that neither Vala nor Elf nor Man was capable of slaying Morgoth,[47] and elsewhere that the only ultimate hope for release from Morgoth's evil would come from beyond the world.[48] Certainly Gúrthang is the only material object in all of Tolkien's writing which is provided with a voice!

Furthermore, the image of the Swordsman of the Sky (Menelmakar), the constellation Orion, was created by the star-strewing goddess Varda during the days of Morgoth's first captivity, as "a sign of Túrin Turambar, who should come into the world, and a foreshadowing of the Last Battle that shall be at the end of Days."[49] In Greek myth, Orion, like Túrin, was a hunter of monsters and a scorner of the gods—he seduced Eos, the goddess of the dawn, causing her to blush. Artemis slew him with an arrow as he fled from a monstrous scorpion, thinking he had seduced one of her maidens also. The two were placed in the sky so that the chase might go on—the scorpion is the constellation Scorpio.[50] These motifs should be very familiar by now! In Hebrew the name of the constellation, *Kesil*, means "the fool" or "the madman," an epithet which fits Túrin very well. It refers to the Mesopotamian king Nimrod, also a hunter, who raised the Tower of Babel in defiance of God.[51]

Varda's prophecy would imply that, although Túrin's destiny seems to be manipulated by Morgoth, Tolkien intended there to be a deeper manipulation going on behind the scenes, as Ilúvatar himself hints at the time of the Creation to Morgoth: "And thou, Melkor, wilt discover all the secret thoughts of thy mind, and wilt perceive that they are but a part of the whole and tributary to its glory."[52]

The only other character in *The Silmarillion* who possesses such a sword is Maeglin,[53] an Elf who brings about the downfall of the hidden kingdom of Gondolin because of his incestuous desire for his first cross-cousin Idril Celebrindal.[54] She, like the heroines of Story Five, rejects him because she has chosen a distant mate, Túrin's cousin Tuor. In fact, the two swords were made by the same smith, Eöl, Maeglin's father. After Maeglin betrays the location of Gondolin to Morgoth, Tuor casts him to his death from a precipice—like the death of Saeros. Tuor and Idril's child, Eärendil, is like Túrin a dragon-slayer, and furthermore like Túrin (and unlike any other character in Tolkien's mythology), he and his wife Elwing are permitted to reach Valinor, whence he sails the skies as the Morning Star in a vessel like those of the Sun and Moon, while she abides in a high tower in the West of the world (Nienna's domain, as well as the location of Morgoth's prison, we may recall), and flies to meet him in bird form.[55]

In Table 2, we have the following parallels between the stories of Túrin and Tuor (or Eärendil):

There are some very curious connections to be noted here. The name of Eärendil is one of the very few Tolkien admitted to borrowing directly from Saxon literature: there, as Earendel or Orendel or Horvandillus (obviously also equivalent to Tolkien's Sun-Maiden, Urwendi), he is still the Morning Star, an object of hymns of praise, the equivalent of Christ or John the Baptist.[56] But in the same Saxon sources, Orendel is the father of Shakespeare's Hamlet (Amlodhi), whose madness marks the transition between two celestial eras, as de Santillana and von Dechend have shown.[57] So we may draw a further astral comparison between Túrin, who goes mad at times, and Eärendil.

While Story Seven is not explicitly cosmogonic, in its earliest versions (apparently abandoned later in the author's conception) it does contain an *eschatology,* the opposite of cosmogony—the collapse of the Universe into a non-dualistic state, in which the original light of the Two Trees is rekindled:

> *and the Mountains of Valinor shall be leveled, so that the light goes out all over the world. In that light the Gods will again grow young, and the Elves awake and their dead arise, and the purpose of Ilúvatar be fulfilled concerning them.*[58]

Table 2: Túrin and Tuor compared: Fallen Man and Redeemed Man

	Túrin	Tuor
Father:	Húrin	Huor (Húrin's brother)
Fostering:	Grey-Elves of Doriath	Grey-Elves of Nevrast
Attitude:	Disrespectful	Respectful
Hidden City:	Nargothrond	Gondolin
Distant Mate:	Finduilas	Idril Celebrindal
Her Role:	Rejected by Túrin	Knowingly accepts Tuor
Close Mate:	Nienor (sister)	Maeglin (parallel cousin)
Mate's Role:	Unknowingly accepts Túrin	Rejected by Idril
Mate's Fate:	Jumps off precipice	Is thrown from precipice
Iron Sword:	Gúrthang	Maeglin's sword
Obtained by:	Murder of friend	Theft from father
Dragon Slain:	Glaurung	Ancálagon (by Eärendil)
Victory:	Slays Morgoth	Defeats Morgoth (Eärendil)
Final Fate:	Transfiguration in Fos'Almir into Orion	Sails the heavens with the Silmaril as Venus (Eärendil)
Mate's Fate:	Reunion in Fos'Almir	Transformation into bird; reunion (Elwing)

In the earliest version of the mythology, the "magic sun" will be rekindled at this time, after Urwendi is released from her prison in Ungoliant's lair.[59]

Ultimately, the "purpose" is the greater glory of Ilúvatar, the Creator, not merely in spite of but *because* of the sufferings and misdeeds of Valar, Elves, and Men.[60] In this post-apocalyptic state, it should by now not surprise us that the brother–sister pair, so tormented by the fate apparently set for them by Morgoth, but really planned by Ilúvatar himself, should dwell in perpetual bliss among the Valar as, in the expectations of their cultures, did the pharaohs, the royal Incas, and the Hawaiian kings and queens after their transition from this mortal plane.

CHAPTER TEN

CLOSING THE CIRCLE

MYTH IN THE MODERN WORLD

A Retrospective Summary

In our pursuit of cross-cultural themes in myth, we now have completed our circumnavigation of the globe and returned to our starting point. In this final chapter, it will be my task to reflect upon the meaning of our mythic journey through space and time, and also upon the implications of that meaning for the present world situation.

Along our way, we have encountered many structures used by myths in all cultures to convey their messages. These include *inversion, free substitution, enantiodromion, disjunction, sequential repetition, ætiology, recombination, transformation, isomorphism, irony, metaphor,* and *displacement.* We have seen that the myths of many cultures lay emphasis on symbolic systems of numbers, colors, parts of the body, horizontal and vertical directions, topographic features, times of year, animals, plants, stones, heavenly bodies, social status, and members of the nuclear family. Often they relate several, or even all of these systems together into a larger synthesis which serves as a model of/model for the world, as the culture as a whole perceives it. In the myths I have chosen to explore, there is an impressive catalogue of common specific motifs: the dog, the stag, the chase, transformation, flight, decapitation and dismemberment, death, the goddess, water, the color white, the serpent/eagle, and, above all, *hybris.* Even without examining the content of the myths, it is striking that cultures all over the world use such similar devices to convey it. This suggests that there is something akin to a universal mythic grammar at work, a "deep structure" similar to that posited by Noam Chomsky for elucidating human language. Chomsky expresses the character of generative grammar in terms strikingly isomorphous to Jung's concept of the collective unconscious:

> A person who knows English has mastered a system of rules which make use of properties of deep and surface structure in determining pronominal reference. Again, he cannot discover these rules by introspection. In fact, these rules are still unknown, though some of their properties are clear.[1]

The conclusion that myth also possesses a "deep" structural grammar will certainly not be a surprise to structural linguists, because myths are essentially products of language itself. The fact that myths are couched in this kind of intentional language has two important consequences: first, because it is different from ordinary discourse, it captures our attention; second, because it is truly transcultural, it is capable of doing this even across the barriers of space, time, culture, and language.

Reaching a Decision: Which Mechanism Best Accounts for the Similarities?

We have also struggled to come to terms with the three most prominent explanations for mythic similarity: diffusion, psychic unity, and independent invention. At the outset, I cautioned the reader not to attempt to decide *in advance* among these three explanations, for that kind of limited thinking has often led to errors in understanding myth. But now that we have completed our journey, I think we can begin to form a judgment about this issue. If indeed there is a universal grammar of myth, no matter how rudimentary, that is rooted in every culture's repertoire, it is evident that it does not function (for most people in the storyteller's audience, at least) on a fully conscious level.

This is much the same as saying that a listener does not need to be familiar with the *sonata allegro* form to appreciate a symphony by Beethoven, although if one does know the form one might be able appreciate it on another level. The forms of Western classical music are themselves cultural expressions quite analogous to myth, linking aesthetic perception and logical thinking, as the quote from Wagner in the last chapter shows he was well aware. He used many of the same devices listed above in constructing musical leitmotivs for his music-dramas, which were portrayals of Germanic and Arthurian myths. It was also for this reason that Lévi–Strauss chose to dedicate the first volume of his *Mythologiques* "To Music," and to use musical forms as the headings of its chapters.[2] This linkage between spoken and musical media of expression is also found in many non-Western forms, especially in the classical music of India.

Thus, we may conclude that wherever and whenever diffusion or independent invention have taken place, they have found a receptive audience primarily because the unconscious ability to apprehend myth at an aesthetic or intuitive level has been universally present. This ability may be somewhat culturally constrained, just as the forms and modes of Western music differ from those of southern Asia. But the primary emotional reactions are likely to cover the same range of responses, and this allows for what musicians today refer to as "crossover."

This is not to say that the other two mechanisms have been unimportant to the historical development of myth. Diffusion has both enriched and impoverished the mythological repertoire: enriched, because contact with other cultures has usually allowed more variety to enter into the corpus of any culture's *mythos;* impoverished, in the case of canon-based cultures which have imposed their rigid written variants upon other cultures and squelched their creativity. Even here, as we saw with the Tzeltal myth of Santo Cristo, the mythic imagination is able to reroot itself in ways that are often slyly subversive of the imposing culture's *mythos.* Independent invention has generally acted to enrich myth, by incorporating new elements that are capable of being integrated into the corpus, and moreover providing mythic endorsement for innovations within the existing structure of the society.

However, it is the opinion of this author that psychic unity, or at least some underlying common human identity operating at an unconscious level, is the *sine qua non* of myth. Without it, there would be no easy way of communicating the innovations introduced by diffusion or independent invention. If myth indeed possesses a "deep structure," it is in the culture's collective unconscious that it resides, and it resonates to incoming ideas only insofar as these correspond to the existing archetypal constructs. These constructs differ somewhat in their *emphasis* from culture to culture: for example, ascribed social status (e.g., Royal Rule) is likely to be of very little importance to hunter–gatherer societies, in which what little differentiation in social status is tolerated is acquired through experience and survival to a respectable age. But I would agree with Jung's statement that the collective unconscious:

> has contents and modes of behaviour that are more or less the same everywhere and in all individuals. It is, in other words, identical in all men and thus constitutes a common psychic substrate of a suprapersonal nature which is present in every one of us.[3]

Essentially, this is in agreement with Tolkien's conclusion that "legends and myths are largely made of 'truth,' and indeed present aspects of it that can only be received in this mode."[4]

Myth in Cross-Cultural Context: A Summary of Common Dynamics

If this conclusion is indeed correct, then it follows logically that the myths of any culture are capable of speaking to members of different cultures across space and time and producing a resonance capable of transforming their lives very much in the same way that their own myths can do. While it is certain that they will resonate more strongly when told in their original languages and cultural contexts, and while we certainly do need to retrieve those contexts for a fuller understanding of their meaning, the act of translating myths into a different language and context does not entirely deprive them of this power. That is precisely what storytellers all over the world have been doing for countless millennia, with all the material they can lay hands upon. To illustrate this, ask yourself whether any of the myths you have read in this book have produced in you a *frisson* of recognition, a realization that the story is not after all alien to you. It is my belief (based upon my own personal appreciation of myth) that this is what has kept myth alive, even through the difficulties posed for it over the past three centuries by the advent of skeptical science. By directing our attention to the commonalities of myth, one of the things we are doing is creating a network of connections in our minds which give each retelling a resonance that builds into a kind of self-organizing pattern, a model of and model for our perceptions, if not of the universe, at least of our own lives. This may have an actual physical correlate in the creation (especially in early childhood) of interconnecting synapses among the brain's neurons, which as we saw in Chapter Two may be the physical correlates of Jung's archetypes. Once these channels are constructed, whenever a neuron is fired communication flows back across the synapses as a line of least resistance.[5] I suggest that this may provide a neurological basis for the mythic literacy that I have advocated throughout this book.

It also follows logically that if we can recognize ourselves in these myths, they may have something as important to say to us as they did to their original audiences. For this reason, we next need to explore the common contents of the myths we have studied. This will lead very directly into a consideration of how myth might be instrumental in reshaping our lives and our society today. Perhaps the easiest way to approach this is to observe that another common structure of the myths we have studied is a tripartite process, consisting of *thesis, antithesis,* and *synthesis.* In other words, the characters we have met in the myths are presented with points of crisis which they may either resolve or fail to resolve. We may then proceed to review the nature of the crises they encountered, and to indicate the ways (if any) in which they overcame their difficulties. This will provide us with a pattern from which we may draw some conclusions. Table 3 should be useful in this regard:

Table 3: A Dynamic Summary of the Myths

Character (Thesis)	Crisis (Antithesis)	Solution (Synthesis)
Bran (the dog)	Drowning	None
Fionn MacCumhaill	Premature aging	Bardic spells
Oisin	The hag	Respect → entry into Tir-na-n'og
Niall	The hag	Respect → Royal Rule
Bran (the king)	Wound in foot	Decapitation → oracle
Actæon	Transformation and dismemberment	None
Kallisto	Rape	Apotheosis into Ursa Major
Izanagi	Pursuit by skeletal sister	Obstacle flight → births
Inanna	Denuding → death	Water and bread of life
Dumuzi	Death	Inanna's tears → seasonal substitution
Persephone	Rape by Hades	Demeter's tears → seasonal return
Antigone	Burial alive	None
Gabricus	Absorption into Beya's womb	Rebirth

(*continued*)

Table 3: (*Continued*)

Character (Thesis)	Crisis (Antithesis)	Solution (Synthesis)
Arisleus and Beya	Imprisonment under sea	Harforetus' rescue
Adonis	Goring to death	Blood → flower
Hainuwele	Burial alive → dismemberment	Parts → plants
Indian gods	Loss of Amrta in sea	Amrtamanthana
Iaça	Decapitation	Head → moon
Arapaho Woman	Marriage to Moon	Fall to her death
Stone Boy	Falling from sky	Meadowlark rescue
Etana's eagle	Entrapment in pit	Rescue by Etana
Etana	Lack of son	Flight to heaven
Tieresias (1)	Gender inversion	Blindness/inner sight
Tieresias (2)	Blindness	Inner hearing
Tlingit boy	Insult of and capture by moon	Obstacle flight from rolling head
Sedna	Loss of fingers → drowning	Control of sea beasts
Little Mermaid	Wounding of feet	Transmutation into air and foam
Inuit sister	Incest with brother	Enflaming → sun
Inuit brother	Denunciation by sister	Lesser light → moon
Kuniba brother	Denunciation by sister; decapitation	Transformation into moon
Cheyenne mother	Dismemberment	Rolling head
Cheyenne siblings	Pursuit by rolling head	Revenge on father → council of chiefs
Psyche	Discovery and loss of Eros	Discriminatory tasks → reunion
Myrrha	Incest with father	Transformation into tree
Allerleirauh	Threat of incest with father	Transformation into tree, beast, heavenly bodies → marriage
Túrin and Nienor	Dragon, incest	Bath in Fos'Almir → Valar
Signy/Sieglinde	Abusive husband → incest with brother	Immolation

The Dilemma of the Present: Two Mythic Predictions

If we look around us, we cannot fail to observe that this entire century has been one of almost incessant crisis, with no clear sign of a synthesis that will bring us out of the problem. At times, it may seem that the only possible solution to the global crisis is a global catastrophe, brought on by any of a number of possible human causes: e.g., nuclear weapons, environmental pollution, overpopulation, global warming, depletion of the ozone layer. Symbolically, each of these may be read in mythological terms: the brandishing of destructive phallic symbols; the Waste Land; the results of an excess of sexuality; the Flood; the cannibal Sun. Some look for a *deus ex machina* in the form of extraterrestrial invasion or asteroid collision, but even here the implication is that, just as for the Inuit, the cause of such a catastrophe would be our own failure to live up to the expectations of a wrathful divinity.

When we examine what myths have to say about the ending of the cosmogonic cycle either projected into the future or retrojected into the past, we often find ourselves on disturbingly familiar ground. I offer two examples out of many. The first is from the Hindu doctrine of the Avatars of Vishnu:

> *At the end of our present age, dharma will vanish from the life of the world, to be replaced by chaos. Men will be motivated by only lust and evil. Sovereigns will set the tone for the final decline; they will be mean-minded and of limited power but during their short reigns they will try to profit to the maximum from their power. They will murder their subjects, and their neighbors will follow their example. The apparent wealth of the materialists will be an empty display, for real worth will have departed from everything. There will no longer be anyone in whom goodness prevails: no one speaking truth and standing by his word. Old people, lacking the wisdom of old age, will try to act like the young, and the young will lack the innocence of youth. The social classes will lose their virtues; princes and servants will sprawl together in general vulgarity. The desire to achieve supreme heights will fail; the bonds of sympathy and love will dissolve; narrow egotism will prevail. At this point of degeneration Vishnu will appear on earth, riding a white horse, Kalki, his tenth incarnation. He will ride through the world, his arm aloft and bearing a drawn sword blazing like a comet. He will consume the world by fire, flood it with water, and dissolve it into the nothingness from which it came, into his own sleeping body, until it is ready to be reborn in the next Mahayuga.*[6]

Much of this description of conditions should sound extremely familiar to us as we approach the close of the millennium. As Vico was aware, the breakdown of the social contract is indicative of the entry of a society into the *Recorso* phase, a return to chaotic conditions from which a new order may emerge. My own view of this is that Vico's stages are not necessarily precisely sequential upon one another; they overlap and one can, if one looks in the right places, see signs of a regeneration even in the midst of the *Recorso* in which we are embroiled.

The second example is from the Book of the Hopi:

> *Now in the third world they multiplied in such numbers and advanced so rapidly that they created big cities, countries, a whole civilization. This made it difficult for them to conform to the plan of Creation and sing praises to Taiowa and Sotúknang. More and more of them became wholly occupied with their own earthly plans.*
>
> *Some of them, of course, retained the wisdom granted them upon their Emergence. With this wisdom they understood that the farther they proceeded on the Road of Life and the more they developed, the harder it was. That was why their world was destroyed so often to give them a fresh start. They were especially concerned because so many people were using their reproductive power in wicked ways. There was one woman who was becoming known throughout the world for her wickedness in corrupting so many people. She even boasted that so many men were giving her turquoise necklaces for her favors she could wind them around a ladder that reached to the end of the world's axis. So the people with wisdom sang louder and longer their praises to the Creator from the tops of their hills.*
>
> *The other people hardly heard them. Under the leadership of the Bow Clan they began to use their creative power in another evil and destructive way. Perhaps this was caused by that wicked woman. But some of them made a patúwvota (shield made of hide) and with their creative power made it fly through the air. On this many of the people flew to a big city, attacked it, and returned so fast no one knew where they came from. Soon the people of many cities and countries were making patúvwotas and flying on them to attack one another. So corruption and war came to the Third World as it had to the others.*
>
> *This time Sotúknang came to Spider Woman and said, "There is no use waiting until the thread runs out this time. Something has to be done lest the people with the song in their hearts are corrupted and killed off too. But I will help them. Then you will save them when I destroy this world with water."*[7]

While this story is retrojected into the past, the Hopi have prophecies which include the possibility that the disaster which overtook the Third

World might be repeated in this, the Fourth World. Their elders refer to Western civilization by the name *Koyaanisqatsi*, denoting "crazy life," "life out of balance," "life ripe for destruction." They warn that if we do nothing to correct it, the oceans may join hands above the North American continent, as they did at the end of the Third World. [8]

Wounded King, Wounded Land

Fundamental to the imbalance of such a "crazy" world is the idea of its *woundedness,* which in myth is symbolized by the wounding of the state's primary member, the King. The nature of this wound is very specific; it is a *morbio inferiore,* a sickness of the "lower" part of the body, as Hermann Hesse termed it in *The Journey to the East.*[9] In the Medieval Grail legends, the Grail King Anfortas (from the Old French *inferteiz,* "infertile") was wounded by a spear thrust through his testicles, and this wound caused his entire land to go waste—like the condition which resulted from Inanna's detention in the underworld. Even worse, it was a wound which would not heal, nor could the king die; so the condition of desolation was rendered potentially permanent.[10] The cause of the wounding was the Grail King's lust for *Amor.* In other words, we have returned to the scene at Diana's grotto. But in Story Two Actæon's fault resulted only in his own destruction; here, the wounding is extended to the king's entire domain.

This problem has certainly not escaped the attention of modern writers. In a late essay, Tolkien described Morgoth in terms entirely isomorphous to the Waste Land King:

> When Melkor was confronted by the existence of other inhabitants of Arda, with other wills and intelligences, he was enraged by the mere fact of their existence, and his only notion of dealing with them was by physical force, or the fear of it. His sole ultimate object was their destruction. Elves, and still more Men, he despised because of their "weakness": that is their lack of physical force, or power over "matter"; but he was also afraid of them. He was aware . . . that he could not "annihilate" them: that is, destroy their being; but their physical "life" and incarnate form became increasingly to his mind the only thing that was worth considering. Or he had become so far advanced in Lying that he lied even to

> himself, and pretended that he could destroy them and rid Arda of them altogether. Hence his endeavour always to break wills and being, before destroying their bodies. This was sheer nihilism, and negation its one ultimate object: Morgoth would no doubt, if he had been victorious, have ultimately destroyed even his own "creatures," such as the Orcs, when they had served his sole purpose in using them: the destruction of Elves and Men. Melkor's final impotence and despair lay in this. . . . Melkor could do nothing with Arda, which was not from his own mind and was interwoven with the work and thoughts of others: even left alone he could only have gone raging on till all was leveled again into a formless chaos. And yet even so he would have been defeated, because it would still have "existed," independent of his own mind, and a world in potential.[11]

And in his novel, *The Last Temptation of Christ,* Nikos Kazantzakis has Rabbi Eliezer give Jesus a very similar description of Herod the Great:

> He killed beautiful Mariana, the woman he loved; killed his friends, his generals, his sons. He conquered kingdoms, built towers, palaces, cities, and the holy Temple of Jerusalem, richer even than Solomon's ancient Temple. He inscribed his name deeply on the stones in bronze and gold: he thirsted for immortality. Then suddenly at the height of his glory God's finger touched him on the neck, and all at once he began to rot . . . His belly, feet, and armpits began to swell. Worms emerged from his testicles—they were the first to rot.[12]

Eliezer, as an itinerant healer, tries to heal the wounded king, but to no avail. The Anfortas wound is deeper than physical healing alone can address, and it consumes the whole being in self-hatred which is projected out on others:

> a devil was still enthroned in that filth and he gave orders. He commanded all the rich and powerful of Israel to assemble, and he penned them up in his courtyard. As he was dying he called for his sister Salome. "As soon as I give up the ghost," he said, "kill them all, so that they won't rejoice at my death."[13]

While the scope of Herod's sway was certainly not as great as Morgoth's (which eventually encompassed nearly all of Middle-Earth except for Valinor), the "nihilism" Kazantzakis has him exhibit in this passage, which is really his own blind selfishness, is clearly the same.

At this point, we must address the question of how it is possible, as the myths depict, for one such corrupted individual, even though he rises to the top of a power structure through his uncontrollable ambition, to create an entire Waste Land. Jung's answer to this is clear: the Tyrant or Waste Land King is an *archetype*, present in the collective unconscious of every person.[14] It is the archetype of James' tough-minded, who can only see the periphery of things and cannot or will not peer through to their source. As we saw in Chapter One, it is also at the root of the materialism which has characterized Western civilization for the past 500 years. To this centrifugal impetus the mathematicians of the seventeenth through the nineteenth centuries, the era of European colonial expansion, graciously obliged, creating differential calculus, which as we have seen reduces curves to their linear components. But to accomplish this, as we have seen, one must cut off the lower half of the circle—as the Valar hewed off the lower half of Morgoth, or Iaça's mother cut off and discarded her lower parts—again, creating a *morbio inferiore.* When actualized in a human being, this wounded archetype appeals to and thus is capable of evoking its correspondence in each one of us: it appeals to that in us which is corruptible, separative, selfish, greedy, morally lazy, and indifferent to the fact that the needs of those around us are the same as our needs. The situation is reminiscent of the dreadful curse placed upon the Ring by the dwarf Alberich in Wagner's *Ring of the Niebelungen:*

> *Whoever possesses it*
> *shall be consumed by care,*
> *And whoever has it not*
> *shall be gnawed by envy!*
> *Everyone shall lust*
> *after its worth,*
> *But no one shall delight*
> *In its use!*
> *Without profit shall its lord guard it;*
> *But it will attract his murderer to him!*
> *Destined to die,*

let fear fetter the coward:
So long as he lives,
Let him die wasting away,
The Lord of the Ring
as the slave of the Ring . . .[15]

The Ring was stolen by Alberich after he dove into the Rhine, where it was being guarded by three female spirits, the Rhinemaidens. To obtain it he had to do what Fionn very nearly had forced upon him—to renounce Love. Possession of the Ring is supposed to give its wearer rule over all the earth, but in this case the price is far too high, and it succeeds in corrupting everyone who touches it until it is returned to its proper owners under the water in the context of a cosmic catastrophe.

The Waste Land King is ego-consciousness personified, and he has cut himself off—or so he thinks—from his untamed, unconscious roots. Thereby he is self-wounded in the "lower" part of his psyche, and this reflects itself in the corruption of the "lower" physical organs too (those most subject to the natural instincts), either in their misuse or their inability to function, or, even, as in the case of Herod, their material substance. It is Nature herself whom he violates, because in his state of alienation anything "natural" is dangerous; he cannot control it, and therefore it can potentially arise to unseat him. He externalizes this fear, not only in terms of a wanton disregard for ecology, but also by suppressing or attempting to destroy all factors that carry any taint of the unconscious with them. Thus we have in the male-dominated, white, wealth- and youth-obsessed, religious and politically conservative elites of our society the desire for the suppression of women (for the feminine is universally a symbol of the natural and of the unconscious), "people of color" (for their color difference reminds the elite of the darkness of the unconscious), the poor (for their persistence in spite of material deprivation reminds us that "man does not live by bread alone"[16]), the old (for, being closer to death they remind the tyrant of his own mortality), and the political "left" (since the lefthand path, the side of the Heart, is that which leads downwards into the unconscious).

The results are certainly not difficult to notice wherever we care to look: the politically motivated rape of Muslim women by Serbs so as to make them unsuitable Muslim wives, precluding a next generation of Muslims in Bosnia; the recently abolished apartheid system in South

Africa and its like; the dehumanizing conditions in "rest homes" in this country and elsewhere; the denial of basic human rights to Native peoples throughout the world; and the virulent anti-Communism which has led to the largest buildup of armaments in history: 70,000 phallic symbols pointed by the superpowers at one another. Even though with the collapse of the Soviet Union their and our missiles have been "detargeted," it would take less than an hour, in a time of crisis, to point them back at the urban centers of Russia and the United States. Carol Cohn has studied the "psychostrategic" language of nuclear defense experts and found it to be full of phallic imagery: "penetration aids," "more bang for the buck," "vertical injector launchers," etc.[17] The awesome power of the atom moved even J. Robert Oppenheimer, father of the atomic bomb, to a mythic allusion to the *Bhagavad Gita* when he witnessed the first nuclear blast at Los Alamos: "I am come as Death, shatterer of the worlds."[18]

All of this concentration of power in the industrialized world has had its deleterious effects upon the myth-based peoples of the world, who are faced with the prospects of subjugation and adaptation, or of using the same kinds of weaponry and regimented organization as their oppressors in a struggle to achieve some degree of autonomy. The Tzeltal Maya, for example, have continued to fight for independence from their Spanish and Mexican overlords. In the early part of this century their great revolutionary leader, Emiliano Zápata, came close to securing them land rights and social justice from the Mexican government, but the United States intervened and helped to establish the political party which still rules the country to this day; Zápata himself was tricked into an ambush and assassinated. But in the early months of 1994, seeing a moment of opportunity due to the weaknesses of the central government in Mexico City, the Tzeltal (calling themselves Zápatistas) rose once again in armed rebellion against it, occupying several towns and demanding, among other things, an end to forced missionization. As of this writing negotiations with the corrupt Mexican government are at a standstill, while massacres of noncombatants by both sides continue. Maybe it's time for all the saints to get together again and tie Santo Cristo tighter? But of course that would once again just be a displacement of the problem. We have to face our civilization's collective Shadow squarely, naming it for what it is, both in the developed and underdeveloped world, and that is no easy task. As Joseph Campbell said of the Tyrant figure in *The Hero with a Thousand Faces:*

> He is the hoarder of the general benefit. He is the monster avid for the greedy rights of "my and mine." The havoc wrought by him is described in mythology and fairy tale as being universal throughout his domain. This may be no more than his household, his own tortured psyche, or the lives that he blights with the touch of his friendship or assistance; or it may amount to the extent of his civilization. The inflated ego of the tyrant is a curse to himself and his world—no matter how his affairs may seem to prosper. Self-terrorized, fear-haunted, alert at every hand to meet and battle back the anticipated aggressions of his environment, which are primarily the reflections of the uncontrollable impulses to acquisition within himself, the giant of self-achieved independence is the world's messenger of disaster, even though, in his mind, he may entertain himself with humane intentions. Wherever he sets his hand there is a cry (if not from the housetops, then—more miserably—within every heart): a cry for the redeeming hero, the carrier of the shining blade, whose blow, whose touch, whose existence, will liberate the land.[19]

A Relevant Example: *Hybris* and the American Presidency

One theme present from the beginning is the idea that individuals cause personal and social disjunction when ego-inflation causes them to seek more than that to which the norms of society entitle them. The universal platitude that overweening pride leads individuals to their inevitable downfall is so often repeated that it is rarely heeded. Yet many myths also speak of the consequences which occur when *hybris* is permitted to continue unchecked—when *hybris* becomes the normative pattern for an entire society rather than a deviant behavior pattern on the part of an individual.

The idea that those in positions of authority are more responsible than ordinary citizens in this regard is one which we find especially emphasized in the myths of *state societies*—societies in which authority is permanently vested in a class of leaders, since the population is too large to govern through the medium of extended kin networks. The danger with ceding power to such authority figures—thereby, psychologically, investing them with the projections of our hopes and fears—is that they may become so inflated with the projection that they are unable to distinguish between their own moral compass and the exalted role which they are privileged to occupy. As Henry Adams wrote in 1928 of the American presidency:

> Power is poison. Its effect on Presidents had been always tragic, chiefly as an almost insane excitement at first, and a worse reaction afterwards; but also because no mind is so well balanced as to bear the strain of seizing unlimited force without habit or knowledge of it; and finding it disputed with him by hungry packs of wolves and hounds whose lives depend on snatching the carrion.[20]

This description, with its mythological overtones of Story Two, has certainly not lost its applicability over the past seventy years. I think of Woodward and Bernstein's descriptions of Richard Nixon's mental degeneration in *The Final Days:* his "darker instincts, his paranoia, the capacity for hatred, the need for revenge, the will to crush anyone he perceived as an enemy."[21] The theme of the tyrant's physical woundedness is not restricted to myth, either; Woodward and Bernstein also recount Richard Nixon's impotence during his final year in office.[22]

As I write this, another American president, having come into the office with what seemed to be the best of intentions, is being pursued like Actæon by the hungry hound packs, because in his youth he was contaminated, through his feminine side, by something known as *Whitewater.* Having a weakness on this side, he has, like Fionn, not been able to summon the moral courage to refrain from jumping into the pool again, nor, like Dumuzi, to put on the requisite sackcloth and ashes, something for which the goddess is unlikely to be forgiving—much of his electoral support comes from American women. A man of large appetites, his hidden "inappropriate" relationship with a woman young enough to be his daughter was only brought to light because the woman produced a stain which, metaphorically, has resulted in a corresponding stain on his character. Nor is there any college of druids (other than the ever-present spin-doctors) in his vicinity who are able to restore his integrity. The concentration of the American media upon the sordid details of the president's peccadillos is a *morbio inferiore* with a vengeance.

In psychological terms, it seems to me that, having deliberately evoked the archetype of the Hero (the man from Hope) without having developed and maintained a sufficiently disciplined personality container to receive it, Mr. Clinton is now experiencing the inevitable consequences of bearing both the positive and negative projections of an entire people—or even of an entire planet. This becomes ever more difficult to bear as his opponents, smelling blood, circle in. Of course, the same charges of *hybris* and hypocrisy may be leveled at the "hounds" as well! The ambiguity of this double-edged *hybris* may remind us of Hainuwele and her treatment by the ancestors of the Wemale. Nietzsche minced no words when he described this state in *Also Sprach Zarathustra:*

> Alas, I knew noble men who lost their highest hope. Then they slandered all high hopes. Then they lived impudently in brief pleasures and barely cast their goals beyond the day. Spirit too is lust, so they said. Then the wings of their spirit broke: and now their spirit crawls about and soils what it gnaws. Once they thought of becoming heroes: now they are voluptuaries. The hero is for them an offense and a fright.[23]

It is certainly not difficult to read the unfolding history of the Clinton White House in mythological terms, nor to predict the range of possible outcomes. And I think it is no accident that this has all caught up to him during his second term of office—for the phrase we use to refer to a politician who is no longer electable is *lame duck!*

Some readers may think that I have set up the entire argument of the book in order to reach the conclusions I have presented above. I would respond that I am only an observer and reteller of events, and that the original drafts of the book contained no references to Mr. Clinton at all but only emphasized the irrational behavior of Nixon's final days. Rationalists, on the other hand, may object that all this is only coincidence ("the moon is like the moon") but, after all, what is history itself other than the working out of human behavior in the field of time? And it is in the description of what is invariant in human behavior that myths have always excelled—as Clifford Geertz' *models for,* in addition to being *models of.* As C. S. Lewis once wrote:

> All that is made seems planless to the darkened mind, because there are more plans than it looked for. . . . There seems to be no plan because it is all plan: there seems to be no centre because it is all centre.[24]

The Promise of the Future: What the Myths Have to Tell Us

By suppressing all the "uncontrollable" factors in his environment, the Waste Land King only succeeds in accomplishing his own overthrow. When the Darkness is most complete, it evokes, by *enantiodromion,* its opposite, the Light. So we must next ask the question, what do the myths tell us about what must be done to reverse the conditions of the Waste Land? How can we once again close the circle?

If we return to Table 3, it will be evident that, just as the crises are largely precipitated as the result of an attitude of exaggerated self-importance, the solutions, such as there are, are brought about in most cases by a reversal of attitudes, a reorientation toward a harmonious interaction with either the natural, supernatural, or larger social worlds. The result of this reorientation, if it occurs within the individual, is something which in turn has the ability to transform those worlds and to provide a new balance which had either been lost or at least was not realized before.

In the view of myth, this kind of reorientation and rebalancing is constantly necessary. As Heinrich Zimmer has suggested:

> The creation of the world is not an accomplished work, completed within a certain span of time . . . but a process continuing throughout the course of history, refashioning the universe without cease, and pressing it on, every moment afresh. Like the human body, the cosmos is in part built up anew, every night, every day; by a process of unending regeneration it remains alive. But the manner of its growth is by abrupt occurrences, crises, surprising events and even mortifying accidents. Everything is forever going wrong; and yet, that is precisely the circumstance by which the miraculous development comes to pass.[25]

This passage sounds almost presciently like the precepts of modern Complexity Theory which would be developed over thirty years after Zimmer's death, in which existence is perpetually balanced on the knife-edge between stagnation and chaos, and must continually readjust to keep pace with changing circumstances.[26] Or, in the words of Joseph Campbell:

> Schism in the soul, schism in the body social, will not be resolved by any scheme of return to the good old days (archaism) or by pro-

> grams guaranteed to render an ideal projected future (futurism), or even by the most realistic, hard-headed work to weld together again the deteriorating elements. Only birth can conquer death—the birth, not of the old thing again, but of something new. Within the soul, within the body social, there must be—if we are to experience long survival—a continuous "recurrence of birth" (*palingenesia*) to nullify the unremitting occurrences of death. For it is by means of our own victories, if we are not regenerated, that the work of Nemesis is wrought: doom breaks from the shell of our very virtue. Peace is then a snare; war is a snare; change is a snare; permanence is a snare. When our day is come for the victory of death, death closes in; there is nothing we can do, except be crucified—and resurrected; dismembered totally, and then reborn.[27]

How is this kind of continuous regeneration possible? Again, we may turn to Jung's idea of the archetypes of the collective unconscious. For if it is true that all of us bear within our psyches the potential for the emergence of the Tyrant archetype, surely we also bear the potential for all the other archetypes as well. These certainly include transformative forces that can radically reorient the personality to a new relationship with both outer and inner reality, with both of Ursula LeGuin's worlds, factuality and truth. This is precisely what Campbell means when he describes the fourth, psychological function of myth:

> To foster the centering and unfolding of the individual in integrity, in accord with d) himself (the microcosm), c) his culture (the mesocosm), b) the universe (the macrocosm), and a) that awesome ultimate mystery which is both beyond and within himself and all things.[28]

Myths about the transformation of the Waste Land, either those which focus on the individual or the larger world, serve as examples which can evoke the more positive archetypal forces within us, and encourage us to act in such a way as to stimulate the emergence of the new balance in others. Just as the Waste Land begins with one individual possessed and corrupted by the Tyrant archetype, so its transformation begins with individuals who have allowed themselves to undergo the frightening, painful, but ultimately healing transformation that integrates them as living personalities with the universal pattern.

The cross-cultural study of myth, then, has the potential to evoke deep-seated common human feelings or archetypes within the consciousness of the hearer or reader. These archetypes, when they rise to the surface of waking consciousness, have the potential for transforming both the life of the individual and that of those in his or her surroundings—for good or for ill, depending on which archetype is evoked.

Jung was quite concerned about the potential negative effects of this reemergence of myth upon Western society:

> I am convinced that the growing impoverishment of symbols has a meaning. It is a development that has an inner consistency. Everything that we have not thought about, and that has therefore been deprived of a meaningful connection with our developing consciousness, has got lost. If we now try to cover our nakedness with the gorgeous trappings of the East, as the theosophists do, we would be playing our own history false. A man does not sink down to beggary only to pose afterwards as an Indian potentate. It seems to me that it would be far better stoutly to avow our spiritual poverty, our symbol-lessness, instead of feigning a legacy to which we are not the legitimate heirs at all. We are, surely, the rightful heirs of Christian symbolism, but somehow we have squandered this heritage. We have let the house our fathers built fall into decay, and now we try to break into Oriental palaces that our fathers never knew. Anyone who has lost the historical symbols and cannot be identified with the substitutes is certainly in a very difficult position today: before him there yawns the void, and he turns away from it in horror. What is worse, the vacuum gets filled with absurd political and social ideas, which one and all are distinguished by their spiritual bleakness . . . It is dangerous to avow spiritual poverty, for the poor man has desires, and whoever has desires calls down some fatality upon himself. . . . Just as in Christianity the vow of worldly poverty turned the mind away from the riches of this earth, so spiritual poverty seeks to renounce the false riches of the spirit in order to withdraw not only from the sorry remnants—which today call themselves the Protestant Church—of a great past, but also from all the allurements of the odorous East; in order, finally, to dwell with itself alone, where, in the cold light of consciousness, the blank barrenness of the world reaches to the very stars.[29]

Jung, however, was writing (in 1954) from a viewpoint strongly conditioned by the old European values of nationalism which have survived on the continent even to the last decade of this century and which produced (among others) the egregious German and Russian experiments in national socialism—in the case of the Nazis, experiments which deliberately evoked mythic images to sway the populace to their cause. He did not live to see the great changes of the last third of the century, in which the new fields of space technology and telecommunications have transformed the world into a single, global community, whether we like it or not. Cultural barriers are becoming more and more blurred, despite the recent resurgence of tribalism in the Third and former Second (and even First, with Native movements active in North America and Australia) Worlds. If we in the West are busily breaking into Oriental palaces, it is partly because the guard on those palaces has been slackened by the Orientals themselves in their desire to ransack the West for its material riches and scientific advances. As I write this, the newly inaugurated Hindu Nationalist government of India has shown its muscle by detonating five nuclear weapons at an underground site, and its Islamic antagonists in Pakistan have responded with several tests of their own—clear evidence that the East has done its share of breaking and entering! And furthermore chillingly reminiscent of the mythic prophecies in both cultures about Kalki and the Imam Mahdi.

Moreover, in America, cultural conglomeration has long been our outstanding sociological feature, with increasing demands by minorities old and new for recognition and equality. Except perhaps for some members of old New England Puritan families, the sort of spiritual poverty to which Jung alludes has never quite applied to Americans. While Europe could perhaps be said to have squandered its spiritual riches, American society has been in a state of spiritual poverty from the colonial period onward, once the founding fathers decided at the outset to reject the considerable spiritual riches the Native peoples had to offer. We are poor in that we never have been wealthy; empty because we have never been filled; and *all* our spiritual movements have been transplants, even those (like Mormonism and Shakerism) which had their origins in American soil. We have consequently never been eager to follow Jung's cautionary advice, and the result in the latter third of this century has been a steady and heady stream of influence from Eastern and tribal wisdom teachings from around the world which is rapidly permeating every level of our culture.

It is apparent that we live today in the midst of a great cross-cultural interchange, in which the myths of all cultures are being grafted onto what we are coming to recognize as our common human heritage. Global communication has made this result inescapable, for we are now able to view images on our television and computer screens from every culture in the world, including those which are long since extinct and can only be reconstructed through archæological research. As we discover our common human heritage, we find that the tales which have been told in different times and in different places are nevertheless about *us*—about the commonalities of the human condition which remain true even when the scenery is changed.

There is, moreover, another aspect of myth which has been too little explored, and that is the cultural context of its transmission, its *Sitz im Leben* as a cultural expression. Today most people obtain their knowledge of myths through reading or passively viewing enactments of them, either as isolated individuals or small knots of people at the cinema or before the television screen. But myth has always been an oral tradition, and its most frequent mode of transmission was by a storyteller to a group of people, sitting in a circle so that all of them can interact dynamically with the narrator, as well as with one another. As Diane Bell has described it among the Walbiri women of Central Australia:

> Storytelling is a group activity: the presence and assistance of an audience ensures that there will always be a number of persons to bear witness to the content of the story and to quell any accusations that the storyteller may have erred or touched on matters which were improper.[30]

Somehow, we need to recapture the ability to tell each other meaningful stories, so that, like Tepeu and Gúcumatz of the Maya creation myth, we can construct together a satisfying model of a world in which we can live productive lives.

If the central problem of our age is the separative ego-consciousness, traditional myth-telling is, by its very form, as well as by its content, a remedy, since it fosters the development of a group consciousness among its hearers. And it retains its potential for this, even though opportunities are more limited—within the rectilinear walls of a classroom or lecture hall, for example.

I would suggest that the fostering of this kind of group consciousness is a vital necessity to the long-term survival of humanity, and for this purpose I consider it appropriate to reintroduce myth in its traditional mode as told tale. It is for this reason that I have written this book. It is my hope that it will play a small part in restoring myth to its rightful place within our culture, for I see myth as a most effective means by which we can all work together to transfigure human consciousness, and, therewith, our world. The deep structure of myth, if we can look beyond the babble of cultural and individual differences which divide the world's peoples, speaks to us in a remarkably unified language. No matter where we look, the Seven Story Tower of myth still stands and invites us to enter it and discover what it has to reveal, particularly about the human condition at all places and times.

BIBLIOGRAPHY

Adams, Henry, *The Education of Henry Adams.* New York: The Book League of America, 1928.

Aldington, Richard and Stanley Weintraub, eds., *The Portable Oscar Wilde.* New York: Viking Penguin, 1981.

Allanby, Michael and James Lovelock, *The Great Extinction.* Garden City, NY: Doubleday Books, 1983.

Andersen, Hans Christian, *The Little Mermaid,* trans. Eva LaGalliene. New York: Harper and Row, 1971.

Apuleius, Lucius, *The Golden Ass,* trans. W. Adlington. London: William Heinemann Ltd., 1915.

Ashe, Geoffrey, *The Dawn behind the Dawn: A Search for the Earthly Paradise.* New York: Henry Holt and Co., 1992.

Axtell, James, *The European and the Indian.* Oxford, England: Oxford University Press, 1981.

Bachofen, Johann Jakob, *Myth, Religion, and Mother Right. Bollingen Series* 84, trans. Ralph Mauhern. Princeton, NJ: Princeton University Press, 1967.

Bailey, Alice, *Discipleship in the New Age* vol. 2. New York: Lucis Publishing Co., 1955.

———, *Esoteric Psychology,* vol. 2. New York: Lucis Publishing Co., 1970.

———, *Telepathy and the Etheric Vehicle.* New York: Lucis Publishing Co., 1950.

Balikci, Asen, *The Netsilik Eskimo.* Prospect Heights, IL: Waveland Press, 1970.

Banton, Michael, ed., *Anthropological Approaches to Religion.* London: Tavistock Publishers, 1965.

Bartholemew, James, *Inside the Tower: A Comprehensive Guide.* New York: New Amsterdam Books, 1990.

Bateson, Gregory, *Mind and Nature: A Necessary Unity.* New York: E.P. Dutton Co., 1979.

Beck, Brenda E., Peter J. Claus, Praphulladatta Goswami, and Jawaharlal Handoo, *Folktales of India.* Chicago: University of Chicago Press, 1987.

Bell, Diane, *Daughters of the Dreaming.* Melbourne, Australia: McPhee Gribble Publishers, 1983.

Bibbey, Jeffrey and P. V. Glob, *Looking for Dilmun.* New York: Alfred E. Knopf, 1969.

Blakeslee, Thomas, *Beyond the Conscious Mind: Unlocking the Secrets of the Self.* New York: Plenum Publishing Co., 1996.

Boas, Franz, "The Central Eskimo," *Sixth Annual Report of the Bureau of American Ethnology* (1888).

———, *The Mind of Primitive Man.* New York: The Free Press, 1965.

Boll, Friedrich, Carl Bezold, and Wilhelm Gundel, *Sternglaube und Sternbedeutung.* Stuttgart, Germany: B.G. Teubner, 1966.

Bowers, A.W., *Mandan Social and Ceremonial Organization.* Chicago: University of Chicago Press, 1950.

Brinton, Daniel G., *American Hero-Myths.* Philadelphia: H.C. Watts and Co., 1882.

Buchanan, Briggs, "A Snake Goddess and Her Companions," *Iraq* 23 (1971). 1–18.

Budge, E. Wallis, *The Egyptian Book of the Dead: The Papyrus of Ani, Scribe and Treasurer of the Temples of Egypt, about B.C. 1450.* New York: Dover, 1967.

Bürger, Gottfried August, "Der Wilde Jäger," *Sämtliche Werke.* Erste Band: *Gedichte.* Göttingen, Germany: Dieterich'chen Buchhandlung, 1844.

Campbell, Joseph, *The Hero with a Thousand Faces. Bollingen Series* 17. Princeton, NJ: Princeton University Press, 1949.

———, *Historical Atlas of World Mythology: The Way of the Animal Powers,* vol. 1. New York: Harper and Row, 1988.

———, *The Masks of God: Primitive Mythology,* vol. 1. New York: Viking Books, 1959.

———, *The Masks of God: Oriental Mythology,* vol. 2. New York: Viking Books, 1962.

———, *The Masks of God: Occidental Mythology,* vol. 3. New York: Viking Books, 1964.

———, *The Masks of God: Creative Mythology,* vol. 4. New York: Viking Books, 1968.

Capra, Fritjof, *The Tao of Physics.* Boulder, CO: Shambhala Books, 1983.

Card, Orson Scott, *Homecoming: Harmony.* New York: Tor Books, 1994.

Carmos, David, *Vitality, Health, and Relaxation through Yoga.* Boston: Kundalic Press, 1968.

Carpenter, Humphrey, ed., *The Letters of J.R.R. Tolkien.* Boston: Houghton Mifflin, 1981.

———, *J.R.R. Tolkien, A Biography.* Boston: Houghton Mifflin, 1977.

Chagnon, Napoleon, *Yanamamö: The Fierce People.* New York: Holt, Rinehart, and Winston, 1968.

Chalmers, David P., *The Conscious Mind: In Search of a Fundamental Theory.* Oxford, England: Oxford University Press, 1996.

Chamberlain, Basil Hall, trans. *Ko-ji-ki: "Records of Ancient Matters," Transactions of the Asiatic Society of Japan* vol. 10, supplement (1882), 1–41.

Chrétien de Troyes, *Arthurian Romances,* trans. W.W. Kibler and C. W. Carroll. Baltimore: Penguin Books, 1991.

Chomsky, Noam, *Language and the Mind.* New York: Harcourt, Brace Jovanovich 1968.

Clendinnen, Inga, *Aztecs: An Interpretation.* Cambridge, England: Cambridge University Press, 1991.

Cohen, Jack, and Ian Stewart, *The Collapse of Chaos: Discovering Simplicity in a Complex World.* New York: Viking Books, 1994.

Cohn, Carol, "Sex and Death in the Rational World of Defense Intellectuals," paper published by the Center for Psychological Studies in the Nuclear Age, Cambridge, MA: 1987.

The Commonwealth Fund Survey of the Health of Adolescent Girls. http://www.cmwf.org/women/abusfact.html, September 1997.

Constable, George, *The Neanderthals.* New York: Time-Life Books, 1973.

Crawford, Michael, *Antropologia Biologica de los Indios Americanos.* Madrid, Spain: Fundacion MAPFRE America, 1992.

Deacon, Terrence, *The Symbolic Species: The Co-evolution of Language and the Brain.* New York: W.W. Norton, 1997.

del Castillo, Bernal Diaz, *The Discovery and Conquest of Mexico.* New York: Farrar, Strauss, and Giroux, 1956.

Delporte, Henri, *L'Image des Animaux dans L'Art Prehistorique.* Paris: Picard Editeur, 1990.

de Santillana, Giorgio, and Hertha von Dechend, *Hamlet's Mill: An Essay on Myth and the Frame of Time.* Boston: Gambit Press, 1969.

Dillehay, Thomas, G. A. Calderon, G. Politis, and M.C. de Beltrao, "Earliest Hunters and Gatherers of South America," *Journal of World Prehistory* 6 (1992).

Dorsey, G. A., *The Arapaho Sun Dance; the Ceremony of the Offerings Lodge. Field Columbian Museum, Publication* 75, *Anthropological Series,* vol. 4. Chicago: Field Museum, 1903.

———, *The Cheyenne.* I. *Ceremonial Organization. Field Columbian Museum, Publication* 99, *Anthropology Series,* vol. 9, No. 1. Chicago: Field Museum, 1905.

Ebeling, Erich, *Tod und Leben nach den Vorstellung der Babylonier.* Leipzig, Germany: de Gruyter, 1931.

Eliade, Mircea, *Shamanism.* Boston: Routledge and Kegan Paul, 1964.

———, *Yoga: Immortality and Freedom. Bollingen Series* 56. trans. Willard R. Trask. Princeton, NJ: Princeton University Press, 1969.

Erdoes, Richard and Alfonso Ortiz, eds., *American Indian Myths and Legends.* New York: Pantheon Books, 1984.

Evans-Pritchard, Edward E., *Nuer Religion.* London: Oxford University Press, 1956.

Fagan, Brian, *Ancient North America: The Archæology of a Continent.* New York: Thames and Hudson, 1991.

Fairservis, Walter, Jr., *The Roots of Ancient India.* New York: Macmillan, 1971.

Feldman, Burton, and Robert D. Richardson, Jr., *The Rise of Modern Mythology, 1680–1860.* Bloomington, IN: Indiana University Press, 1972.

Fernea, Elizabeth Warnock, *Guests of the Sheikh.* Garden City, NY: Doubleday Books, 1969.

Fire, John, and Richard Erdoes, *Lame Deer: Seeker of Visions.* New York: Pocket Books, 1972.

Firster, R.L., *Akkadian Hymns and Prayers to the Goddess Ishtar.* Philadelphia: Dropsie College, 1970.

Fox, Robin, *The Red Lamp of Incest.* Notre Dame, IN: University of Notre Dame Press, 1983.

Frankfort, Henri, *Kingship and the Gods.* Chicago: Chicago University Press, 1948.

Frazer, Sir James, *The Golden Bough: A Study in Magic and Religion.* (abridged edition) New York: Macmillan Company, 1951.
Freuchen, Peter, *The Book of the Eskimos.* New York: Fawcett Books, 1965.
Freud, Sigmund, "A Case of Hysteria," *The Standard Edition of the Complete Psychological Works of Sigmund Freud,* vol. 7, trans. James Strachey. London: The Hogarth Press, 1953.
———, *Totem and Taboo and Other Works. The Standard Edition of the Complete Psychological Works of Sigmund Freud,* vol. 13, trans. James Strachey. London: The Hogarth Press, 1953.
Frobenius, Leo, *Schicksalskunde im Sinne des Kulturwerdens.* Leipzig, Germany: R. Voigtlanders Verlag, 1932.
Gantz, Jeffrey, trans., *The Mabinogion.* New York: Viking Penguin, 1976.
Geertz, Clifford, "Religion as a Cultural System," in Banton, Michael, ed., *Anthropological Approaches to Religion.* London: Tavistock Publishers, 1965, 1–46.
Gell-Mann, Murray, *The Quark and the Jaguar: Adventures in the Simple and the Complex.* New York: W. H. Freeman, 1994.
Gibbs, W. Wayt, "Beyond Physics: Renowned Scientists Contemplate the Evidence for God," *Scientific American* 279(2) (1998).
Gifford, Edward W., *Tongan Myths and Tales.* Honolulu, HI: Bernice *Pauahi Bishop Museum Bulletin* 8 (1924).
Gimbutas, Marija, *The Language of the Goddess.* New York: Thames and Hudson, 1989.
Goethe, Johann Wolfgang, "Euphrosyne," *Selected Poems,* ed. Christopher Middleton. Boston: Suhrkam/Insel Publishing, 1983.
Goodall, Jane, *In the Shadow of Man.* Boston: Houghton Mifflin, 1971.
Goodchild, Peter, J., *Robert Oppenheimer: Shatterer of Worlds.* Boston: Houghton Mifflin, 1981.
Gordon, Cyrus H., *Before Columbus: Links between the Old World and Ancient America.* New York: Crown Books, 1971.
Gowlett, John, *Ascent to Civilization: The Archæology of Early Man.* New York: Alfred A. Knopf, 1984.
Graves, Robert, *The Greek Myths,* 2 vols. Baltimore, MD: Penguin Books, 1955.
———, *The White Goddess.* New York: Vintage Books, 1960.
Graves, Robert, and Raphael Patai, *Hebrew Myths.* Garden City, NY: Doubleday, 1963.
Gregor, Thomas, *Mehinaku: The Drama of Daily Life in a Brazilian Indian Village.* Chicago: University of Chicago Press, 1977.
Grimal, Pierre, *LaRousse World Mythology,* trans. Patricia Beardsworth. London: Paul Hamlyn, 1965.
Grinnell, George Bird, *Blackfoot Lodge Tales.* New York: Charles Scribner's Sons, 1892.
———, "Cheyenne Obstacle Myths," *Journal of American Folklore* 16 (1903), 108–115.
Guidon, N. and B. Arnaud, "The Chronology of the New World: Two Faces of One Reality," *World Archæology* 23 (2) (1991).
Guillaumont, A., H. Ch. Puech, G. Quispel, W. Till, and Yassah 'Abd al-Masih, trans., *The Gospel According to Thomas.* New York: Harper and Row, 1959.

Gutstein, Harry Z., trans., *Passover Haggadah.* New York: Ktav Publishing House, Inc., 1949.

Halevi, Z'ev ben-Shamir, *Tree of Life: An Introduction to the Cabala.* London: Rider and Company, 1972.

Hallo, William W., and William K. Simpson, *The Ancient Near East: A History.* New York: Harcourt Brace Jovanovich, 1971.

Hallo, William W., and J.J.A. Van Dijk, *The Exaltation of Inanna.* New Haven, CT: Yale University Press, 1968.

Harris, Marvin, *Cows, Pigs, Wars, and Witches.* New York: Random House, 1974.

Hartner, Willy, "The Earliest History of the Constellations in the Near East and the Motif of the Lion-Bull Combat." *Journal of Near Eastern Studies* 24 (1965).

Hawkins, Gerald, *Stonehenge Decoded.* Garden City, NY: Doubleday Books, 1965.

Heine-Geldern, Robert, "The Origin of Ancient Civilizations and Toynbee's Hypothesis," *Diogenes* 13. Chicago: University of Chicago Press, 1956.

Heine-Geldern, Robert, and Gordon F. Eckholm, "Significant Parallels in the Symbolic Arts of Southern Asia and Middle America," *Papers of the 29th International Congress of Americanists,* vol. 1: *The Civilization of Ancient America.* Chicago: University of Chicago Press, 1951.

Hennig, R., "Beitrag zur kulturgeschichtlichen Bedeutung der Sternbilder," *Zeiss Nachrichten,* Sonderheft 2 (1937).

Hesse, Hermann, *The Journey to the East.* trans. Hilda Rosner. New York: Farrar, Strauss, and Giroux, 1956.

Hewitt, J. N. B, "Iroquois Myths and Legends," *Bureau of American Ethnology Twenty-first Annual Report* (1903), 255–339.

Hoagland, Kathleen, ed., *A Thousand Years of Irish Poetry.* Old Greenwich, CT: Devin-Adair Co., 1957.

Hoebel, E. Adamson, *The Cheyenne: Indians of the Great Plains.* New York: Holt, Rinehart, and Winston, 1960.

Hoffman, Curtiss, "Dumuzi's Dream," *Dream Network Journal* 13 (4), 10–11.

———, *The Lion, the Eagle, the Man, and the Bull in Mesopotamian Glyptic.* Doctoral dissertation. Ann Arbor, MI: University Microfilms, 1974.

———, *People of the Fresh Water Lake: A Prehistory of Westborough, Massachusetts.* Bern, Switzerland: Peter Lang Publishing, 1991.

———, "Shadow and Substance," in Donald Y. Gilmore and Linda S. McElroy, eds., *Across Before Columbus? Evidence for Transoceanic Contact with the Americas Prior to 1492.* Edgecomb, ME: The New England Antiquities Research Association, 1998, 97–103.

Hogbin, Ian, *The Island of the Menstruating Men: Religion in Wogeo, New Guinea.* Scranton, PA: Chandler Publishing Co., 1970.

The Holy Bible, King James Version. Nashville, TN: Thomas Nelson, 1972.

Homer, *The Odyssey,* trans. Richard Latimore. New York: Harper and Row, 1967.

Howitt, A. W., *The Native Tribes of South-East Australia.* London: Macmillan and Co., 1904.

Huxley, Aldous, *The Perennial Philosophy.* Freeport, NY: Books for Libraries Press, 1972.

Ions, Veronica, *Indian Mythology.* London: Paul Hamlyn, 1967.

Jacobsen, Thorkild, *The Treasures of Darkness*. New Haven, CT: Yale University Press, 1971.

Jacoby, Felix, *Die Fragmente der griechischen Historiker,* Dritter Teil, C. New York: E. J. Brill, 1993.

James, William, *Pragmatism*. New York: Longmans, Green, and Company, 1907.

Jensen, Adolf, *Myth and Cult among Primitive Peoples,* trans. Marianna Tax Choldin and Wolfgang Weissleder. Chicago: University of Chicago Press, 1963.

———, *Das religiose Weltbild einer frühen Kultur*. Stuttgart, Germany: August Schröder Verlag, 1949.

Jeremias, Alfred, *Handbuch der altorientalische Geisteskultur*. Leipzig, Germany: J.C. Hinrisch'sche Buchhandlung, 1913.

Jett, Stephen, "Precolumbian Transatlantic Contacts," in Jesse Jennings, ed., *Ancient North Americans*. San Francisco: W.H. Freeman Co., 1983, 557–613.

Joyce, James, *Finnegans Wake*. New York: Viking Press, 1959.

Jung, Carl G., *Aion. Collected Works* vol. 9_2. *Bollingen Series* 20. trans. R.F.C. Hull. Princeton, NJ: Princeton University Press, 1969.

———, *The Archetypes and the Collective Unconscious. Collected Works* vol. 9_1. *Bollingen Series* 20, trans. R.F.C. Hull. Princeton, NJ: Princeton University Press, 1969.

———, *Memories, Dreams, Reflections*. New York: Random House, 1961.

———, *Psychology and Alchemy. Collected Works* vol. 12. *Bollingen Series* 20, trans. R.F.C. Hull. Princeton, NJ: Princeton University Press, 1969, 107.

———, *Symbols of Transformation, Collected Works* vol. 8. *Bollingen Series* 20, trans. R.F.C. Hull. Princeton, NJ: Princeton University Press, 1969.

Kazantzakis, Nikos, *The Last Temptation of Christ,* trans. P. A. Bien. New York: Bantam Books, 1971.

———, *The Odyssey: A Modern Sequel,* trans. Kimon Friar. New York: Simon and Schuster, 1958.

Katz, Richard, *Boiling Energy: Community Healing among the Kalahari Kung*. Cambridge, MA: Harvard University Press, 1982.

Kehoe, Alice Beck, *The Ghost Dance Religion: Ethnohistory and Revitalization*. New York: Holt, Rinehart and Winston, 1989.

Kensinger, Kenneth M., *How Real People Ought to Live: The Cashinahua of Eastern Peru*. Prospect Heights, IL: Waveland Press, 1995.

Koestler, Arthur, *The Sleepwalkers*. New York: Grosset and Dunlap, 1963.

Kramer, Samuel N., *The Sacred Marriage Rite*. Bloomington, IN: University of Indiana Press, 1969.

———, *The Sumerians: Their History, Culture, and Character*. Chicago: University of Chicago Press, 1963.

Kuhn, Thomas Y., *The Structure of Scientific Revolutions*. Chicago: University of Chicago Press, 1960.

Labat, René, *Manuel d'Epigraphie Akadienne*. Paris: Impremerie Nationale, 1963.

Lafaye, Jacques, *Quetzalcoatl and Guadelupe,* trans. Benjamin Keene. Chicago: University of Chicago Press, 1976.

Lambert, William G., *Enuma Elish: The Babylonian Epic of Creation*. Oxford, England: Oxford University Press, 1966.

———, "A Part of the Ritual for the Substitute King," *Archiv für Orientforschung* 18 (1957), 109–112.

Lambert, William G. and A. R. Millard, *Atra-hasis*. Oxford, England: Clarendon Press, 1969.

Landersdorfer, P., *Der Baal Tetramorphos und die Kerube von Ezekiel (Studien zur Geschichte und Kultur des Altertums* vol.9, no.3). Paderborn, Germany: Verlag von Ferdinand Schöningh, 1918.

Lanier, Sterling, *Hiero's Journey*. New York: Bantam Books, 1973.

LeGuin, Ursula K., *The Language of the Night: Essays on Fantasy and Science Fiction*. New York: Berkley Books, 1982.

Leroi–Gourhan, Andre, *Les Religions de la Prehistoire: le Paleolithique*. Paris: Presses Universitaires de France, 1971.

Lévi–Strauss, Claude, *The Elementary Structures of Kinship*, trans. James Bell and John von Strome. Boston: Beacon Press, 1969.

———, *From Honey to Ashes. Introduction to a Science of Mythology*, vol. 2, trans. John and Doreen Weightman. New York: Harper and Row, 1973.

———, *The Naked Man. Introduction to a Science of Mythology*, vol. 4, trans. John and Doreen Weightman. New York: Harper and Row, 1981.

———, *The Origin of Table Manners. Introduction to a Science of Mythology*, vol. 3, trans. John and Doreen Weightman. New York: Harper and Row, 1978.

———, *The Raw and the Cooked: Introduction to a Science of Mythology*, vol. 1, trans. John and Doreen Weightman. New York: Harper and Row, 1969.

———, *The Savage Mind*. Chicago: University of Chicago Press, 1966.

———, "The Structural Study of Myth," in T. A. Sebeok, ed., *Myth: A Symposium*. Bloomington, IN: University of Indiana Press, 1955.

———, *Totemism*, trans. Rodney Needham. Boston: Beacon Press, 1963.

Lewis, C. S., *Perelandra*. New York: Collier Books, 1962.

———, *The Last Battle*. New York: Macmillan, 1956.

Lindsay, David, *A Voyage to Arcturus*. New York: Ballantine Books, 1963.

Little, Barbara J., "Consider the Hermaphroditic Mind: Comment on 'The Interplay of Evidential Constraints and Political Interests: Recent Archæological Research on Gender,' *American Antiquity* vol. 59 (3) (1994), 439–544.

Lommel, Andreas, *Die Unumbal: Ein Stamm in Nordwest-Australia*. Hamburg, Germany: Museum für Völkerkunde, 1962.

Luckenbill, Daniel D., *Ancient Records of Assyria and Babylonia*. Chicago: University of Chicago Press, 1926.

Mannoni, Octave, "Psychoanalysis and the Decolonization of Mankind," in Jonathan Miller, ed., *Freud, the Man, His World, His Influence*. Boston: Little, Brown, 1972.

Marshack, Alexander, *The Roots of Civilization*. New York: McGraw Hill, 1972.

Marshall, Lorna, *The !Kung of Nyae Nyae*. Cambridge, MA: Harvard University Press, 1976.

Matthews, Caitlin, and John Matthews, *Ladies of the Lake*. London: Aquarian Press, 1992.

Metraux, Andre, "Tribes of the Jurua-Purus Basins," *Handbook of South American Indians. Bulletin of the Bureau of American Ethnology* 143 (1948).

Moortgat, Anton, *The Art of Ancient Mesopotamia*. London: Phaedon Press, 1969.

Moss, Robert, *Conscious Dreaming: A Spiritual Path for Everyday Life*. New York: Crown Books, 1996.
Munch, Peter Andreas, *Norse Mythology: Legends of Gods and Heroes,* trans. Sigurd Bernard Hustvedt. New York: American Scandinavian Foundation, 1926.
Myss, Caroline, *Anatomy of the Spirit*. New York: Harmony Books, 1996.
Naso, Publius Ovidius (Ovid), *Metamorphoses,* trans. Frank Justus Miller. Cambridge, MA: Harvard University Press, 1977.
National Oceanic and Atmospheric Administration, World Map. http://www.ogp.noaa.gov/.
Neihardt, John, *Black Elk Speaks*. New York: Pocket Books, 1972.
Nietzsche, Friedrich Wilhelm, *The Portable Nietzsche,* trans. and ed. Walter Kaufmann. New York: Viking Press, 1954.
Neumann, Ernst, *The Life of Richard Wagner, 1813–1848,* vol. 1. New York: Alfred A. Knopf, 1933.
Newton, Sir Isaac, *The Correspondence of Isaac Newton,* vol. 1, ed. H.W. Turnbull. Cambridge, England: Cambridge University Press, 1959.
Nicolis, Gregoire and Ilya Prigogine, *Exploring Complexity: An Introduction*. New York: W. H. Freeman and Co., 1989.
Opie, Iona and Peter, *The Classic Fairy Tales*. New York: Oxford University Press, 1974.
Opler, Morris E., *Myths and Tales of the Jicarilla Apache Indians. Memoirs of the American Folklore Society,* vol. 31 (1938).
Osborne, Harold, *South American Mythology*. London: Paul Hamlyn Publishing Co., 1968.
Ostermann, H., *The Alaskan Eskimos, as Described in the Posthumous Notes of Dr. Knud Rasmussen. Report of the Fifth Thule Expedition 1921–24,* vol. 10, no. 3. Copenhagen: Nordisk Verlag, 1952.
Pennick, Nigel, *Celtic Sacred Landscapes*. London: Thames and Hudson, 1996.
Pfeiffer, John, *The Emergence of Society: A Prehistory of the Establishment*. New York: McGraw Hill, 1977.
Penrose, Roger, *Shadows of the Mind: A Search for the Missing Science of Consciousness*. Oxford, England: Oxford University Press, 1994.
Plato, *Symposium,* in Benjamin Jowett, trans., *The Dialogues of Plato*. New York: Random House, 1937.
Pratt, Jane Austen, *Consciousness and Sacrifice. Contributions to Jungian Thought*. New York: Analytic Psychology Club of New York, 1967.
Pope, Alexander, *The Thickenham Edition of the Poems of Alexander Pope,* ed. Maynard Mack. London: Methuen and Co., Ltd., 1950.
Publius Ovidius Naso (Ovid), *Metamorphoses,* trans. Frank Justus Miller. Cambridge, MA: Harvard University Press, 1977.
Rassmussen, Knud, *Across Arctic America*. New York: G. Putnam and Sons, 1927.
———, *Report of the Fifth Thule Expedition 1921–24,* vol. 7, no. 1. Copenhagen: Nordisk Verlag, 1929.
———, "A Shaman's Journey to the Sea Spirit Takanakapsaluk," in Dennis and Barbara Tedlock, eds., *Teachings from the American Earth*. Los Angeles: Livewright, 1973.

Recinos, Adrian, *Popol Vuh: The Sacred Book of the Ancient Quiche Maya.* From the translation by Delia Goetz and Sylvanus Morley. Norman, OK: University of Oklahoma Press, 1950.

Reiner, Erica, "The Etiological Myth of the 'Seven Sages,'" *Orientalia* n.s. 30 (1961), 1–11.

Róheim, Géza, *The Eternal Ones of the Dream.* New York: International Universities Press, 1945.

Roszak, Theodore, *Where the Waste Land Ends.* Garden City, NY: Doubleday Books, 1972.

Saggs, H. W. F., *The Greatness That Was Babylon.* New York: Hawthorn Books 1962.

Sakellariou, M. B., "Linguistic and Ethnic Groups in Prehistoric Greece," in George Christopoulus, ed., *History of the Hellenic World: Prehistory and Protohistory.* University Park, PA: Pennsylvania State University Press, 1974.

Shakespeare, William, *Hamlet,* in Hardin Craig, ed., *The Complete Works of Shakespeare.* Chicago: Scott, Foresman and Company, 1951.

Shalvey, Thomas, *Claude Lévi–Strauss: Social Psychotherapy and the Collective Unconscious.* Amherst, MA: University of Massachusetts Press, 1979.

Sieveking, Ann, *The Cave Artists.* London: Thames and Hudson, 1979.

Sophocles, "Antigonæ," trans. Friedrich Hölderlin. In *Hölderlin: Sämtliche Werke.* Frankfurt am Main: Insel Verlag, 1961.

Speiser, Ephraim, trans., "Akkadian Myths and Epics," in James B. Pritchard, ed., *Ancient Near Eastern Texts Relating to the Old Testament.* Princeton, NJ: Princeton University Press, 1969.

Spencer, Baldwin, and F. J. Gillen, *The Native Tribes of Central Australia.* London: Macmillan and Company, 1899.

Stephen, Michele, *A'aisa's Gifts.* Berkeley, CA: University of California Press, 1995.

Stevens, Anthony, *Private Myths.* Englewood Cliffs, NJ: Bowker–Ingram, 1996.

Sturluson, Snorri, "Gylfaginning," *The Prose Edda,* trans. Arthur Brodeur. New York: American–Scandinavian Foundation, 1929.

Suetonius, Gaius Tranquillus, *The Twelve Caesars,* trans. Robert Graves. Baltimore, MD: Penguin Books, 1957.

Swanton, John, *Tlingit Myths and Texts. Bureau of American Ethnology Bulletin* 39. Washington, DC: U.S. Government Printing Office, 1909.

Tessman, Günter, *Die Pangwe,* vol. 2. Berlin, Germany: E. Wasmuth, 1913.

Thoreau, Henry David, *Walden.* New York: New American Library, 1960.

Tolkien, John Ronald Reuel, *The Adventures of Tom Bombadil.* New York: Ballantine Books, 1966.

———, *The Book of Lost Tales. The History of Middle Earth,* vol. 2., ed. Christopher Tolkien. Boston: Houghton Mifflin, 1984.

———, *The Hobbit.* New York: Ballantine Books, 1966.

———, *The Lost Road. The History of Middle Earth,* vol. 5., ed. Christopher Tolkien. Boston: Houghton Mifflin, 1987.

———, *Morgoth's Ring. The History of Middle-Earth,* vol. 10., ed. Christopher Tolkien. Boston: Houghton Mifflin, 1993.

———, *The Shaping of Middle-Earth. The History of Middle Earth,* vol. 4., ed. Christopher Tolkien. Boston: Houghton Mifflin, 1986.

———, *The Silmarillion*, ed. Christopher Tolkien. Boston: Houghton Mifflin, 1979.
———, *Sauron Defeated. The History of Middle Earth*, vol. 9, ed. Christopher Tolkien. Boston: Houghton Mifflin, 1992.
———, *The Return of the King*. New York: Ballantine Books, 1965.
———, *Unfinished Tales*. Boston: Houghton Mifflin, 1980.
Tonkinson, Robert, *The Mardudjara Aborigines: Living the Dream in Australia's Desert*. New York: Holt, Rinehart, and Winston, 1978.
Toor, Frances, *A Treasury of Mexican Folkways*. New York: Crown Publishing, 1947.
Turnbull, Colin, *The Forest People*. New York: Simon and Schuster, 1962.
———, *The Mbuti Pygmies: Change and Adaptation*. New York: Holt, Rinehart and Winston, 1983.
Turner, Victor, "Betwixt and Between: The Liminal Period in *Rites de Passáge*," in June Helm, ed., *Proceedings of the 1964 Annual Spring Meeting of the American Ethnological Society*. Seattle, WA: University of Washington Press, 1964, 4–20.
———, "Colour Classification in Ndembu Ritual," in Michael Banton, ed., *Anthropological Approaches to the Study of Religion*. London: Tavistock Publishers, 1966, 47–84.
Van Buren, E. Douglas, "The Dragon in Ancient Mesopotamia," *Orientalia* n.s. 16 (1947).
———, *The Flowing Vase and the God with Streams*. Berlin, Germany: Hans Schök & Co., 1933.
———, "The Sacred Marriage in Early Times in Mesopotamia," *Orientalia* n.s. 13 (1944), 1–72.
Velikovsky, Immanuel, *Oedipus and Akhnaton*. New York: Doubleday, 1960.
Vermeule, Emily, *Greece in the Bronze Age*. Chicago: University of Chicago Press, 1964.
Volk, Tyler, *Gaia's Body: Toward a Physiology of Earth*. New York: Copernicus Books, 1998.
———, *Metapatterns: Across Space, Time, and Mind*. New York: Columbia University Press, 1995.
von Eschenbach, Wolfram, *Parzival*, ed. Karl Lachmann. Berlin and Leipzig, Germany: Walter de Gruyter, 1926.
von Strassburg, Gottfried, *Tristan*, trans. A. T. Hatto. Baltimore, MD: Penguin Books, 1960.
Wagner, Richard, *Der Ring des Niebelungen*, edited by F. Riedel. Leipzig, Germany: Max Beck Verlag, 1945.
Waldrop, M. Mitchell, *Complexity: The Emerging Science at the Edge of Order and Chaos*. New York: Simon and Schuster, 1992.
Wardwell, Allen, ed., *Native Paths*. New York: Metropolitan Museum of Art, 1998.
Warner, W. Lloyd, *A Black Civilization: A Social Study of an Australian Tribe*. New York: Harper and Row, 1958.
Waters, Frank, *The Book of the Hopi*. New York: Viking Press, 1963.
Watson, Lyall, *Gifts of Unknown Things*. New York: Bantam Books, 1978.
Weidner, Ernst, *Handbuch der babylonischen Astronomie*. Leipzig, Germany: J. C. Hinrisch'sche Buchhandlung, 1915.
Wensinck, Arent J., "The Semitic New Year and the Origin of Eschatology." *Orientalia* n.s. 1 (1923).

Wilde, Lady Francesca, *Ancient Legends, Mystic Charms, and Superstitions of Ireland.* Boston: Ticknor Publishers, 1887.

Wilhelm, Richard, *The I Ching. Bollingen Series* 19, trans. Cary F. Baynes. Princeton, NJ: Princeton University Press, 1950.

Will, C. F. and H. J. Spinden, *The Mandans: A Study of Their Culture, Archæology and Language. Papers of the Peabody Museum of American Archæology and Ethnology,* vol. 3, No. 46. Millwood, NY: Kraus Reprint Co.,1974.

Williams, Mentor L., ed., *Schoolcraft's Indian Legends.* East Lansing, MI: Michigan State University, 1956.

Willoya, William and Vinson Brown, *Warriors of the Rainbow.* Healdsburg, CA: Naturegraph Publishers, 1962.

Wolkstein, Diane and Samuel N. Kramer, *Inanna: Queen of Heaven and Earth.* New York: Harper and Row, 1983.

Woodman, Marion, *Leaving My Father's House: A Journey to Conscious Femininity.* Boulder, CO: Shambhala Books, 1992.

———, *The Pregnant Virgin: A Process of Psychological Transformation.* Toronto, Canada: Inner City Books, 1985.

Woodman, Marion, and Elinor Dickson, *Dancing in the Flames: The Dark Goddess in the Transformation of Consciousness.* Boston: Shambhala Publications, 1996.

Woodward, Robert, and Carl Bernstein, *The Final Days.* New York: Simon and Schuster, 1976.

Woolley, Sir Leonard, *Ur Excavations* vol. 2. *The Royal Cemetery.* London: Clarendon Press, 1934.

Zimmer, Heinrich, *Myths and Symbols of Indian Art and Civilization. Bollingen Series* 6. Princeton, NJ: Princeton University Press, 1946.

———, *The King and the Corpse: Tales of the Soul's Conquest of Evil. Bollingen Series* 11. Princeton, NJ: Princeton University Press, 1957.

Zipes, Jack, *The Trials and Tribulations of Little Red Riding Hood.* South Hadley, MA: Bergin and Garvey Publishers, Inc., 1983.

ENDNOTES

Preface

[1] David Lindsay, *A Voyage to Arcturus* (New York: Ballantine Books, 1963), 281–287.
[2] C.G. Jung, *Memories, Dreams, Reflections* (New York: Random House, 1961), 84–85.
[3] Curtiss Hoffman, *People of the Fresh Water Lake: A Prehistory of Westborough, Massachusetts* (Bern, Switzerland: Peter Lang Publishing, 1991), 256.
[4] Curtiss Hoffman, "The Lion, the Eagle, the Man, and the Bull in Mesopotamian Glyptic" (Ph.D. dissertation, Yale University, 1974), 856–895.
[5] Claude Lévi-Strauss, "The Structural Study of Myth," in T. Sebeok, ed., *Myth: A Symposium* (Bloomington, IN: University of Indiana Press, 1955), 440.

Chapter One

[1] Delia Goetz and Sylvanus G. Morley, *Popol Vuh: The Sacred Book of the Ancient Quiche Maya,* from the translation of Adrian Récinos (Norman, OK: University of Oklahoma Press, 1950), 81–84.
[2] Harry Z. Gutstein, trans., *Passover Haggadah* (New York: Ktav Publishing House, Inc., 1949), 10.
[3] Joseph Campbell, *The Masks of God: Occidental Mythology,* vol. 3 (New York: Viking Books, 1964), 520.
[4] 1 Corinthians 13:11.
[5] David Chalmers, *The Conscious Mind: In Search of a Fundamental Theory* (Oxford, England: Oxford University Press, 1996), 5.
[6] John Gowlett, *Ascent to Civilization: The Archæology of Early Man* (New York: Alfred A. Knopf, 1984), 120–133.
[7] Gregory Bateson, *Mind and Nature: A Necessary Unity* (New York: E. P. Dutton Co., 1979), 31–38.

[8] Burton Feldman and Robert D. Richardson, Jr., *The Rise of Modern Mythology, 1680–1860* (Bloomington, IN: Indiana University Press, 1972), 8–9.
[9] James Frazer, *The Golden Bough: A Study in Magic and Religion,* 1-volume abridged edition (New York: Macmillan Company, 1951), 824–825.
[10] Jack Cohen and Ian Stewart, *The Collapse of Chaos: Discovering Simplicity in a Complex World* (New York: Viking Books, 1994), 364–365.
[11] Arthur Koestler, *The Sleepwalkers* (New York: Grosset and Dunlap, 1963), 191–219.
[12] Isaac Newton, Letter to R. Hooke, February 5, 1675. *The Correspondence of Isaac Newton,* vol. I. ed. H. W. Turnbull (Cambridge, England: Cambridge University Press, 1959), 416.
[13] Thomas S. Kuhn, *The Structure of Scientific Revolutions* (Chicago: University of Chicago Press, 1960), *passim.*
[14] Brian Goodwin, *How the Leopard Changed its Spots: The Evolution of Complexity* (New York: Charles Scribner's Sons, 1994), 42–76.
[15] Michael Allaby and James Lovelock, *The Great Extinction* (Garden City, NY: Doubleday Books, 1983), 46–47.
[16] Cohen and Stewart, 209–212.
[17] Joseph Campbell, *The Masks of God: Creative Mythology,* vol. 4 (New York: Viking Press, 1968), 609–624.
[18] Carl G. Jung, *Psychology and Alchemy, Collected Works,* vol. 12, Bollingen Series 20, trans. R. F. C. Hull (Princeton, NJ: Princeton University Press, 1969), 107.
[19] Joseph Campbell, *Creative Mythology,* 586.
[20] Claude Lévi–Strauss, *The Raw and the Cooked: Introduction to a Science of Mythology,* vol.1, trans. John and Doreen Weightman (New York: Harper and Row, 1969), 240.
[21] Lévi–Strauss, "A Structural Study of Myth," 443.
[22] Claude Lévi–Strauss, *The Naked Man: Introduction to a Science of Mythology,* vol. 4, trans. John and Doreen Weightman (New York: Harper and Row, 1981), 639.
[23] Theodore Roszak, *Where the Waste Land Ends* (Garden City, NY: Doubleday Books, 1972), 220–264.
[24] Henry David Thoreau, *Walden* (New York: New American Library, 1960), 10.
[25] Jung, *Psychology and Alchemy,* 230–232.
[26] M. Mitchell Waldrop, *Complexity: The Emerging Science at the Edge of Order and Chaos* (New York: Simon and Schuster, 1992), 11–13.
[27] Gregoire Nicolis and Ilya Prigogine, *Exploring Complexity: An Introduction* (New York: W. H. Freeman and Co., 1989), 44.
[28] Roger Penrose, *Shadows of the Mind: A Search for the Missing Science of Consciousness* (Oxford, England: Oxford University Press, 1994), 371–376.
[29] Chalmers, 93–122.
[30] Fritjof Capra, *The Tao of Physics* (Boulder, CO: Shambhala Books, 1976), 245.
[31] W. Wayt Gibbs, "Beyond Physics: Renowned Scientists Contemplate the Evidence for God," *Scientific American* 279(2) (August 1998), 20–22.
[32] Barbara J. Little, "Consider the Hermaphroditic Mind: Comment on 'The Interplay of Evidential Constraints and Political Interests: Recent Archæological Research on Gender,'" *American Antiquity* 59(3) (1994), 439–544.
[33] Lévi–Strauss, *The Raw and the Cooked,* 6.

[34] Ursula K. LeGuin, "Why Americans Are Afraid of Dragons," in *The Language of the Night: Essays on Fantasy and Science Fiction* (New York: Berkley Books, 1982), 34–35.
[35] Orson Scott Card, *Homecoming: Harmony* (New York: Tor Books, 1994), 607.
[36] Alexander Pope, *An Essay on Man. The Thickenham Edition of the Poems of Alexander Pope,* ed. Maynard Mack (London: Methuen and Co., Ltd., 1950), 53.

Chapter Two

[1] Bernal Diaz del Castillo, *The Discovery and Conquest of Mexico* (New York: Farrar, Strauss, and Giroux, 1956), 222–223.
[2] Jacques Lafaye, *Quetzalcoatl and Guadelupe,* trans. Benjamin Keene (Chicago: University of Chicago Press, 1976), 179–181.
[3] James Axtell, *The European and the Indian* (Oxford, England: Oxford University Press, 1981), 45–47.
[4] Feldman and Richardson, 15.
[5] Ibid., 53.
[6] Ibid., 416–419.
[7] Frazer, 705.
[8] Feldman and Richardson, 480–483.
[9] Sigmund Freud, *Totem and Taboo and Other Works, The Standard Edition of the Complete Psychological Works of Sigmund Freud,* vol. 13, trans. James Strachey (London: The Hogarth Press, 1953), 64–65.
[10] Carl G. Jung, *The Archetypes and the Collective Unconscious, Collected Works,* vol. 9, Bollingen Series 20, trans. R. F. C. Hull (Princeton, NJ: Princeton University Press, 1969), 43.
[11] Marvin Harris, *Cows, Pigs, Wars, and Witches* (New York: Random House, 1974), 35–57.
[12] Claude Lévi-Strauss, *The Savage Mind* (Chicago: University of Chicago Press, 1966), 35–74; *Totemism,* trans. Rodney Needham (Boston: Beacon Press, 1963), 89.
[13] George Bird Grinnell, *Blackfoot Lodge Tales* (New York: Charles Scribner's Sons, 1892), 137–142.
[14] E. E. Evans–Pritchard, *Nuer Religion* (London: Oxford University Press, 1956), 20–21.
[15] Adolf Jensen, *Myth and Cult among Primitive Peoples,* trans. Marianna Tax Choldin and Wolfgang Weissleder (Chicago: University of Chicago Press, 1963), 182.
[16] James Joyce, *Finnegans Wake* (New York: Viking Press, 1958), 193–195.
[17] Thomas Gregor, *Mehinaku: The Drama of Daily Life in a Brazilian Indian Village* (Chicago: University of Chicago Press, 1977), 255.
[18] Ian Hogbin, *The Island of the Menstruating Men: Religion in Wogeo, New Guinea* (Scranton, PA: Chandler Publishing Co., 1970), 100–101.
[19] Colin Turnbull, *The Forest People* (New York: Simon and Schuster, 1962), 144–146.
[20] Ibid., 150.
[21] Gregor, 255.
[22] Hogbin, 134–135.

[23] Géza Róheim, *The Eternal Ones of the Dream* (New York: International Universities Press, 1945), 165.
[24] Colin Turnbull, *The Mbuti Pygmies: Change and Adaptation* (New York: Holt, Rinehart and Winston, 1983), 51–54.
[25] e.g., Robert Heine-Geldern, "The Origin of Ancient Civilizations and Toynbee's Hypothesis," *Diogenes* 13 (1956), 90–99.
[26] Franz Boas, *The Mind of Primitive Man* (New York: The Free Press, 1965), 147.
[27] Frances Toor, *A Treasury of Mexican Folkways* (New York: Crown Publishing, 1947), 482–485.
[28] Genesis 7:11–24; 9:20–24.
[29] Octave Mannoni, "Psychoanalysis and the Decolonization of Mankind," in *Freud: The Man, His World, His Influence,* ed. Jonathan Miller (Boston: Little, Brown, 1972), 90.
[30] Daniel G. Brinton, *American Hero-Myths* (Philadelphia: H. C. Watts and Co., 1882), 65–67; Inga Clendinnen, *Aztecs: An Interpretation* (Cambridge, England: University of Cambridge Press, 1991), 35–37.
[31] Lafaye, 179–181.
[32] Goetz and Morley, 50–52.
[33] Jung, *The Archetypes and the Collective Unconscious,* 4–6.
[34] Alice A. Bailey, *Telepathy and the Etheric Vehicle* (New York: Lucis Publishing Co., 1950), 1–4.
[35] Anthony Stevens, *Private Myths* (Englewood Cliffs, NJ: Bowker-Ingram, 1996), 184–189.
[36] Thomas Blakeslee, *Beyond the Conscious Mind: Unlocking the Secrets of the Self* (New York: Plenum Publishing Co., 1996), 175–177, 195–198.
[37] Clifford Geertz, "Religion as a Cultural System," in *Anthropological Approaches to the Study of Religion,* ed. Michael Banton (London: Tavistock Publishers, 1965), 7–8.
[38] Carl. G. Jung, *Symbols of Transformation, Collected Works,* vol. 8, Bollingen Series 20, trans. R. F. C. Hull (Princeton, NJ: Princeton University Press, 1969), 417–519.
[39] Jung, *The Archetypes and the Collective Unconscious,* 344.
[40] Frazer, 825.
[41] Lévi–Strauss, *The Savage Mind,* 1–33.
[42] Thomas Shalvey, *Claude Lévi–Strauss: Social Psychotherapy and the Collective Unconscious* (Amherst, MA: University of Massachusetts Press, 1979), 114–115.

Chapter Three

[1] Lévi–Strauss, *The Naked Man,* 609–611.
[2] Lady Francesca Wilde, *Ancient Legends, Mystic Charms, and Superstitions of Ireland* (Boston: Ticknor Publishers, 1887), 6–7.
[3] The original for Franck's composition is a poem by Gottfried August Bürger, "Der Wilde Jäger," *Sämtliche Werke,* Erste Band: *Gedichte* (Göttingen, Germany: Dieterich'chen Buchhandlung, 1844), 313–322.

[4] Joseph Campbell, *The Hero with a Thousand Faces,* Bollingen Series 17 (Princeton, NJ: Princeton University Press, 1949), 221–223.
[5] Robert Graves, *The White Goddess* (New York: Vintage Books, 1960), 228.
[6] Campbell, *The Hero with a Thousand Faces,* 116–118.
[7] Ibid., 245–251.
[8] Jung, *The Archetypes and the Collective Unconscious,* 166.
[9] Graves, *The White Goddess,* 136–137, 222.
[10] Johann Jakob Bachofen, *Myth, Religion, and Mother Right,* Bollingen Series 84, trans. Ralph Mauhern (Princeton, NJ: Princeton University Press, 1967), 76–80.
[11] Marija Gimbutas, *The Language of the Goddess* (New York: Thames and Hudson, 1989), xix–xxi.
[12] Graves, *The White Goddess,* 425.
[13] Ibid., 364.
[14] Frazer, 1–12.
[15] Campbell, *The Hero with a Thousand Faces,* 114.
[16] Jung, *Psychology and Alchemy,* 436–437.
[17] Graves, *The White Goddess,* 425–426.
[18] Jeffrey Gantz, trans., *The Mabinogion* (New York: Viking Penguin, 1976), 164–166.
[19] Henri Frankfort, *Kingship and the Gods* (Chicago: Chicago University Press, 1948), 45.
[20] Jung, *The Archetypes and the Collective Unconscious,* 17.
[21] Ibid., 40.
[22] Victor Turner, "Betwixt and Between: The Liminal Period in *Rites de Passáge,*" in *Proceedings of the 1964 Annual Spring Meeting of the American Ethnological Society,* ed. June Helm (Seattle, WA: University of Washington Press, 1964), 6–7.
[23] Graves, *The White Goddess,* 110–120.
[24] Ibid., 68.
[25] Joyce, 1.
[26] Gantz, 81.
[27] James Bartholemew, *Inside the Tower: A Comprehensive Guide* (New York: New Amsterdam Books, 1990), 99.
[28] Graves, *The White Goddess,* 188.
[29] Frazer, 1–12.
[30] John 12:24.
[31] Heinrich Zimmer, *The King and the Corpse: Tales of the Soul's Conquest of Evil,* Bollingen Series 11 (Princeton NJ: Princeton University Press, 1957), 67–76.
[32] Gantz, 49–51.
[33] Caitlin Matthews and John Matthews, *Ladies of the Lake* (London: Aquarian Press, 1992), 48–50.
[34] Gowlett, 106, 160–161.
[35] Nigel Pennick, *Celtic Sacred Landscapes* (London: Thames and Hudson, 1996), 68–78.
[36] Ibid., 70–71.
[37] Matthews and Matthews, xxviii–xxx.
[38] Ibid., 110.

Chapter Four

[1] Robert Graves, *The Greek Myths*, vol. 1 (Baltimore, MD: Penguin Books, 1955), 84–85.
[2] Publius Ovidius Naso (Ovid), *Metamorphoses*, trans. Frank Justus Miller (Cambridge, MA: Harvard University Press, 1977), Book 3, ls. 173–193.
[3] Homer, *The Odyssey*, trans. Richard Latimore (New York: Harper and Row, 1967), 158–161.
[4] Pierre Grimal, *LaRousse World Mythology*, trans. Patricia Beardsworth (London: Paul Hamlyn, 1965), 125.
[5] E. Adamson Hoebel, *The Cheyenne: Indians of the Great Plains* (New York: Holt, Rinehart, and Winston, 1960), 95.
[6] Hogbin, 86.
[7] Lévi–Strauss, *The Savage Mind*, 51–52.
[8] Leviticus 15:19–24.
[9] Lorna Marshall, *The !Kung of Nyae Nyae* (Cambridge, MA: Harvard University Press, 1976), 226.
[10] Ann Sieveking, *The Cave Artists* (London: Thames and Hudson, 1979), 77–78.
[11] Alexander Marshack, *The Roots of Civilîzation* (New York: McGraw Hill, 1972), 147–168.
[12] Andre Leroi-Gourhan, *Les Religions de la Prehistoire: le Paleolithique* (Paris: Presses Universitaires de France, 1971), 124.
[13] Henri Delporte, *L'Image des Animaux dans L'Art Prehistorique* (Paris: Picard Editeur, 1990), 264.
[14] Sieveking, 82.
[15] Graves, *The White Goddess*, 274.
[16] Ovid, Book 2, ls. 409–528.
[17] George Constable, *The Neanderthals* (New York: Time-Life Books, 1973), 108–113.
[18] Campbell, *The Hero with a Thousand Faces*, 204–206.
[19] Graves, *The Greek Myths*, vol. 1, 112–113.
[20] Ibid., 105.
[21] Ibid., 278.
[22] Ibid., 103–104.
[23] Graves, *The White Goddess*, 355–356.
[24] Ibid., 361–365.
[25] Baldwin Spencer and F. J. Gillen, *The Native Tribes of Central Australia* (London: Macmillan and Company, 1899), 523–525.
[26] Mircea Eliade, *Shamanism* (Boston: Routledge and Kegan Paul, 1964), 110–144.
[27] William James, *Pragmatism* (New York: Longmans, Green, and Company, 1907), 12.
[28] Michele Stephen, *A'aisa's Gifts* (Berkeley, CA: University of California Press, 1995), 230–292.
[29] Ibid., 23.
[30] I am indebted to Sterling Lanier's novel, *Hiero's Journey* (New York: Bantam Books, 1973), 13–15 for this image.
[31] Lévi–Strauss, *The Raw and the Cooked*, 8–9.

[32] Gerald Hawkins, *Stonehenge Decoded* (Garden City, NY: Doubleday Books, 1965), 45.
[33] Ibid., 29–31.
[34] The Commonwealth Fund Survey of the Health of Adolescent Girls (http://www.cmwf.org/women/abusfact.html), September 1997.

Chapter Five

[1] The Sumerian version of the text is paraphrased and greatly synopsized from the verse translation in Diane Wolkstein and Samuel N. Kramer, *Inanna: Queen of Heaven and Earth* (New York: Harper and Row, 1983), 51–89.
[2] Murray Gell-Mann, *The Quark and the Jaguar: Adventures in the Simple and the Complex* (New York: W.H. Freeman, 1994), 292–296.
[3] Ezekiel 8:14.
[4] I personally collected this story from Iranian informants in 1969.
[5] Elizabeth Warnock Fernea, *Guests of the Sheikh* (New York: Doubleday Anchor, 1969), 241–245.
[6] The most complete canonical account of John's execution is in Mark 6:22, but more elaborate, apocryphal folktales about it survived for centuries.
[7] Matthew 26:14–16.
[8] Oscar Wilde, "Salome," in *The Portable Oscar Wilde,* eds. Richard Aldington and Stanley Weintraub (New York: Viking Penguin, 1981), 407.
[9] Ovid, Book 5, ls. 385 ff.
[10] Thorkild Jacobsen, *The Treasures of Darkness* (New Haven, CT: Yale University Press, 1971), 36.
[11] Anton Moortgat, *The Art of Ancient Mesopotamia* (London: Phædon Press, 1969), 45.
[12] Samuel Noah Kramer, *The Sumerians, Their History, Culture, and Character* (Chicago: University of Chicago Press, 1963), 329.
[13] E. Douglas Van Buren, "The Sacred Marriage in Early Times in Mesopotamia," *Orientalia* n.s. 13 (1944), 1–72.
[14] Moortgat, 70.
[15] Jacobsen, 39.
[16] Ephraim Speiser, trans., "Akkadian Myths and Epics," in *Ancient Near Eastern Texts Relating to the Old Testament,* ed. James B. Pritchard (Princeton, NJ: Princeton University Press, 1969), 119.
[17] Arent J. Wensinck, "The Semitic New Year and the Origin of Eschatology," *Orientalia* n.s. 1 (1923), 184.
[18] Jacobsen, 39.
[19] Leo Frobenius, *Schicksalskunde im Sinne des Kulturwerdens* (Leipzig, Germany: R. Voigtlanders Verlag, 1932), 127.
[20] William G. Lambert, "A Part of the Ritual for the Substitute King," *Archiv für Orientforschung* 18 (1957), 111.
[21] Henri Frankfort, *Kingship and the Gods* (Chicago: University of Chicago Press, 1948), 263–264.

[22] Lambert, "A Part of the Ritual for the Substitute King," 110.
[23] Daniel D. Luckenbill, *Ancient Records of Assyria and Babylonia,* vol. 1 (Chicago: University of Chicago Press, 1926), 254.
[24] Wolkstein and Kramer, 104.
[25] Jacobsen, 179.
[26] Campbell, *The Hero with a Thousand Faces,* 19.
[27] Genesis 40–41.
[28] Jacobsen, 120.
[29] Moortgat, 45.
[30] Sir Leonard Woolley, *Ur Excavations,* vol. 2: *The Royal Cemetery* (London: Clarendon Press, 1934), 46–56.
[31] Some of this material was previously published in Curtiss Hoffman, "Dumuzi's Dream," *Dream Network Journal* 13(4), 10–11.
[32] This section is a synopsis of the conclusions of my doctoral dissertation (Hoffman, *The Lion . . . ,* 594–632).
[33] Ezekiel 1:10; Revelations 4:7.
[34] Landersdorfer, *Der Baal Tetramorphos und die Kerube von Ezekiel, Studien zur Geschichte und Kultur des Altertums* 9:3 (Paderborn, Germany: Verlag von Ferdinand Schöningh, 1918), 8.
[35] Willy Hartner, "The Earliest History of the Constellations in the Near East and the Motif of the Lion-Bull Combat," *Journal of Near Eastern Studies* 24 (1965), 15–16.
[36] Alfred Jeremias, *Handbuch der altorientalischen Geisteskultur* (Leipzig, Germany: J. C. Hinrich'sche Buchhandlung, 1913), 35.
[37] Hartner, 8–9.
[38] Ibid., 3.
[39] Wolkstein and Kramer, 12–27.
[40] Geoffrey Ashe, *The Dawn behind the Dawn: A Search for the Earthly Paradise* (New York: Henry Holt and Co., 1992), 82.
[41] Weidner, 66.
[42] William W. Hallo and William K. Simpson, *The Ancient Near East: A History* (New York: Harcourt Brace Jovanovich, 1971), 37–38, 90–91.
[43] E. Douglas Van Buren, *The Flowing Vase and the God with Streams* (Berlin: Hans Schötz & Co., 1933), 12–15.
[44] Kramer, *The Sumerians,* 239.
[45] Ibid., 179.
[46] R. L. Firster, *Akkadian Hymns and Prayers to the Goddess Ishtar* (Philadelphia: Dropsie College, 1970), Text A, ls. 31, 51.
[47] R. Hennig, "Beitrag zur kulturgeschichtlichen Bedeutung der Sternbilder," *Zeiss Nachrichten,* Sonderheft 2 (1937), p. 4.
[48] Van Buren, "The Sacred Marriage in Ancient Mesopotamia," 33–34.
[49] Ernst Weidner, *Handbuch der babylonischen Astronomie* (Leipzig, Germany: J. C. Hinrisch'sche Buchhandlung, 1915), 66.
[50] Johann Wolfgang Goethe, "Euphrosyne," *Selected Poems,* ed. Christopher Middleton (Boston: Suhrkam/Insel Publishing, 1983), 151.
[51] Sophocles, "Antigonæ," trans. Friedrich Hölderlin, in *Hölderlin: Sämtliche Werke* (Frankfurt am Main Germany: Insel Verlag, 1961), 1223. Translation from the German by the author.

[52] Samuel Noah Kramer, *The Sacred Marriage Rite* (Bloomington, IN: University of Indiana Press, 1969), 103.
[53] Wolkstein and Kramer, 79–80.
[54] William W. Hallo and J.J.A. Van Dijk, *The Exaltation of Inanna* (New Haven, CT: Yale University Press, 1968), 51.
[55] H. W. F. Saggs, *The Greatness That Was Babylon* (New York: Hawthorn Books 1962), 402.
[56] William G. Lambert and A.R. Millard, *Atra-hasis* (Oxford, England: Clarendon Press, 1969), 109.
[57] William G. Lambert, *Enuma Elish: The Babylonian Epic of Creation* (Oxford, England: Oxford University Press, 1966), 1, l.5.
[58] Erich Ebeling, *Tod und Leben nach den Vorstellung der Babylonier* (Berlin and Leipzig, Germany: de Gruyter, 1931), 36.
[59] Genesis 1:1–8.
[60] Feldman and Richardson, 481.
[61] Jacobsen, 201–202.
[62] Giorgio de Santillana and Hertha von Dechend, *Hamlet's Mill: An Essay on Myth and the Frame of Time* (Boston: Gambit Press, 1969), 405.
[63] Hallo and Van Dijk, 14.
[64] Tyler Volk, *Metapatterns: Across Space, Time, and Mind* (New York: Columbia University Press, 1995), viii–ix.
[65] Van Buren, "The Sacred Marriage in Ancient Mesopotamia," 33–34.
[66] Robert Graves and Raphael Patai, *Hebrew Myths* (Garden City, NY: Doubleday, 1963), 128–129.
[67] Lévi–Strauss, *The Raw and the Cooked,* 240.
[68] Richard Katz, *Boiling Energy: Community Healing among the Kalahari Kung* (Cambridge, MA: Harvard University Press, 1982), 41–42.
[69] Frank Waters, *The Book of the Hopi* (New York: Viking Press, 1963), 9–10.
[70] Genesis 3:22.
[71] Z'ev ben-Shamir Halevi, *Tree of Life: An Introduction to the Cabala* (London: Rider and Company, 1972), 33–50.
[72] Geoffrey Bibbey and V. Glob, *Looking for Dilmun* (New York: A. E. Knopf, 1969), 257–261.
[73] Kramer, *The Sumerians,* 47–49.
[74] Genesis 2:10–14. The idea that this location is equivalent to Dilmun is from David Neimann, personal communication.
[75] Mircea Eliade, *Yoga: Immortality and Freedom,* Bollingen Series 56, trans. Willard R. Trask (Princeton, NJ: Princeton University Press, 1969), 241–243.
[76] Briggs Buchanan, "A Snake Goddess and Her Companions," *Iraq* 23 (1971), 1–18. Compare this figure to the photograph in David Carmos, *Vitality, Health, and Relaxation through Yoga* (Boston: Kundalic Press, 1968), 165, center.
[77] Eliade, *Yoga: Immortality and Freedom,* 355.
[78] Wolkstein and Kramer, 72–73.
[79] Jacobsen, 138.
[80] Kramer, *The Sumerians,* 198–199.
[81] Ebeling, 102.
[82] Saggs, 459–471.

[83] Feldman and Richardson, 55.
[84] Emily Vermeule, *Greece in the Bronze Age* (Chicago: University of Chicago Press, 1964), 189.
[85] Ovid, Book 2, ls. 833–875; Book 3, ls. 1–137.
[86] M. B. Sakellariou, "Linguistic and Ethnic Groups in Prehistoric Greece," in George Christopoulus, ed., *History of the Hellenic World: Prehistory and Protohistory* (University Park, PA: Pennsylvania State University Press, 1974), 366.
[87] Matthews and Matthews, 127.
[88] de Santillana and von Dechend, 321.
[89] Ovid, Book 10, ls. 533–553, 708–724.
[90] René Labat, *Manuel d'Epigraphie Akadienne. Quatrieme Edition* (Paris: Impremerie National, 1963), 174–175.
[91] Graves, *The Greek Myths,* vol. 1, 70.
[92] Graves, *The White Goddess,* 221.
[93] Victoria Rourke, personal communication, 1997.
[94] Pennick, 75.
[95] Song of Songs 4:1–16.
[96] Feldman and Richardson, 13.
[97] Jung, *The Archetypes and the Collective Unconscious,* 187.
[98] Wolkstein and Kramer, 46.

Chapter Six

[1] Adolf Jensen, *Das religiose Weltbild einer frühen Kultur* (Stuttgart: August Schröder Verlag, 1949), 34–38.
[2] Lyall Watson, *Gifts of Unknown Things* (New York: Bantam Books, 1978), 52–53.
[3] Joseph Campbell, *The Masks of God: Primitive Mythology,* vol. 1 (New York: Viking Press, 1959), 189.
[4] Jensen, *Myth and Cult among Primitive Peoples,* 121.
[5] Jensen, *Das religiose Weltbild einer frühen Kultur,* 66–77.
[6] Robert Heine-Geldern and Gordon F. Eckholm, "Significant Parallels in the Symbolic Arts of Southern Asia and Middle America," *Papers of the 29th International Congress of Americanists,* vol. 1: *The Civilization of Ancient America* (Chicago, IL: University of Chicago Press, 1951).
[7] John Pfeiffer, *The Emergence of Society: A Prehistory of the Establishment* (New York: McGraw Hill, 1977), 304.
[8] Jensen, *Myth and Cult among Primitive Peoples,* 90.
[9] Campbell, *Occidental Mythology,* 519.
[10] For a definition of these terms, see Robert Tonkinson, *The Mardudjara Aborigines: Living the Dream in Australia's Desert* (New York: Holt, Rinehart, and Winston, 1978), 15–17.
[11] Watson, 221–231.
[12] Lévi–Strauss, "The Structural Study of Myth," 440.
[13] Jensen, *Myth and Cult among Primitive Peoples,* 244, 315.

[14] Jensen, *Das religiose Weltbild einer frühen Kultur,* 39.
[15] Campbell, *Primitive Mythology,* 185–187.
[16] Claude Lévi-Strauss, *The Elementary Structures of Kinship,* trans. James Bell and John von Strome (Boston: Beacon Press, 1969), 490–492.
[17] Jensen, *Das religiose Weltbild einer frühen Kultur,* 46 ff.
[18] Heinrich Zimmer, *Myths and Symbols of Indian Art and Civilization,* Bollingen Series 6 (Princeton, NJ: Princeton University Press, 1946), 175–176.
[19] Frazer, 447.
[20] Aldous Huxley, *The Perennial Philosophy* (Freeport, NY: Books for Libraries Press, 1972), *passim.*
[21] Frazer, 420–426.
[22] E. Wallis Budge, *The Egyptian Book of the Dead: The Papyrus of Ani, Scribe and Treasurer of the Temples of Egypt, about B.C. 1450* (New York: Dover, 1967), *passim.*
[23] Jacobsen, 36.
[24] G.A. Dorsey, *The Cheyenne,* vol. 1: *Ceremonial Organization,* Field Columbian Museum, Publication 99, Anthropology Series, vol. 9, no. 1 (Chicago: Field Museum, 1905), 75, 79–80, 87, 89.
[25] Ashe, 16–17.
[26] Sophocles, 1213–1219.
[27] 1 Samuel 28:7.
[28] Homer, 169.
[29] Kramer, *The Sumerians,* 198–200.
[30] Jensen, *Das religiose Weltbild einer frühen Kultur,* 34.
[31] Eliade, *Yoga: Immortality and Freedom,* 134.
[32] Jung, *Psychology and Alchemy,* 232.
[33] Jung, *The Archetypes and the Collective Unconscious,* 38–39.
[34] Campbell, *Primitive Mythology,* 71.
[35] Plato, "Symposium," in *The Dialogues of Plato,* trans. Benjamin Jowett (New York: Random House, 1937), ls. 189D ff.
[36] Graves and Patai, 66–67.
[37] Campbell, *Primitive Mythology,* 177.
[38] Jensen, *Myth and Cult among Primitive Peoples,* 200–201.
[39] Ibid., 92. I suspect that the use of the male gender in this passage is a mistranslation: in German the phrase would probably have read *"verwandelt sich";* the reflexive pronoun in German is not gender-specific.
[40] Genesis 3–4.
[41] 1 Peter 1:19–20.
[42] Mentor L. Williams, ed., *Schoolcraft's Indian Legends* (East Lansing, MI: Michigan State University, 1956), 58–60.
[43] Hoffman, *The Lion, the Eagle, the Man, and the Bull,* 840–842.
[44] Capra, 198.
[45] For the Big Bang, see Cohen and Stewart, 240–241; for the rise of eukaryotes see Tyler Volk, *Gaia's Body: Toward a Physiology of Earth* (New York: Copernicus Books, 1998), 224–229.
[46] Goetz and Morley, 84.
[47] Jensen, *Myth and Cult among Primitive Peoples,* 197.

[48] John Neihardt, *Black Elk Speaks* (New York: Pocket Books, 1972), 36.
[49] Alice Beck Kehoe, *The Ghost Dance Religion: Ethnohistory and Revitalization* (New York: Holt, Rinehart and Winston, 1989), 64.
[50] Ashe, 111–113.
[51] Mircea Eliade, *Yoga: Immortality and Freedom*, 235–236.
[52] Jane Austen Pratt, *Consciousness and Sacrifice, Contributions to Jungian Thought* (New York: Analytic Psychology Club of New York, 1967), 23–24.
[53] Jensen, *Myth and Cult among Primitive Peoples*, 200.

Chapter Seven

[1] Claude Lévi–Strauss, *The Origin of Table Manners. Introduction to a Science of Mythology*, vol. 3, trans. John and Doreen Weightman (New York: Harper and Row, 1978), 97.
[2] Feldman and Richardson, 53.
[3] Ibid., 99–102.
[4] Kenneth Kensinger, *How Real People Ought to Live: The Cashinahua of Eastern Peru* (Prospect Heights, IL: Waveland Press, 1995), 122.
[5] Marion Woodman, *The Pregnant Virgin: A Process of Psychological Transformation* (Toronto, Canada: Inner City Books, 1985), 1–18.
[6] Isaiah 7:14.
[7] Lévi–Strauss, *The Raw and the Cooked*, 50–51.
[8] Kensinger, 11–28.
[9] Richard Erdoes and Alfonso Ortiz, eds., *American Indian Myths and Legends* (New York: Pantheon Books, 1984), 46–47.
[10] Kensinger, 259.
[11] Lévi–Strauss, *The Origin of Table Manners*, 97.
[12] Kensinger, 104.
[13] Terrence Deacon, *The Symbolic Species: The Co-evolution of Language and the Brain* (New York: W.W. Norton, 1997), 448–449.
[14] Friedrich Boll, Carl Bezold, and Wilhelm Gundel, *Sternglaube und Sternbedeutung* (Stuttgart, Germany: B.G. Teubner, 1966), 54; Jeremias, 85.
[15] Kathleen Hoagland, ed., *A Thousand Years of Irish Poetry* (Old Greenwich, CT: Devin-Adair Co., 1957), 132.
[16] Jung, *Psychology and Alchemy*, 229.
[17] Levi–Strauss, *The Origin of Table Manners*, 96, 110.
[18] Frazer, 824–825.
[19] Victor Turner, "Colour Classification in Ndembu Ritual," in *Anthropological Approaches to the Study of Religion*, ed. Michael Banton (London: Tavistock Publishers, 1966), 47–48.
[20] Ibid., 58–61.
[21] Andreas Lommel, *Die Unumbal: Ein Stamm in Nordwest-Australia* (Hamburg, Germany: Museum für Volkerkunde, 1962), 10–12.
[22] A. W. Howitt, *The Native Tribes of South-East Australia* (London: Macmillan and Co., 1904), 493.

[23] Genesis 6:1–3, 9:1–4,11–16.
[24] Graves and Patai, 71–72.
[25] Synopsis based upon W. Lloyd Warner, *A Black Civilization: A Social Study of an Australian Tribe* (New York: Harper and Row, 1937), 240–249.
[26] Kensinger, 220–222.
[27] Jung, *The Archetypes and the Collective Unconscious*, 18–19.
[28] Speiser, 114.
[29] Snorri Sturluson, "Gylfaginning," *The Prose Edda*, trans. Arthur Brodeur (New York: American–Scandinavian Foundation, 1929), 61.
[30] Morris E. Opler, *Myths and Tales of the Jicarilla Apache Indians, Memoirs of the American Folklore Society*, vol. 31 (1938), 26.
[31] John Swanton, *Tlingit Myths and Texts*, Bureau of American Ethnology Bulletin 39 (Washington, DC: U.S. Government Printing Office, 1909), 209–212.
[32] Campbell, *The Hero with a Thousand Faces*, 201–207.
[33] Jung, *Psychology and Alchemy*, 57–58.
[34] Bailey, Alice, *Discipleship in the New Age*, vol. 2 (New York, Lucis Publishing Co., 1955), 408.
[35] Alice Bailey, *Esoteric Psychology*, vol. 2 (New York: Lucis Publishing Co., 1970), 69–70.
[36] Eliade, *Yoga: Immortality and Freedom*, 196.
[37] H. Ostermann, *The Alaskan Eskimos, as Described in the Posthumous Notes of Dr. Knud Rasmussen, Report of the Fifth Thule Expedition 1921–24*, vol. 10, no. 3 (Copenhagen: Nordisk Verlag, 1952), 99.
[38] Ashe, 92–95.
[39] Knud Rassmussen, *Across Arctic America* (New York: G.P. Putnam's Sons, 1927), 82–84.
[40] Ashe, 28.
[41] Diane Bell, *Daughters of the Dreaming* (Melbourne, Australia: McPhee Gribble, 1983), *passim*.
[42] Kensinger, 217–220.
[43] Speiser, 102.
[44] Kramer, *The Sumerians*, 198–200.
[45] Graves and Patai, 62–68.
[46] Speiser, 116.
[47] Caroline Myss, *Anatomy of the Spirit* (New York: Harmony Books, 1996), *passim*.
[48] Ovid, Book 3, ls. 316–338.
[49] Matthew 6:22.
[50] Graves, *The Greek Myths*, vol. 2, 10.
[51] Ibid., vol. 1, 96–98.
[52] C. F. Will and H. J. Spinden, *The Mandans: A Study of Their Culture, Archæology and Language, Papers of the Peabody Museum of American Archæology and Ethnology*, vol. 3, no. 46 (Millwood, NY: Kraus Reprint Co., 1974), 121–122.
[53] G. A. Dorsey, *The Arapaho Sun Dance; the Ceremony of the Offerings Lodge. Field Columbian Museum, Publication* 75, *Anthropological Series*, vol. 4 (Chicago: Field Museum, 1903), 212–221.
[54] John Fire and Richard Erdoes, *Lame Deer: Seeker of Visions* (New York: Pocket Books, 1972), 191.

[55] A. W. Bowers, *Mandan Social and Ceremonial Organization* (Chicago: University of Chicago Press, 1950), 110–115.
[56] Fire and Erdoes, 252.
[57] Claude Lévi–Strauss, *From Honey to Ashes: Introduction to a Science of Mythology,* vol. 2, trans. John and Doreen Weightman (New York: Harper and Row, 1973), 59–68.
[58] Lévi–Strauss, *The Origin of Table Manners,* 237–238.
[59] Brian Fagan, *Ancient North America: The Archæology of a Continent* (London: Thames and Hudson, 1991), 174–177.
[60] Variants of this myth are found in Franz Boas, "The Central Eskimo," *Sixth Annual Report of the Bureau of American Ethnology* (1888), 175; Peter Freuchen, *The Book of the Eskimos* (New York: Fawcett Books, 1965), 174–175; and Asen Balikci, *The Netsilik Eskimo* (Prospect Heights, IL: Waveland Press, 1970), 206.
[61] Knud Rasmussen, "A Shaman's Journey to the Sea Spirit Takanakapsaluk," in *Teachings from the American Earth,* eds. Dennis and Barbara Tedlock (Los Angeles: Livewright, 1973), 13–19.
[62] Jensen, *Myth and Cult among Primitive Peoples,* 145–146.
[63] Boas, "The Central Eskimo," 178.
[64] Knud Rasmussen, "Iglulik Eskimos," *Report of the Fifth Thule Expedition 1921–24,* vol. 7, no. 1 (Copenhagen: Nordisk Verlag, 1929), 63.
[65] Günter Tessman, *Die Pangwe,* vol. 2 (Berlin: E. Wasmuth, 1913), 199 ff.
[66] Erdoes and Ortiz, 34–37.
[67] Lambert and Millard, 113–115.
[68] Jung, *Psychology and Alchemy,* 327–331, 346–348.
[69] Ibid, 329, fn. 37.
[70] Ibid., 355.
[71] Boas, "The Central Eskimo," 195–196.
[72] Allen Wardwell, ed., *Native Paths* (New York: Metropolitan Museum of Art, 1998), 105.
[73] Boas, "The Central Eskimo," 199.
[74] Hans Christian Andersen, *The Little Mermaid,* trans. Eva La Gálliene (New York: Harper and Row, 1971), *passim.*
[75] Jung, *The Archetypes and the Collective Unconscious,* 24–25.
[76] Marion Woodman and Elinor Dickson, *Dancing in the Flames: The Dark Goddess in the Transformation of Consciousness* (Boston: Shambhala Publications, 1996), 75–86.
[77] Felix Jacoby, *Die Fragmente der griechischen Historiker,* Dritter Teil, C. (New York: E. J. Brill, 1993), 369–370.
[78] Erica Reiner, "The Etiological Myth of the 'Seven Sages,'" *Orientalia* n.s. 30 (1961), 6.
[79] Jacoby, 371.
[80] Immanuel Velikovsky, *Oedipus and Akhnaton* (New York: Doubleday, 1960), 57.
[81] William Shakespeare, *Hamlet,* in Hardin Craig, ed., *The Complete Works of Shakespeare* (Chicago: Scott, Foresman and Company, 1951), Act 1, Scene 2, ls. 129–130.
[82] Campbell, *Creative Mythology,* 3–8.
[83] Campbell, *Primitive Mythology,* 64–65.

Chapter Eight

[1] Freuchen, 172–173.
[2] Boas, "The Central Eskimo," 196–199.
[3] Lévi–Strauss, *The Origin of Table Manners,* 94.
[4] Ibid., 42.
[5] Michael Crawford, *Antropologia Biologica de los Indios Americanos* (Madrid, Spain: Fundacion MAPFRE America, 1992), 144–147.
[6] Evidence for occupation of South America as early as 35,000 B.C. is presented in Thomas Dillehay, G. A. Calderon, G. Politis, and M.C. de Beltrao, "Earliest Hunters and Gatherers of South America," *Journal of World Prehistory* 6 (1992), 185–186; and N. Guidon and B. Arnaud, "The Chronology of the New World: Two Faces of One Reality," *World Archæology* 23(2) (1991), 167–178.
[7] The evidence for trans-Pacific contact is summarized in Stephen Jett, "Precolumbian Transatlantic Contacts," in *Ancient North Americans,* ed. Jesse Jennings (San Francisco: W. H. Freeman, 1983), 557–613.
[8] Edward W. Gifford, *Tongan Myths and Tales. Bernice Pauahi Bishop Museum Bulletin* 8, (1924), 183.
[9] Cyrus H. Gordon, *Before Columbus: Links between the Old World and Ancient America* (New York: Crown Books, 1971), 120–127.
[10] My views on this subject may be found in Curtiss Hoffman, "Shadow and Substance," in Donald Y. Gilmore and Linda S. McElroy, eds., *Across Before Columbus? Evidence for Transoceanic Contact with the Americas Prior to 1492* (Edgecomb, ME: The New England Antiquities Research Association, 1998), 97–103.
[11] Fagan, 172–177.
[12] Lévi–Strauss, *The Naked Man,* 581–624.
[13] Andre Metraux, "Tribes of the Jurua-Purus Basins," *Handbook of South American Indians, Bulletin of the Bureau of American Ethnology* 143 (1948), 677.
[14] Kensinger, 109–111.
[15] Balikci, 107, 153.
[16] Freud, *Totem and Taboo,* 141–146.
[17] Jane Goodall, *In the Shadow of Man* (Boston: Houghton Mifflin, 1971), 187–188.
[18] Lévi–Strauss, *Totemism,* 40–41.
[19] Frankfort, 43–44.
[20] Harold Osborne, *South American Mythology* (London: Paul Hamlyn Publishing Co., 1968), 51–52.
[21] Robin Fox, *The Red Lamp of Incest* (Notre Dame, IN: University of Notre Dame Press, 1983), 12–14.
[22] Goodall, 182.
[23] Marion Woodman, *Leaving My Father's House: A Journey to Conscious Femininity* (Boulder, CO: Shambhala Books, 1992), 351–366.
[24] For a remarkably narrow-minded example of this, see Sigmund Freud, "A Case of Hysteria," *The Standard Edition of the Complete Psychological Works of Sigmund Freud,* vol. 7, trans. James Strachey (London: The Hogarth Press, 1953), 64–93.
[25] Lévi–Strauss, *The Savage Mind,* 35–74.

[26] Joseph Campbell, *Historical Atlas of World Mythology: The Way of the Animal Powers,* vol. 1 (New York: Harper and Row, 1988), 133.
[27] Lévi-Strauss, *The Raw and the Cooked,* 268–269.
[28] Lévi-Strauss, *Totemism,* 42.
[29] Erdoes and Ortiz, 161–162.
[30] Graves, *The Greek Myths,* vol. 2, 124–125.
[31] Lévi-Strauss, *The Origin of Table Manners,* 96.
[32] Gregor, 255.
[33] Kensinger, 65–66
[34] Spencer and Gillen, 269.
[35] Napoleon Chagnon, *Yanamamö: The Fierce People* (New York: Holt, Rinehart, and Winston, 1968), 47–48.
[36] Jung, *The Archetypes and the Collective Unconscious,* 185.
[37] Graves and Patai, 66.
[38] Ovid, Book 3, ls. 310–312.
[39] Frobenius, 127.
[40] e.g., Fire and Erdoes, 138.
[41] Kensinger, 35.
[42] George Bird Grinnell, "Cheyenne Obstacle Myths," *Journal of American Folklore* 16 (1903), 108–115.
[43] Adamson Hoebel, 39–44.
[44] Fire and Erdoes, 227.
[45] Adamson Hoebel, 27.
[46] Balikci, 207.
[47] Jack Zipes, *The Trials and Tribulations of Little Red Riding Hood* (South Hadley, MA: Bergin and Garvey Publishers, Inc., 1983), 5–6.
[48] J. N. B. Hewitt, "Iroquois Myths and Legends," *Bureau of American Ethnology Twenty-first Annual Report* (1903), 255–339.
[49] Joyce, 193–195.
[50] Basil Hall Chamberlain, trans. *Ko-ji-ki: "Records of Ancient Matters," Transactions of the Asiatic Society of Japan,* vol. 10, supplement (1882), 28.
[51] Lambert and Millard, 103.
[52] Evans-Pritchard, 6.
[53] Jung, *The Archetypes and the Collective Unconscious,* 20–21.
[54] Richard Wilhelm, *The I Ching,* Bollingen Series 19, trans. Cary F. Baynes (Princeton, NJ: Princeton University Press, 1950), 167.
[55] Lévi-Strauss, *The Origin of Table Manners,* 42.
[56] Ibid., 217.
[57] Dorsey, *The Arapaho Sun Dance,* 220.
[58] Campbell, *Primitive Mythology,* 393–394.
[59] Bell, 167–168.
[60] Spencer and Gillen, 463–464.
[61] Joseph Campbell, *The Masks of God: Oriental Mythology,* vol. 2 (New York: Viking Press, 1962), 352.
[62] Jacobsen, 103–104.
[63] Ibid, 112–113.

[64] Paraphrased from Brenda E. Beck, *et al.*, *Folktales of India* (Chicago: University of Chicago Press, 1987), 7–9.
[65] Graves, *The Greek Myths.* vol. 1, 78.
[66] Ibid., vol. 2, 22.
[67] Feldman and Richardson, 480–483.
[68] Lucius Apuleius, *The Golden Ass,* trans. W. Adlington (London: William Heinemann Ltd., 1915), 201–285.
[69] Campbell, *The Hero with a Thousand Faces,* 31–33.
[70] Ovid, Book 10, ls., 298–518.
[71] Gaius Suetonius Tranquillus, *The Twelve Caesars,* trans. Robert Graves (Baltimore, MD: Penguin Books, 1957), 161, 198, 223–224.
[72] Genesis 19:30–38.
[73] Ovid, Book 10, ls. 708–724.
[74] A. Guillaumont, *et al.*, trans., *The Gospel According to Thomas* (New York: Harper and Row, 1959), 43.
[75] Graves, *The Greek Myths,* vol. 1, 69–70.
[76] Matthew 3:11.
[77] Lévi–Strauss, "The Structural Study of Myth," 443.
[78] Graves, *The White Goddess,* 238.
[79] Graves, *The Greek Myths,* vol. 1., 199.
[80] Ibid., vol. 2, 22.
[81] Woodman, *Leaving My Father's House,* 10–19, 109–118, 199–209.
[82] Woodman, *The Pregnant Virgin,* 13–20.
[83] Woodman, *Leaving My Father's House,* 29.
[84] Chrétien de Troyes, "Eric and Enide," in *Arthurian Romances,* trans. W.W. Kibler and C. W. Carroll (Baltimore, MD: Penguin Books, 1991), cited in Matthews and Matthews, 143.
[85] Matthews and Matthews, 143.
[86] Ibid., 118–120.
[87] Ibid., 135–139.
[88] Genesis 3:16.

Chapter Nine

[1] Graves, *The White Goddess,* 136.
[2] J.R.R. Tolkien, *Unfinished Tales* (Boston: Houghton Mifflin, 1980), 68–71, 111–115, 129–130.
[3] J.R.R. Tolkien, "On Fairy Stories," in *The Adventures of Tom Bombadil* (New York: Ballantine Books, 1966), 37.
[4] Ernst Neumann, *The Life of Richard Wagner, 1813–1848,* vol. 1 (New York: Alfred A. Knopf, 1933), 451.
[5] Humphrey Carpenter, ed., *The Letters of J.R.R. Tolkien* (Boston: Houghton Mifflin, 1981), 147.
[6] Clive Staples Lewis, *The Last Battle* (New York: Macmillan, 1956), 144–146.

[7] Humphrey Carpenter, *J.R.R. Tolkien, A Biography* (Boston: Houghton Mifflin, 1977), 13.
[8] Carpenter, *The Letters of J.R.R. Tolkien,* 217.
[9] Ibid., 412–413.
[10] J.R.R. Tolkien, "The Notion Club Papers, Part Two," *Sauron Defeated. The History of Middle Earth,* vol. 9, ed. Christopher Tolkien (Boston: Houghton Mifflin, 1992), 222–307 (especially 250–253).
[11] Graves, *The White Goddess,* 378–380.
[12] Robert Moss, *Conscious Dreaming: A Spiritual Path for Everyday Life* (New York: Crown Books, 1996), 150–153.
[13] Carpenter, *The Letters of J.R.R. Tolkien,* 213.
[14] Peter Andreas Munch, *Norse Mythology: Legends of Gods and Heroes,* trans. Sigurd Bernard Hustvedt (New York: American-Scandinavian Foundation, 1926), 152–158.
[15] Richard Wagner, *Der Ring des Niebelungen,* ed. F. Riedel (Leipzig: Max Beck Verlag, 1945), 61–62. This and all subsequent passages from this source translated by the author.
[16] Clendinnen, 177.
[17] Goetz and Morley, 82, fn. 3.
[18] E. Douglas Van Buren, "The Dragon in Ancient Mesopotamia," *Orientalia* n.s. 16 (1947), 7.
[19] Jung, *Psychology and Alchemy,* 292–294.
[20] Ibid., 395.
[21] Tolkien, *Unfinished Tales,* 64.
[22] Gottfried von Strassburg, *Tristan,* trans. A. T. Hatto (Baltimore, MD: Penguin Books, 1960), 130.
[23] J.R.R. Tolkien, *The Hobbit* (New York: Ballantine Books, 1966), 212–217.
[24] Wagner, 109.
[25] J.R.R. Tolkien, "The Etymologies," *The Lost Road. The History of Middle Earth,* vol. 5, ed. Christopher Tolkien (Boston: Houghton Mifflin, 1987), 353.
[26] Ibid., "Quenta Silmarillion," 240–241.
[27] J.R.R. Tolkien, "Myths Transformed," *Morgoth's Ring. The History of Middle Earth,* vol. 10., ed. Christopher Tolkien (Boston: Houghton Mifflin, 1993), 381.
[28] J.R.R. Tolkien, *The Book of Lost Tales. The History of Middle Earth,* vol. 2., ed. Christopher Tolkien (Boston: Houghton Mifflin, 1984), 187–188.
[29] Clendinnen, 197–198.
[30] J.R.R. Tolkien, "Akallabeth," in *The Silmarillion,* ed. Christopher Tolkien (Boston: Houghton Mifflin, 1979), 273–274.
[31] Tolkien, *The Book of Lost Tales,* 281.
[32] Tolkien, *Unfinished Tales,* 66.
[33] Wagner, 58.
[34] Campbell, *The Hero with a Thousand Faces,* 77–89.
[35] Ibid., 51.
[36] Wagner, 58.
[37] Tolkien, *The Silmarillion,* 80–81.
[38] Tolkien, "Valaquenta," in *The Silmarillion,* 28.
[39] Tolkien, The Annals of Aman," in *Morgoth's Ring,* 93.

[40] Friedrich Wilhelm Nietzsche, "Contra Wagner," *The Portable Nietzsche,* trans. and ed. Walter Kaufmann (New York: Viking Press, 1954), 673.
[41] Carpenter, *The Letters of J.R.R. Tolkien,* 145.
[42] Ibid., 115–116.
[43] Tolkien, *The Book of Lost Tales,* 33–38.
[44] Tolkien, "Laws and Customs among the Eldar," *Morgoth's Ring,* 210–234.
[45] Ibid., "Athrabeth Finrod Ah Andreth," 308.
[46] J.R.R. Tolkien, "The Quenta," *The Shaping of Middle-Earth, The History of Middle Earth,* vol. 4, ed. Christopher Tolkien (Boston: Houghton Mifflin, 1986), 165.
[47] Tolkien, "The Annals of Aman," *Morgoth's Ring,* 80.
[48] Ibid., "Athrabeth Finrod Ah Andreth," 322.
[49] Ibid., 71.
[50] Graves, *The Greek Myths,* vol. 1, 151–152.
[51] Graves and Patai, 125–126.
[52] Tolkien, "Ainulindalë," *Morgoth's Ring,* 11.
[53] Tolkien, *The Silmarillion,* 201–202.
[54] Ibid., 139.
[55] Ibid., 250.
[56] Carpenter, *The Letters of J.R.R. Tolkien,* 385.
[57] de Santillana and von Dechend, 354–359.
[58] Tolkien, "The Quenta," 165.
[59] Tolkien, *The Book of Lost Tales,* 286.
[60] Tolkien, "Ainulindalë," *Morgoth's Ring.* 36.

Chapter Ten

[1] Noam Chomsky, *Language and the Mind* (New York: Harcourt, Brace Jovanovich 1968), 110.
[2] Lévi–Strauss, *The Raw and the Cooked,* 14–26.
[3] Jung, *The Archetypes and the Collective Unconscious,* 4.
[4] Carpenter, ed., *The Letters of J.R.R. Tolkien,* 147.
[5] Blakeslee, 182–183.
[6] Zimmer, *Myths and Symbols of Indian Art and Civilization,* 35–36; Veronica Ions, *Indian Mythology* (London: Paul Hamlyn, 1967) 72.
[7] Waters, 17–18.
[8] These prophecies are discussed in William Willoya and Vinson Brown, *Warriors of the Rainbow* (Healdsburg, CA: Naturegraph Publishers, 1962), 54–55.
[9] Hermann Hesse, *The Journey to the East,* trans. Hilda Rosner (New York: Farrar, Strauss, and Giroux), 37–49.
[10] Wolfram von Eschenbach, *Parzival,* ed. Karl Lachmann (Berlin and Leipzig, Germany: Walter de Gruyter, 1926), 478–479.
[11] J.R.R. Tolkien, "Myths Transformed," in *Morgoth's Ring,* 395–396.
[12] Nikos Kazantzakis, *The Last Temptation of Christ,* trans. A. Bien (New York: Bantam Books, 1971), 395–396.

[13] Ibid., 396.
[14] Carl G. Jung, *Aion, Collected Works* vol. 9, Bollingen Series 20, trans. R.F.C. Hull (Princeton, NJ: Princeton University Press, 1969), 8–10.
[15] Wagner, 44–45.
[16] Luke 4:4.
[17] Carol Cohn, "Sex and Death in the Rational World of Defense Intellectuals," Center for Psychological Studies in the Nuclear Age, Cambridge, MA (1987), 16, cited in Woodman and Dickson, 97–99.
[18] Peter Goodchild, *J. Robert Oppenheimer: Shatterer of Worlds* (Boston: Houghton Mifflin, 1981), 162.
[19] Campbell, *The Hero with a Thousand Faces,* 15–16.
[20] Henry Adams, *The Education of Henry Adams* (New York: The Book League of America, 1928), 418.
[21] Robert Woodward and Carl Bernstein, *The Final Days* (New York: Simon and Schuster, 1976), 329.
[22] Ibid., 405.
[23] Friedrich Wilhelm Nietzsche, *Thus Spake Zarathustra,* in Walter Kaufmann, ed. and trans., *The Portable Nietzsche* (New York: Viking Press, 1954), 156.
[24] Clive Staples Lewis, *Perelandra* (New York: Collier Books, 1962), 217.
[25] Zimmer, *The King and the Corpse,* 251.
[26] Cohen and Stewart, 430–431.
[27] Campbell, *The Hero with a Thousand Faces,* 16–17.
[28] Campbell, *Creative Mythology,* 6.
[29] Jung, *The Archetypes and the Collective Unconscious,* 14–15.
[30] Bell, 44.

GLOSSARY

(Note: Boldface terms within definitions refer to other items in the glossary)

Aetiology: A **myth** that describes the origins of something in the natural or **cultural** world.

Alchemy: The Medieval (and earlier) craft of transmuting base metals, which metaphorically also was a form of psychological self-**transformation.** A precursor of modern chemistry.

Alienation: The inability to fit within a **cultural** framework that leads either to destructive or creative **transformations.**

Alpha male: The leading adult male of a primate band, who in some species maintains exclusive access to females—unlike any hominid society we can document!

Analeptic trance: A method of exploring **myths** and dreams by quieting the intellect and stimulating the creative imagination.

Anality: In Freudian psychology, a stage of child development in which there is a fixation on the process and products of elimination, and a confusion between them and sexuality.

Anima: In Jungian psychology, the feminine aspect of a man's psyche, often projected by him onto women with whom he becomes emotionally involved.

Animus: In Jungian psychology, the masculine aspect of a woman's psyche, often projected by her onto men with whom she becomes emotionally involved.

Anorexia: A condition in which a person deliberately refuses nourishment; the individual often has feelings of inadequacy and self-destructive tendencies; frequently a long-term consequence of **incest.**

Anthropic principle: The **scientific** theory that the universe is a locus for information flow, that its fundamental constants are just right for life, and that the human ability to communicate is predetermined in its structure.

Archetype: In Jungian psychology, an energy quantum within the **collective unconscious,** that may rise to the surface of consciousness and influence an individual's behavior.

Astrology: A system of correspondences (see **Doctrine of Signatures**) in which associations or analogies are made between the positions of the stars and planets and events on earth.

Big man: In **chiefdoms,** an influential leader, often with hereditary status. In Sumerian, a literal translation of the word for "king."

Caduceus: A **symbol** borne by the Greek god Hermes, consisting of a pair of serpents intertwined about a winged pole, with a ball at the top. It has become the symbol of the medical profession, and probably refers to the **kundalini.**

Cannibalism: The consumption of human flesh, usually something attributed **ethnocentristically** as a sign of inferior status by one **culture** or subculture to another. A **metaphor** for **incest.**

Canonical: Refers to **myths** or religious ideas that have been written down and thereby frozen into a fixed form.

Chakra: In the **kundalini** system of India, a center or vortex of energy within the body. There are seven major chakras and many subsidiary ones.

Chaos theory: A development of late twentieth century **science** which posits that small perturbations from the orderly rules of nineteenth century science can produce very large effects.

Chiefdom: A **culture** organized around a hereditary leader, whose status is very different from that of most members. Usually found in groups of ten thousand or more.

Chrysalis phase: A stage of recovery from a traumatic episode, such as **incest**, prior to the **transformation** of the trauma's energy into something creative.

Classification system: A means by which any **culture** comes to understand both the natural and social world by creating categories and assigning persons and objects into them.

Collective unconscious: In Jungian psychology, the substrate of the **unconscious** that is common to all humans, regardless of **culture.**

Comparative mythology: A method of mythological analysis in which similar **myths** from different **cultures** are juxtaposed to come to a better understanding of their common meaning.

Complexity theory: In late twentieth century **science**, a theory which posits that complexity emerges on the border between order and **chaos** and is necessary for life.

Cosmological function: In the writings of Joseph Campbell, the role that **myth** plays in explaining the world around us.

Creation through the word: A common mythological motif, in which the speaking of the name of an object magically brings it into existence.

Cross cousins: Individuals related to one another through parents who are siblings of opposite sex. In many **tribal societies,** cross-cousin marriage is preferred because it crosses **moieties**.

Cult of personality: The overemphasis upon the importance of prominent individuals, to the detriment of citizen responsibility.

Cultural hearth: For **diffusionists,** a center of "high" civilization from which cultural traits diffused to supposedly less advanced **cultures.**

Cultural materialism: The theory that everything that happens in **culture** is the result of an adaptation to environmental conditions.

Cultural relativism: The concept that all **cultures** are equally valid for their own members, and therefore no culture has the right to impose its values upon another.

Culture: A group of individuals who share a significant number of agreed upon norms of behavior; or, the norms of behavior which characterize such a group of individuals.

Culture hero: A mythological figure who is credited with having introduced some important innovation to a **culture,** usually in the distant past (see **dream-time**).

Cuneiform: The system of writing used in ancient Mesopotamia.

Diffusion: The spread of traits—objects, methods, or ideas—from one **culture** to another.

Disjunction: In **myth,** a separation of something that was originally unitary into disparate parts.

Displacement: The shunting of responsibility for something undesirable onto another person or group, often as a result of **Shadow** projection.

Doctrine of signatures: An idea whose popularity peaked in the Middle Ages, in which any system in nature or **culture** could be mapped onto any other; e.g., **astrology.**

Dream-time: In Australian aboriginal belief, a "time before time" when the ancestral beings were actively creating the current world conditions. The concept has been extended to include concepts of a precultural state in the **myths** of many **cultures.**

Dualism: The concept that all things are divided into opposing pairs, sometimes out of a **primal unity.**

Electra complex: In Freudian psychology, the attraction to the father-imago in the psyche of a woman.

Enantiodromion: In Jungian psychology, the interplay of the opposites that leads to balance.

Endogamy: Marriage within the local group or family, especially within royal families in **state societies,** to keep power and wealth within the group.

Eschatology: A **myth** about the end state of things, the opposite of an **aetiology**.

Ethical dualism: A concept especially strong in Western religions, in which the individual is presented with an ethical choice between good and evil actions.

Ethnocentrism: The deeply ingrained idea that the values of one's own **culture** are superior to those of any other. This leads to clear self-identification, but also to discrimination.

Exogamy: Marriage out of the local group or **moiety,** in order to promote **reciprocity.**

Factuality: Ursula LeGuin's term to describe the tangible, measurable world, as distinguished from "truth."

Free substitution: In **myth,** the ability to replace one member of a category with another without altering the sense of the story.

Gift exchange: A principal of **reciprocity,** upon which much **cultural** interaction is based.

Hætera: An "**anima**-woman," who takes on the preferred behavior of whatever man she is with.

Hendiadys: A literary device in which the same thing is said twice, using synonyms. This is one way of determining the rules of **free substitution** in a **culture's classification system.**

Hero: An individual who sacrifices his or her self interest on behalf of the greater whole. A perennially popular theme of **myth.**

Hieros gamos or Sacred Marriage: A ceremony in **state societies** in which the ruler engages in ritual intercourse with a representative of the goddess, in order to ensure the fertility of the land.

Holistic: Tending to think of the big picture, synthesizing rather than analyzing.

Iconography: The consistent use within a **culture** of a **symbol** or set of symbols to represent important ideas.

Incest: Marriage, or sexual relations, between persons whom a culture considers to be too close relatives.

Incubation: A method of dream instruction in which the individual seeks guidance about a problem by thinking about it before going to sleep, sometimes in a location designed for the purpose.

Independent invention: The idea that **cultures** are likely to come up with similar results under similar environmental conditions, without being in contact with one another, because the possibilities are limited.

Individuation: In Jungian psychology, the process by which an individual appropriates all of the potentials of the psyche through relationship with the inner **Self.**

Initiation: A process of ritual **transformation** from one state to another, often accompanied by physical or psychological stress as a means of forcing the change.

Inversion: The **transformation** of something into its opposite, either in form or in order.

Isomorphism: An observed similarity of form, irregardless of scale or causality.

Kundalini: A system of yoga based upon the raising of energies along the spinal column, through the energy centers or **chakras,** in order to attain enlightenment.

Liminal state: A borderline condition, especially during **initiation,** when the individual has died to their previous state of consciousness but has not yet attained to the next state.

Mandala: A radially symmetrical diagram, originally from India; in Jungian psychology a **symbol** of wholeness or the **Self.**

Matrilineal descent group: An extended family within a **culture** in which membership is determined through the female line.

Melusina: A mermaid, a tempting manifestation of the **anima** that is delusional because it is of a presexual nature.

Metaphor: A broad comparison or **isomorphism** which is the basis for much **mythological** imagery. In a larger sense, everything in **culture** could be interpreted as a metaphor.

Mischwesen: A "mixed beast," a monster made up of parts of two or more animals.

Models for: In Clifford Geertz's terminology, the function of **myths** and religions as determinants of how **culture,** or the Universe, should be.

Models of: In Clifford Geertz's terminology, the function of **myths** and religions as descriptions of how **culture,** or the Universe, actually is.

moiety: A group consisting of about half the members of a **culture,** which has a **reciprocal** relationship with the other half, especially in terms of feasting, marriage, and burial.

Morbio inferiore: A sickness of the lower part of the body, either actual or metaphorical, that characterizes the Waste Land king.

Motif: Any element of a **myth** that can be identified.

Myth: A told tale; a story containing something essentially true about the human condition, whatever else it has to say.

Mythic literacy: A familiarity with the processes by which **myth** operates, and an appreciation of its importance as a determinant of human behavior.

Mythology: The study of **myths,** under any number of theoretical perspectives; or, the body of **myths** of a particular **culture.**

Mythopoeia: The conscious creation of **myths,** especially by modern artists.

N/um: In !Kung Bushman **culture,** an energy analogous to **kundalini** that is used for healing.

New year's festival: In agriculturally-based societies, a celebration often tied to the planting calendar in which the fertility of the land is reenergized by ritual acts.

Numerology: The use of numbers as **symbols,** often similar across **cultures** due to the structural properties inherent in the numbers, e.g., **dualism.**

Obstacle flight: A chase scene in **myth** in which the pursued casts obstacles behind to deter the pursuer.

Occam's razor: The principle in **science** that "essences should not be multiplied beyond the necessary"; i.e., the simplest explanation of a phenomenon is most likely to be the correct one.

Oedipus complex: In Freudian psychology, the attraction to the mother-imago in the psyche of a man.

Oral tradition: The means of transmission of most **myths** prior to the introduction of **canonical** texts.

Orthodoxy: A group within a **culture** that insists that only the literal interpretation of the **canon** is correct.

Paradigm: In **science,** a **model of** some aspect of the universe that is internally consistent and (for a time) intellectually satisfying. Paradigms are subject to change, however, especially if it is discovered that they have become **models for.**

Parallel cousins: Individuals related to one another through parents who are siblings of the same sex. In many **tribal societies,** parallel-cousin marriage is forbidden because it fails to cross **moieties.**

Paranatellon: In **astrology,** a constellation adjacent to the zodiacal band which is associated with the zodiacal constellation to which it is closest and may be a **free substitution** for it.

Parsimony: In **science,** the preference for simple, elegant explanations of phenomena over complex, convoluted ones. See **Occam's razor.**

Patriarchy: The domination of **culture** by its male members, especially in political, economic, and religious terms. Those who believe in the existence of a **primordial matriarchy** consider patriarchy to have replaced it by violence during the Late Bronze Age.

Perennial philosophy: So named by Aldous Huxley, the idea system of **"primitive"** peoples, which is perennial both in that it endures for a long time and in that it is based upon the cycle of growth, death, and regrowth of plants (see **vegetative analogy**)

Precession of the equinoxes: The apparent backward motion through the zodiac of the stars rising with the Sun at the time of the spring equinox, caused by the wobble of the Earth's axis. The movement from one sign of the zodiac to another through precession is believed to herald major changes in **culture,** for example, the current transition from the Age of Pisces to the Age of Aquarius.

Primal father: In Freudian psychology, the **alpha male** in a band of ape-men, who was killed and eaten by his sons, thereby occasioning the inception of **culture.**

Primal unity: A state alleged by **myth** to be antecedent to the present **dualism** of the universe, often a paradisal state of innocence. The **scientific** equivalent is the state prior to the Big Bang. In both cases the state is almost unimaginable.

Primitive: A pejorative term applied to technologically simple **cultures** by **state societies** who conquer them. This is often an **ethnocentristic** rationalization for conquest. When it comes to kinship systems or **myths,** technologically simple **cultures** are anything but simple!

Primogeniture: A principle of inheritance in which the eldest son is the major or sole inheritor of his father's wealth, position, and status; especially found in **state societies.**

Primordial matriarchy: A theory that **myths** reflect a historical condition in which women were once the principal rulers (or at least that female divinities were the principal objects of worship) of **cultures** throughout the world.

Psychic unity: A theory that the similarities between **myths** of **cultures** distant from one another is due to either a common psychological substrate (the **collective unconscious**) or ongoing psychic communication across cultural boundaries.

Psychological function: In the writings of Joseph Campbell, the role which **myth** plays in establishing the individual psyche within the framework of **culture.**

Qabbalah: A branch of Jewish mysticism based upon the ascension of the **Tree of Life.**

Reality principle: In Freudian psychology, the hard facts of life to which the individual must make a psychological adjustment.

Reciprocity: The establishment of reliable back-and-forth exchange between two or more parties, especially **moieties,** that ensures the harmonious functioning of **culture.**

Recombination: A process whereby parts of **myths** may be broken up and reworked (sometimes via **inversion**) into other myths, sometimes without changing their original meaning. This is **isomorphous** to the recombination process in DNA.

Reductionism: The principle in **science** that complex phenomena are capable of being broken down into their constituent parts and thereby understood: the whole is equal to the sum of its parts.

Ritual regicide: The practice of ritually killing the king, common in early **state societies** and possibly a reflection of social tension between Church and State.

Sacred mountain: In **myths,** an elevated place which is often the abode of divinities, and represents the **Self** in Jungian psychology.

Science: The pursuit of knowledge about the universe through its tangible qualities (though the qualities of twentieth century physics are not very tangible!).

Self: In Jungian psychology (where it is always capitalized when it has this meaning), the central core of being within the individual psyche.

Self-representation, self-similarity: The ability of a complex system to produce images of itself; sometimes held to be a determinant of consciousness.

Sequential repetition: A device in **myth** whereby a section is repeated, with incremental changes in one direction or another, both for emphasis and to tie in to **numerology.**

Shadow: In Jungian psychology, that portion of a person's psyche which is contrary to what one represents oneself to be, and therefore refuses to acknowledge. The Shadow is often projected onto others, as a form of **displacement.**

Shaman: In **tribal** societies, a specialist in the sacred, who has achieved this position through a critical **initiatory** experience. Shamans function as ritual directors as well as medical practitioners and psychological counselors for their people, but they are often marginalized because ordinary people fear their powers.

Sitz im Leben: (German for situation in life) The context within **culture** into which a **myth** fits.

Sociological function: In the writings of Joseph Campbell, the role which **myth** plays in describing and justifying the structures of society.

State society: A **culture** based upon agricultural surplus and urbanism, with a permanent central political authority which often needs to justify its existence by conquering its neighbors. Societies of this sort usually have more than one hundred thousand members.

Stimulus diffusion: A method of **cultura**l transmission that does not require direct contact but works through intermediaries.

Structuralism: The theory that **culture** is largely determined by the mental structure of its members, and that **myths** are primarily mental constructs of reality.

Substitute king: In incipient **state societies,** a ritual exchange of the responsibilities of kingship with a commoner, who is sacrificed as a means of avoiding the **ritual regicide** of the real king.

Supervenience: In **science,** the concept that one level of interpretation is causally dependent upon another; for example, biology is supervenient upon chemistry, which is supervenient in turn upon physics.

Swidden horticulture: A simple method of cultivating vegetable crops that keeps the ground fertile by periodically burning off the vegetative cover.

Sylviculture: The cultivation of trees, especially for their fruit.

Symbol: Any token which can be said to represent another, either in the tangible world or in the imagination. Symbols are usually consistent among members of the same **culture,** and may be consistent **cross-culturally,** or even for all cultures.

Synchronicity: In Jungian psychology, an acausal connecting principle which links events which happen at the same time even though they have no apparent causal relationship. Much of **Doctrine of Signatures** is based upon this concept. Then again, there is strong evidence that this works for subatomic particles, too.

Tender-minded: William James' term for individuals in all societies (the minority) who by temperament are not satisfied with normative **culture** and who seek reality beyond its confines.

Totemism: The attribution of common ancestry between a subgroup within a **culture** and a species in the natural world. The common ancestor is called a totem. Totemism often implies **reciprocity,** since members of one totemic group are expected to provide their totem animal (which they often are forbidden to consume) to the members of the other totemic groups within the society.

Tough-minded: William James' term for individuals in all societies (the majority) who by temperament are satisfied with normative **culture** and who see no need to seek reality beyond its confines.

Transcendent function: In the writings of Joseph Campbell, the role which **myth** plays in relating the members of a **culture** to the essential mystery of being, which can never be fully explained.

Transformation (or metamorphosis): A change of form for a character in a **myth** to something other than what he or she was. Transformations can often be profoundly disturbing, but they offer the possibility of enlarging the psyche if they can be accepted.

Tree of Life: In **Qabbalah,** the tree which grew within the Garden of Eden from which the primordial pair were not permitted to partake lest they become as gods. But the Qabbalist, through earnest study and meditation, seeks to ascend this tree and its ten branches or Sephiroth in order to approach God. The concept has been extended to tree motifs in other **mythologies,** which often encompass the entire conceptual system of the **culture.**

Tribal society: A **culture** of usually fewer than ten thousand members, which is organized around the principle of relative egalitarianism of inherited status. Leadership is usually attained through personal merit and democratic selection.

Triune goddess: A set of feminine divinities **symbolic** of the three major phases of a woman's life: Maiden, Matron, and Crone.

Unconscious: That part of the psyche which is not readily accessible during waking life. It is accessed during sleep, in trance, and in near-death states. In Freudian psychology, the unconscious (Id) is the seat of all desires and its manifestations are detrimental to sanity and society. In Jungian psychology, the unconscious is a source of wisdom and of the potential **transformation** of society.

Unilineal kinship system: A system of reckoning membership in a subset of a **culture** through only one gender of ancestors; e.g., a **matrilineal descent group.**

Universal grammar: In the writings of Noam Chomsky, the underlying structural principles which exist below the level of consciousness in all cultures upon which linguistic communication is based. This may be the same as Jung's **collective unconscious,** in which case it may be said that **myths** possess a universal grammar.

Variant: Any alternative form of a **myth,** usually within the same **culture** or group of cultures.

Vegetative analogy: The persistent idea, among horticulturalists, that human life is like that of the plants, with phases of living, dying, and resurrection.

Virgin birth: The idea, prevalent in many cultures, that the **Hero** must spring from a mother who is not dominated by **patriarchal cultural** values.

Waste Land: A condition of **alienation** that characterizes a whole society. It is caused by the loss of **Self** and rejection of **Shadow** within the psyche of its members, but particularly in **myth** through the laming of its ruler. The Waste Land can only be healed through **enantiodromion:** through the appearance of the **Hero,** the opposite **archetype** of connection to the Self.

Yoga: The Indian science of union with divinity, through various physical, emotional, and mental methods.

INDEX